the Unofficial Guide® to Landing a Job

L. Michelle Tullier, PhD

D1260870

WILEY

Wiley Publishing, Inc.

For Alexandra

Acknowledgements

This is the eighth book I've written, and by now, my family, friends, and professional colleagues know that I could not finish any book without their help. As always, my husband, Michael Gazelle, along with my parents, friends, and neighbors provided all sorts of emotional and logistical support from "meals-on-wheels" and childcare to encouragement when deadlines were nipping at my heels. On the professional front, colleagues enriched this book with valuable input, ideas, and quotes. You are too numerous to cite by name, but you know that I am grateful to you–particularly my pals in the Atlanta office of Right Management Consultants. I do, however, want to acknowledge by name Richmond Fourmy, Bob Carlson, and John Williams for granting me the flexibility and freedom to accomplish this project.

I also want to thank the clients I have worked with during the past two decades, particularly the job seekers who've passed through the doors of Right Management since I began there in the Spring of 2001. You are the brave souls who endured job hunting during one of the toughest employment markets in history. I have learned so much from all of you–not just about dotting the i's and crossing the t's on résumés or what's being asked in job interviews these days–but about the human spirit.

Finally, I am very grateful to the folks at Wiley. Roxane Cerda had the vision to see this book as more than just a revision of my 1999 *Unofficial Guide* on interviewing but as a comprehensive job search guide. Marcia Johnson has been a pleasure to work with through the editing process, and I thank her and all of the editing and production staff for their excellent work.

Contents

As a career counselor for more than 20 years, Michelle Tullier has seen it all when it comes to job hunting. She knows what it takes to land not just a job, but the right job. Michelle is the Vice President of Career Consulting in the Atlanta office of the global career transition firm Right Management Consultants. At Right, she and her colleagues coach thousands of job seekers each year, helping them develop the best strategies, write powerful resumes, and learn to network and interview effectively.

Prior to joining Right, Michelle ran a successful independent career consulting practice in New York City, attracting clients from across the United States and abroad, and facilitated seminars in Fortune 500 companies on career development topics. Michelle also served as a career coach for Monster.com, taught career development at New York University, and served as a career counselor at Barnard College, Columbia University. Her work in career counseling is complemented by management roles in e-commerce during the dot-com boom of the late 1990s and dot-com bust of the early 2000s—a harrowing, thrill-a-minute experience that she wouldn't trade for anything.

Michelle's expertise has been quoted or published in numerous magazines and newspapers, including *Fortune, Chicago Tribune,* and *The New York*

Times, and she is the author of seven books, including *Networking for Job Search and Career Success* (JIST, 2004), *The Unofficial Guide to Acing the Interview* (Wiley, 1999), and *The Complete Idiot's Guide to Overcoming Procrastination* (Alpha, 1999). Michelle holds a Ph.D. in counseling psychology from UCLA and a bachelor's degree from Wellesley College. She resides in Atlanta with her husband and daughter.

What is it about a job search that can overwhelm and frustrate even the savviest of professionals, from hot-shot recent grads to seasoned executives? Having worked with tens of thousands of job seekers over the past twenty-plus years, I have witnessed the struggles that go hand-in-hand with job hunting. Whether the economy is in a boom, bust, or bound-for-recovery mood, and whether you're seeking your dream job or any old position to pay the bills, landing a job is a challenging task.

One reason for the challenge is that it can be so difficult to know what employers are looking for and what they're thinking. Even if you've been in a position to read résumés , interview candidates, and hire employees yourself and have learned what you like and don't like in an applicant, how could you possibly be certain about what any given employer on any given day will want from *you*?

Will the employers you're targeting, for example, actually read your three-page resume, or must you slash it down to one page before they'll give it the time of day? Did you provide the answers they wanted to hear in the interview or were you just listening to yourself talk? Are they not calling you back because they're truly busy or because they're giving you the brush-off? Searching for a job can feel at times like picking numbers for a lottery ticket. You might have a method to your madness, but is it the winning method or just madness?

How this book will help you

If there is one universal key to a successful job hunt, it is to put yourself in the employer's shoes. The *Unofficial Guide to Landing a Job* does just that. Beginning with the inside scoop on how hiring decisions are made and what makes some job seekers more successful than others, this book shifts your approach from the passive, "I need a job," to the strategic, "What does the marketplace need, and how can I meet those needs?"

On these pages you'll find insiders' tips on every aspect of a job search, including

- How to market yourself effectively and why that old advice, "You gotta sell yourself," is a myth
- What is really meant by the term "hidden job market" and how to crack it
- Why networking is so important, but why networking the wrong way is worse than not networking at all
- How anthropology—yes, I said anthropology—helps us work with headhunters and other types of recruiters
- How to make yourself stand out from the millions of Internet job seekers without spending every waking hour at the computer
- Why direct mail campaigns may or may not be a waste of time and how to decide whether they'll work for you
- How to ace the interview every time and follow up to clinch the deal, not your teeth
- Ways to troubleshoot and jumpstart a search that's going nowhere
- How to ensure after you land your dream job that the next job search will be much easier!

Why you need the inside scoop

Competition for jobs is stiffer than ever before. No matter what the economic headlines happen to be on the day you read this book—whether the news is positive, doom-and-gloom, or somewhere in between—landing a job is going to be much more of a challenge than it was at earlier points in your own career or in your parents' careers.

To gain an advantage over increased competition

Employers have access to candidates like never before due to the emergence of online recruiting, the globalization of the workplace, and increased use of contract workers and outsourcing. Similarly, job seekers have more ways, and more convenient ways, to apply for jobs down the street or across the globe with the explosion of career-related Web sites. If you had gone online to look for work during one particular week of August, 2003, for example, you would have been competing with 4,609,000 pairs of eyeballs visiting just five of the thousands of career sites online (U.S. Department of Labor, Monster.com, Yahoo!, HotJobs, AOL Careers & Work, and CareerBuilder) according to Forrester Research. Remember, that's more than four million people in just a *week*!

In addition to the competition online, more people are out on the market than in the past. Continual corporate downsizings and reorganizations have poured huge numbers of people into the job market. What this means is that for any given advertised position for which you might apply, you are likely to be competing with hundreds, if not thousands, of other applicants, many of whom may be just as qualified as you are. The competition is tough, and you must learn how to get the edge.

To get past more stringent hiring methods

Employers are more strategic and sophisticated in their recruiting and hiring methods these days. Many carefully plot the qualifications needed in a new employee, use formal assessment tools, and employ rigorous behavior-based interviewing formats. Organizations must be leaner and meaner to survive and compete in today's world, so their hiring approach is a razor-sharp, cautious one designed to uncover only the highest quality candidates. Employers must ensure that every person on the payroll is a human resource, not human surplus. As a result, you are likely to be screened more carefully and find that your search takes longer than it might have in the past.

To prove your value, not just show that you're qualified

For the most part, organizations are interested in hiring only people who can help them fulfill a bottom-line, dollars-and-cents mission rather than simply fill a seat. You must show how, when, and where you can add value. You must also show that you are versatile, flexible, adaptable, and able to take on any responsibility that a changing workplace demands because the needs of the employer and demands of the marketplace are likely to change frequently—sometimes on a daily basis. You are not being hired just to do a particular job but are being hired for your ability both to contribute to an organization's long-range vision and to put out the fires in the short term. As a result, you have to know what your value is and be able to articulate it.

To use technology and the Internet wisely in your search

Web sites that advertise job openings are only the tip of the iceberg when it comes to ways you can spend time online during your job search. There are also online opportunities for networking, research databases for uncovering the hidden market, and scores of career coaching or job placement experts hawking their wares online. All of this makes it both easier and more confusing to find a job. It can be hard to know where to begin digging, how deep to dig, and where it's safe to dig. For example, posting your resume online or applying for positions through Internet-based job boards is incredibly convenient, but these methods are not without their pitfalls. You must master the logistics and technicalities of job searching online to make it work, while being very wary of personal security risks that range from merely annoying spam email to very serious identity theft potential.

To accept the reality that some jobs are gone forever

Some jobs are hard to land because they don't really exist anymore, or at least don't exist in the geographic location where you need them, or because it's a type of job that's on the brink of extinction. This is a harsh reality that may affect your ability to replace a job you've lost or may limit your ability to move voluntarily to a new company when you get tired of the old one. In some cases, it's a matter of globalization. American businesses have found that it is more cost-effective to outsource entire functions, such as information technology, payroll, customer service, and more, to other countries. Many American workers have seen their jobs go to highly skilled English-speaking professionals overseas who will work for dramatically lower wages than their American counterparts.

According to research and advisory firm Gartner, Inc., by the year 2010, up to 25 percent of information technology (IT) jobs in developed countries, including the United States, will be lost to emerging IT markets, such as India, China, Russia, Eastern European countries, Ireland, and Israel. Regardless of how you feel about this phenomenon from a political or personal point of view, this trend is one to be taken seriously as it's much more than a passing fad.

In other cases, lost jobs are a matter of some industries having undergone dramatic changes, whether through technological advances (such as computers doing humans' work) or the tragic 9/11 event in this country and the dot.com bust of the 1990s. Industries that were hardest hit by 9/11, such as airlines and travel, will never do business in the same way again, or employ the same numbers and types of people again. This book offers guidance for accepting this reality and moving on to something new.

To compete with a cheaper, more agile free agent workforce

There is a growing pool of free agents in this country—temporary employees, freelancers, contractors, independent consultants, and micro business owners (very small businesses usually with no more than one or two employees). Free agents who work as contractors or freelancers can meet an organization's needs at any given point in time and then be off on their merry way when those needs change rather than hanging around as dead weight on the payroll. According to FreeAgentNation.com, an estimated one in four Americans is a free agent. That's about 33 million people! Many employers are converting formerly permanent jobs to contract positions to save money on benefits, which often are not paid to contract or temporary workers, and to remain more flexible.

To find not just a job, but the right job

Forget about the problem of keeping up with the competition for a moment, and look at what's in your best interest. You owe it to yourself to find the job that's really right for you. You want—and deserve—the one that will make you the most satisfied, whether that's one with the highest salary, most appealing location, most interesting responsibilities, best work-life balance, or whatever it is that's important to you. Can't be choosy in a tight job market, you say? Having the mindset that you must go after any old job you can get is not only selling yourself short, it's also the kiss of death for a job search. The more focused you are on what you want and the more strategic you are about going after it, the more successful and expedient your search will be.

Take it from one who knows firsthand

Although I've worked with job seekers and career changers over my entire career, I've spent the past several years most intensively on the front lines of the job search "war" in my role as a senior career management consultant with one of the world's leading career transition firms. The work we do is commonly known as "outplacement." Companies big and small, as well as nonprofit organizations, purchase our services as part of the severance packages of their departing employees. It's a goodwill gesture to help the terminated employees get on the right track as they search for new work. We don't place people in jobs; we coach them on the best ways to find and land jobs, and everyday we learn what works and what doesn't when it comes to job hunting.

My colleagues and I work with hundreds of men and women each month from all walks of life, industries, functional special-ties, educational backgrounds, ages, races, ethnicities, and career levels, from blue collar to the most senior executives. These are people who have lost their jobs usually through no fault of their own. They've been the victims of organizational downsizing, restructuring, mergers, or acquisitions. They've seen their positions eliminated as companies tighten their belts and shrink their workforces or even close whole facilities such as manufacturing plants or field offices. Others have witnessed their positions evaporating as the work of an entire department is outsourced overseas. Still others have voluntarily chosen to leave their employers, seeing the opportunity to "take a pack-age" (get paid to leave their job) as a great way to make a fresh start with a new employer or even to change career fields or start a business.

Some are fairly new to the work world and were just starting to get some traction in their careers when the rug was pulled out from under them. Others have been with the same employer for 20 or 30 years or more and haven't written a resume or looked for a job in all that time. Some have been living paycheck to paycheck and need a new job yesterday, and others have generous severance packages, plus savings and stock out the wazoo, and can take all the time they want to find the next perfect challenge.

Whoever the job seeker is and whatever his or her situation may be, there are market-tested strategies, tools, and resources that make the job search go more smoothly and reach a successful conclusion more quickly. The sad reality is that these methods and tools are usually unknown to the average job seeker. It is those *secrets* that I share with you in this book.

Making the most of this book

The *Unofficial Guide to Landing a Job* can be used in either of two ways. First, if you're in a hurry to find a job or need quick advice about a situation you're currently facing in your search, refer to the relevant chapter to find the answers you need. If you don't have any particular urgent need but want to get off on the right foot in your search, make sure that you're on the right track in an active search, or troubleshoot an unsuccessful search, then I recommend you start with Chapter 1 and read the entire book in order. The way this book is organized from the parts, to the chapter order, to the content within each chapter, is based on tried-and-true approaches to job hunting that I know can and do lead to success. Happy hunting.

Special Features

Every book in the Unofficial Guide series offers the following four special sidebars that are devised to help you get things done cheaply, efficiently, and smartly.

1. **Moneysaver:** Tips and shortcuts that will help you save money.

2. **Watch Out!:** Cautions and warnings to help you avoid common pitfalls.

3. **Bright Idea:** Smart or innovative ways to do something; in many cases, the ideas listed here will help you save time or hassle.

4. **Quote:** Anecdotes from real people who are willing to share their experiences and insights.

We also recognize your need to have quick information at your fingertips, and have provided the following comprehensive sections at the back of the book:

1. **Appendix:** Lists of Action Verbs and some Sample Resumes to help you make the best impression possible.

2. **Index**

More information online

In addition to the special features listed above, we have posted additional useful information online at www.wiley.com/go/ michelletullier.

1. **Getting Organized and Planning Your Action:** Information about separating friend from foe as you assemble a job search support team, why you need a financial plan for your search, how to set up "job search central," and making the most of your time.

2. **Honing Your Communication Skills and Tools:** Learn about the power of language in your search, managing your mouth to deliver the right message, presenting your image from the inside out, business etiquette in brief, writing in plain English, and making the most of email communication.

3. **More Self-Marketing Tools:** Find out about why you need a business card even when you're not employed, making your references work for you in more ways than you thought, biographies and marketing briefs for the executive edge, and making a splash with a job search portfolio.

4. **What to Do When Nothing Seems to Work:** Learn how to develop a cast-iron stomach for rejection, troubleshoot a job search that's going nowhere, recharge a stalled search even when you think you've completely run out of fuel, and go to Plan B.

5. **After Landing:** Read about why how you leave your old job is as important as how you start the new one, the importance of updating your network and keeping it going, practical tips for shutting down "job search central," ways to transition smoothly into your new role, and critical things to do in the first 90 days of your new job.

6. **Passing Muster: Tests, Observation, and Other Ways You'll Be Assessed:** Information on observation assessment, phychological testing, drug testing, and physical examinations.

7. **Resource Guide:** Names and addresses to enhance your job search.

8. **Recommended Reading List:** A comprehensive bbiliography on such topics as career choice, communication, negotiation, portfolios, and much more.

9. **Professional and Trade Associations:** Names, phone numbers, and websites where you can find additional profession-specific information.

PART I

What You Need to Know About Getting Hired

Twenty Secrets of Successful Job Seekers

What is it that makes some job searches hum along as well as a finely tuned sports car while others cough and sputter, barely lurching out of the driveway? In the career transition firm where my colleagues and I coach thousands of job seekers each year, we see all kinds of searches. We see job seekers who secure so many interviews they can barely juggle the scheduling and who end up with multiple offers to choose from in no time. We see others whose searches drag on with no end in sight. They struggle to get even one interview; their phone calls don't get returned; and when they do finally land interviews, no offers materialize. Are these job seekers less qualified than the more successful ones? Usually not. Is it just lousy luck? Not really. The disparity often is linked to critical differences in the attitude, focus, tools, and strategies (or lack thereof) of the two types of job seekers.

A (True) Tale of Two Job Seekers

Melinda was a technology trainer with strong credentials seeking a position in software training. Donna was a technology trainer with strong credentials seeking the same. Every time Melinda came in for career coaching to help with her search, she was glum, negative, unkempt in her appearance, and never smiled. Her search dragged on for months, and she became increasingly worried about money. She kept plugging away, sending unsolicited résumés to companies and tossing résumés onto the Internet, but nothing came of her efforts. Every suggestion from myself or my fellow consultants for how to jumpstart Melinda's search, including networking more, was met with a "yeah, but." Meanwhile, Donna's search had been dragging on even longer—over a year—and she, too, was worried about money. Even though she had her down moments as anyone would, Donna tried to stay positive. She smiled. She accepted advice willingly and thanked people for their help. She networked. She kept herself well groomed even when she didn't feel like looking good. Well, Donna and Melinda happened to end up interviewing with the same company—a software developer looking to hire several new trainers. Who landed one of those jobs? Donna, of course. Melinda eventually did land a position elsewhere but wasn't particularly happy with it. Moral of the story? Attitude, courtesy, proactive strategy, and willingness to accept feedback are often more important than credentials and timing.

Certainly economic, geographic, and industry-specific factors also make some job searches more difficult and lengthier than others. In the post-9/11 era, a laid-off middle manager from the airline industry faces a much tougher search than an agile Web developer who's worked for all types of companies from start-up to Fortune 100. Similarly, after the downturn of such industries as telecommunications and manufacturing in the late 1990s and early 2000s, job seekers with all their experience in those sectors would take longer to find work than someone coming out of the more vibrant healthcare field, for example. In any economy a senior executive coming from the narrow tip of the organizational pyramid with a compensation level high in the six-figures, will be at it longer than a more junior job seeker who just needs any old job to pay the rent.

Online Bonus Chapter 4, "What to Do When Nothing Seems to Work," addresses ways to cope with these and other major obstacles that can slow down—or even completely stall—a job search. (Find it at www.wiley.com/go/michelletullier.) Meanwhile, however, let's take an "all things being equal approach." Let's assume that you have two job seekers with similar backgrounds looking for the same type of position at about the same compensation level in the same industries. What makes one more successful than the other? That's where attitude, focus, tools, and strategy come in.

Job seekers with a positive attitude who are confident in their ability to find work no matter what the odds, who know what they want and can make a case for why they deserve it, who equip themselves with all the best marketing tools and use a smart strategy—those are the ones who are successful. The remainder of this chapter lets you in on 20 secrets of successful job seekers, grouped into the four categories of attitude, focus, tools, and strategy.

Successful job seekers have the right attitude

Countless studies examining the impact of attitude on emotional and physical health have shown that a positive attitude works wonders at reducing stress and staying healthy. In fact, a recent study out of Carnegie-Mellon University even found that people with positive attitudes—energetic, happy, and relaxed—are less likely to catch colds than those who are depressed, nervous, or angry. What do the common cold and a job search have in common? Well, a lot, come to think of it. Both can be stressful, annoying nuisances that won't ever seem to go away.

I've seen so many discouraged job seekers let the process get to them by becoming negative, bitter, and lacking in confidence, which only ends up making the job search last longer and be less successful. However, those who maintain as much of a positive attitude as possible, who feel confident and powerful, and who relax about the whole thing, find that their job hunts go more smoothly and often reach a successful conclusion more quickly.

In addition to problems with a negative attitude or pessimism, some searchers have what might be thought of as simply a "bad attitude." Some job seekers feel a sense of entitlement—the world "owes" them a good job—and may be unrealistic about what type of position they can land and how soon they will find it. These types also don't always show appreciation for the kindness and generosity of others who take time to help them. Even worse are those searchers who go so far as to be dishonest—embellishing their résumés or lying in interviews—to get what they want.

Ways to avoid these common attitudinal pitfalls are covered in the first six of the twenty secrets of successful job seekers, which are as follows:

- Positive in the face of adversity
- I've got the power
- Doin' what comes naturally
- Honesty is the only policy
- I'd like to thank the Academy...
- Realistic expectations are great expectations

Bright Idea

Cognitive psychologists advocate the use of positive "self-talk" to lift your spirits and confidence during rough times. Repeating phrases like, "I am talented and capable" or "I am strong and get results" can reverse feelings of negativism, pessimism, or any other "isms" that might creep into your mind.

#1 Positive in the face of adversity

No one likes a whiner, or someone who even hints at being negative, angry, or bitter. No matter how irritated you are that you've lost your job and are having to look for a new one, you must try to project a positive attitude. If job loss is not the issue, you might be annoyed that you're currently employed in a dull job or lousy company, have a nightmare boss, or whatever circumstance is causing you to have to get out there and pound the pavement. Under those circumstances, too, you must try to embark on your search with energy and enthusiasm.

> 66 Candidates who are considerate, well-prepared, flexible, and positive have many more opportunities available to them. They present themselves as committed to working with me and realistic of what it takes to find a job. 99
>
> —*Lauren Sacks, Managing Partner, CitiStaffing, LLC, New York City*

Still another situation is that of the job seeker who starts out with high hopes and enthusiasm but finds all that waning as the search drags on with no results. Negativism starts to creep in and sabotages a formerly productive job hunt. No matter which situation resonates with you, if any, it is critical that you make every effort to have a positive outlook.

I know how easy it is to say, "Oh, just put on a happy face and be positive," and how much harder it is to actually do it. I've been in your shoes, looking for work when I resented having to do so, and tired of a search that was taking too long and not turning out how I wanted it to. I know how easy it is to slip into a negative mode. It's easy to lose energy, hope, and any sense of enthusiasm. The first secret of successful job seekers, however, is that they are more positive than their counterparts. They project enthusiasm, confidence, and an interest in what they're doing.

How do they do it? There are four tricks to becoming and staying positive, even when you don't feel like it:

Give yourself time to transition

If you're angry, disappointed, or demoralized as you embark on your search, recognize that making a transition into a more positive place in your life takes time. Don't deny the negative feelings. Go ahead and cry, scream, hide under the covers, vent, punch the wall (not too hard!), or do whatever you need to do to get it out. Only then can you start to feel ready to move forward and take action in your search.

Take baby steps

Don't dive headlong into a job hunt expecting to accomplish great things from day one and every day after that. You do have to take action—don't sit back and do nothing—but take action that is realistic and manageable given your less-than-motivated state of mind. Successfully completing one or two things each day—a draft of your résumé or a couple of networking phone calls—is more motivating than overloading your to-do list and not getting enough of it done.

Keep your eye on the prize

Always keep your goals in sight. Of course, your primary goal is to land a new job, a good job. You will most likely have interim goals, however, such as choosing a career direction before you fully launch your search. You may also have goals beyond the new job. You might be aspiring to reach a certain point in your career or to transition into a new industry or field, and the new job you're seeking now will serve as a bridge to that longer term goal. Keeping any of these goals in mind will help motivate you and remind you what all the hard work is for.

Maintain balance in your life

Nothing sends attitude into a tailspin like burnout. Although your job hunt will demand large amounts of your time, make sure to take time to have some fun, relax, and spend time with friends and family. Don't forget about exercise also, which has been proven to serve as nature's own antidepressant. Exercise brings about chemical changes in the brain that relax you and improve your mood, so if you're not doing it already, start now!

#2 I've got the power

The second secret of a successful job search is to realize that you have more power in the process than you think. Most job seekers fall into the trap of thinking that the employers have all the power. After all, they're the ones who make the decision to return your calls or not, to invite you to interview or not, and, of course, to offer you a job or not. Although there's no arguing with those realities, the reality most job seekers aren't aware of is that they, the job seeker, hold much more power over the outcome of those "or not" situations.

You see, employers want to find the right person for the job as badly as you want to find the right job. Even though a given prospective employer, meaning an organization for which you would like to work, might seem like the almighty Oz, the reality is that the human beings responsible for hiring in that organization are worried that they'll choose the wrong person or that

 Watch Out!

Don't get caught in "revision paralysis," thinking that your search will be more successful if only you revise your résumé yet again, practice interviewing one more time, or have yet another person critique your cover letters. It's more likely to be an attitude adjustment that you need.

Bright Idea

To increase your power in interviews, don't wait until the end to ask all your questions. Inquiring about an employer's needs, challenges, and goals enables you to convey how you could be an asset to the organization. The more you ask throughout the interview, the more leverage you acquire.

they won't find the right person quickly enough. They're human beings who lie awake at night worrying that they're costing their employers thousands of dollars in lost productivity by not having an open position filled or worrying that the decision they made that day to hire a certain candidate could be a big mistake. And, you thought you were the only one lying awake at night worried about making a match! They're not Oz, and you're not a girl with ruby slippers. You are both human beings who share a balance of power in the job search-candidate search process.

#3 Doin' what comes naturally

Employers like to hire people they know. That means that getting to an employer through a mutual acquaintance, for example, by networking, is the best way to go. But, it also means something you might not have thought of. It means that even if the employer got to you in the completely opposite way, say through a random search on the Internet, you still must make an effort to have that employer end up feeling like they know you. That may sound like an impossible task, but it's really quite simple: Be yourself.

Most job seekers go into networking appointments and interviews on their best behavior. With shoes polished, smile fresh, and a firm handshake, they greet the prospective employer with a proper, professional demeanor. They start the meeting with polite conversation, dutifully answer questions throughout the meeting, sit with an erect posture, and try to do everything just right. Although there's certainly nothing wrong with being cordial and professional and following the rules, there is a downside. You might come across as insincere, aloof, distant, or just hard to get a read on. You might even appear downright robotic.

Every time you leave a networking meeting or interview, or even when someone finishes reading a job search letter you've written, you want the person you just interacted with to feel like they got to know you. That doesn't mean letting down your guard so much that you come across as too casual or cavalier. It simply means being down-to-earth, personable, genuine, and even humorous when appropriate. Assuming the real you is a nice person, let the real you come through!

#4 Honesty is the only policy

Setting and maintaining the highest standards for personal integrity throughout your job search is not optional. Every move you make during your search is a reflection of how you would operate as an employee if hired. Do not even think about lying or merely stretching the truth, whether in your résumé, on an employment application, in an interview, or during a networking conversation. In recent years a number of stories have made the headlines about prominent figures lying on their résumés and then enduring the embarrassing situation of having their lies revealed after they're on the job. As a result, employers have become more stringent than ever about checking references to verify that your claims are true.

Even if you could never imagine committing such an egregious sin as claiming a degree you never earned or listing a job you never held, it's very easy for people who are usually honest and sincere to get caught up in the "I-must-land-a-job-at-all-costs" mentality and find themselves embellishing the truth to a dangerous level. If you can't back up facts and figures on your résumé and can't live up to claims you make in interviews, you will sorely regret your lapses of integrity. It just isn't worth it. Stick with the high road.

Watch Out!

Just because I advocate total honesty in your search, don't go so far as to shoot yourself in the foot by volunteering negative information about your past unnecessarily. Stay tight-lipped about any skeletons in your career history closet until someone makes a direct inquiry into them. Then be candid about them.

#5 I'd like to thank the Academy...

If you do your search right, you'll end up having a lot of people to thank, both throughout the search and after landing. The reason I say, "if you do it right," is that the best way to conduct a search is to involve large numbers of people. From the family and friends who will be your support system, to the career coaching professionals who'll provide advice, to the recruiters who'll connect you to job leads, to the many and varied people who make up the professional network that you will tap into, your search will be far from a solitary effort.

You will be amazed how helpful most people will be in your search. The old idea of "what goes around comes around" is very much at work when you set out to look for a job. Chances are, the people you seek help from got a leg up themselves when they were last in need of career assistance. They know what it's like to be in need of ideas and leads, not to mention a shoulder to lean on, when looking for a job and are usually more than happy to be on the giving end of the support this time.

Many of the people who help you will be very busy and have lots of higher priorities on their plate than your job hunt. Nevertheless, they will go out of their way to find the time to help you. No one owes you a job, no one is obligated to help you, but they will. I can make few guarantees when dispensing job search advice, but one I have no qualms about making is that I guarantee you will be incredibly amazed and pleased by how many people—many of whom barely know you—will be willing to go out on a limb to help with your job search. These people deserve your thanks. No question about it.

Moneysaver

When you want to send a gift to someone who has gone above and beyond to help with your search but money's tight, consider sending a basket of gourmet food or luxurious bath products from Wine Country Gift Baskets (www.wine countrygiftbaskets.com or 800-324-2793). Their site is unique in that it has a broader range of sizes and prices than most, and the quality is great.

Showing your appreciation can be as simple and quick as a brief note sent by email or a typed or handwritten letter or note sent by mail. For cases in which someone has really gone beyond the call of duty, you might want to send a small gift to show an extra degree of appreciation. Detailed suggestions for thank you notes and appropriate gifts are discussed in both Chapter 9, "Networking," and Chapter 15, "Clinching the Deal."

#6 Realistic expectations are great expectations

Successful job seekers are realistic about what they can land and when they'll find it. That doesn't mean they can't set the bar high, aiming for the best possible job in the best possible time-frame. I would never advocate that you settle for second best. The mistake too many job seekers make, however, is to be unrealistic about what they can get and when, as well as who's going to get it for them.

In an effective job hunt, you conduct sufficient research to know which industries or specific employers in the marketplace need what you have to offer. Through that research, you learn what is realistic for you to expect in the way of salary and other forms of compensation as well as level of position or title you could expect. You'll also become better informed about how long it is likely to take you to find work in a particular industry, functional area, or type of employer. Ways to conduct this research online, through print resources, and by talking to people are discussed in Chapter 9 and in Chapter 7, "Where Will You Find Your Job?" with salary research discussed specifically in

Chapter 15. Through all this, as a successful job seeker, you will always remember that *you* are the only person who can get you a job. Expecting anyone else to do it for you is unrealistic.

Successful job seekers have focus

Focus is one of the most misunderstood concepts in job searching. Most people assume that being focused means having a very precise job target in mind. They equate focus with knowing exactly what you want to do, right down to a label. "I'm seeking a position as a Director of Product Development," for example. Well, what happens if a particular company needs a Vice President of Product Management, and you would be well qualified for the position? Or, what if another employer uses the term "business development" or "marketing" for what you think of as product development? There is such a thing as being too focused. Whether you communicate your focus through an objective statement on your résumé, in a cover letter, or when speaking with people, there is a danger in labeling your focus too narrowly.

Instead, you need to define focus more broadly, but at the same time very precisely. I know that sounds confusing, so allow me to explain. Having focus in a job search simply means that you know what you have to offer and what you are looking for. It means that you can communicate in your résumé, letters, networking, and interviews exactly what marketable assets you offer to an employer and exactly what you are looking for in a job, a work environment, and an organization. You don't have to put a label on it. You don't have to be able to say, "I want to be a [fill in the blank]." You do have to have a laser sharp focus on what you bring to the table and what you need. That's where the precision comes in. The focus is broad in that you might be open to a few different job titles, types of employers, or sets of responsibilities.

#7 Know what you want

A critical step in attaining focus is to know what you want. Keeping in mind that you don't need to put narrow labels on what you're seeking, your task is to paint a general picture of what you're seeking. You must identify the types of responsibilities and activities that you want your new job to encompass and to be able to describe the type of work environment, organizational culture, colleagues, and bosses with whom you will best function. Your task is also to take stock of the internal and external rewards you need—things like moral fulfillment, a short commute, work-life balance, or a certain level of compensation, to name only a few examples.

In Chapter 3, "Marketing You, the Product," you'll have an opportunity to do some self-assessment to take an inventory of your interests, motivated skills, values, needs, and more. From there, you'll be better able to answer the question you're likely to face often while networking and interviewing: "So, what are you looking for?"

#8 Stand out from the pack

Successful job seekers know how to set themselves apart from the pack. When networking and interviewing, they know how to describe their background and strengths in a way that not only doesn't make the listener's eyes glaze over but causes people to sit up and listen. They distinguish themselves. As a career counselor, I often begin sessions by having clients tell me a little about themselves—particularly their work history—so I can know enough about them to help them. I consistently find that even the most articulate, personable people unwittingly describe their qualifications in a jargon-laden, detached manner, forcing me to ask the follow-up question, "Yes, but what do you do?" I get no sense of who they are—their passions, proficiencies, and preferences. I can't tell what makes them uniquely them. When talking about their work history, they often sound as if they're reading an official job description straight out of human resources, not describing an endeavor in which they have spent most of their waking hours.

The same is true in written communication as well. Too many cover letters focus on how someone meets the basic qualifications

The Power of a Customized Résumé

Distinguishing yourself from the competition is often a matter of going the extra mile to tailor your marketing materials to each targeted job or organization. Take the case of Frank, a job seeker with a background as a lawyer, corporate trainer, and human resources manager. Frank was downsized from his position in human resources with a major company. As he began his search, he was open to any position related to any aspects of his background, as long as the work involved managing diversity programs or preventing or fighting employment discrimination, as that was his primary area of expertise and something he believed strongly about. To market himself best, Frank created five versions of his résumé. There was the résumé for legal positions in corporations; one for work as a lawyer in a law firm; one focusing solely on corporate training; one emphasizing human resources; and another with equal emphasis on training and HR. Even beyond those five basic versions, Frank often tailored the content of each slightly to highlight or de-emphasize various aspects of his background as relevant to the job or employer at hand. He consistently received positive feedback about how focused his résumés were and ended up landing a position with which he was very happy (in human resources, managing diversity programs).

rather than making the letter stand out with its tone and marketable content. In the online Bonus Chapter 3, "More Self-Marketing Tools," you can learn the best ways to distinguish yourself in your written marketing tools.

A final way to distinguish yourself is with your strategy. Job seekers who make the extra effort to be innovative and resourceful in the way in which they look for jobs and approach employers are the ones who stand out from the pack. Take online job hunting, for example. Most jobs posted online are likely to draw hundreds, if not thousands, of applicants. Lazy job hunters apply for lots of positions online and sit back waiting for the offers to pour in. But, resourceful job hunters distinguish themselves from the competition by trying to network their way into an organization in addition to applying online. They also take the time to include a cover letter customized to that position and employer and to tailor their résumé to fit the situation. These and other strategies are discussed in more depth in Chapter 10, "Online Job Hunting."

#9 Build a case with asset statements

Although employers are certainly interested in knowing what your responsibilities and day-to-day tasks are or have been on past jobs, which skills and abilities you have, and what credentials you hold, such as degrees or certifications, they are usually more interested in hearing about your accomplishments. They care more about your past performance at a given task and the results you brought about, than about the task itself. By hearing about the outcomes of your past efforts, they can envision how you could be of benefit to them in the future. It's about showing off your assets.

In Chapter 4, "Your Marketing Plan's Secret Weapon," you'll learn how to put together asset statements that help you convey your skills, knowledge, and positive personal qualities in a way that is relevant and meaningful for a prospective employer.

Successful job seekers have the best tools

Whether it's a home repair project or open heart surgery, everyone knows how important it is to have tools that are handy, in good working order, and are the right ones for the job. Well, a job search is the same. Too many job seekers slap together a quick résumé and call it a day. But, there's much more to effective job hunting than a slipshod résumé. Not only does the résumé need to be a powerful marketing document, a host of other self-marketing tools also go into your job search toolkit. By taking care of these from the outset, you'll get off to the right start in your search and won't find yourself playing catch-up as the need for each arises.

Checklist 1.1 shows what a complete job search toolkit would contain. You won't necessarily need to use all items on the list, but you'll need most. (The optional items tend to be a bio, which is usually required only for executives; letters of recommendation, which are not necessary if you have a list of references who can be reached by telephone; and a portfolio, which is helpful but not essential.) All of these items are discussed in Chapter 5, as well as defined briefly later in this chapter.

Checklist 1.1. A Complete Job Search Toolkit

- Resumé(s)
- Self-marketing sound bite—written
- Self-marketing sound bite—spoken
- Job seeker business card
- Reference list
- Letters of recommendation
- Bio
- Marketing brief
- Approach letter / Cover letter template(s)
- Follow-up letter template(s)
- Portfolio

#10 Make your résumé a marketing document

Chapter 5 covers résumés in depth, including the best overall strategies for developing a résumé as well as a step-by-step guide to creating one. For now, you need to be aware only that a strong résumé can make or break your search if you end up using many nonpersonal job search methods, such as direct mail campaigns, answering ads online or in newspapers, or circulating the résumé at job fairs or among recruiters. In those cases, you are not already a known quantity to the reader, so your résumé serves as the only introduction of you. It, therefore, must be easy to read, hit only the highlights (not every detail of your career history), and present information that is relevant to the employer and the position in question.

> **❝** If a candidate can't get his or her point across concisely in a résumé, or if the résumé is too cluttered and long, I won't read it. I receive so many résumés that I must be able to skim it in 10–20 seconds and glean the most critical information. **❞**
>
> —*John, Senior Corporate Recruiter*

If you find that most of your job search activities center around networking, your résumé is important but becomes a little less critical. You are more likely to be introducing yourself to new people by phone, email, or in person, or re-introducing yourself to people who already know you and don't need to see your résumé right away, if at all. In those cases, a marketing brief can be more effective. Marketing briefs are defined in the "Assemble a Complete Self-Marketing Package" section of this chapter and are discussed in more detail in online Bonus Chapter 3.

 Watch Out!

Résumés for electronic transmission (sent within an email rather than as an attachment, or uploaded to a Web site) are often referred to as "text only" résumés. This is a dangerous misnomer. There's much more to creating an eRésumé than saving it in text-only format. Be sure to read Chapter 10 for more information.

Successful job seekers also have an electronic résumé, or "eRésumé." The eRésumé is in a different technical format than the traditional résumé, a format that ensures the content will be readable when it is transmitted electronically. You'll need an eRésumé whenever someone says they won't accept an attached document and must receive the résumé within the body (the message field) of the email. The eRésumé is also used when you post your résumé online in a résumé bank or upload it to a Web site to apply for a position in a job bank. The eRésumé also works well when you know, or suspect, that your résumé will be scanned electronically to go into a résumé database rather than read initially by a person. When and how to use an eRésumé, not to mention how to develop one, can be confusing, but everything you need to know to demystify the process is discussed in Chapter 5.

#11 Assemble a complete self-marketing package

Effective job seekers realize that there is more to self-marketing than a résumé. Depending on the type of search you conduct and the type of positions you're seeking, you will also need some other self-marketing tools.

Job seeker business card

Every job seeker needs a business card to distribute their names and contact information to people they meet during the search. It's tacky to use the card from your former employer, and going out without any card means that you end up scribbling your name and contact information on scraps of paper. Not only is that not very convenient or professional, those scraps of paper are more likely to get lost than a business card would. Your job seeker business card makes it easier for people to get in touch with you and can serve as a mini-résumé if you add a tagline under your name or some brief text on the back that highlights what you have to offer and what you're seeking.

Reference list and/or letters of recommendation

You definitely will need a list of people who can be contacted to serve as references for you, to verify your past employment, and if company policy permits, to comment on what you were like as an employee. You might also have letters of recommendation from past bosses, coworkers, customers, or others who have been pleased with your work. These are wonderful to have, but you'll find most prospective employers will not put much stock in the letters and instead will want to speak directly to those giving the recommendations. If you do have a lot of strong letters of recommendation, you may want to develop a portfolio to keep them in (see "Portfolios" later in this list).

Bio

For more senior-level positions, you might find that a biography written in the third person is an effective way to communicate your qualifications and credentials. Some prospective employers might even ask for a bio, so it's a good idea to have one on hand if you are among the senior management or executive ranks.

Marketing brief

While networking to explore the market or generate job leads, you might find that a marketing brief is more useful than your résumé. The marketing brief contains elements of your résumé, such as a summary of qualifications and brief overview of your work history, as well as a few examples of accomplishment statements. But, it also includes information that the résumé doesn't cover, such as specific organizations you're targeting or examples of types of industries, positions, or employers you're targeting. Whereas a résumé is a document that is most often used to screen you in or out, the marketing brief is a document that the reader can use to see how he or she can best help you in your search.

Letter template(s)

You'll undoubtedly be writing a lot of letters throughout your job search. Some will be brief emails, others formal printed letters, and some casual handwritten notes. Some will serve as approach letters that introduce you to a networking contact or prospective employer, proposing that they speak with you about opportunities in a given field, educate you about the marketplace, or give advice about your search. Other letters will be what are usually known as cover letters—written correspondence that accompanies your résumé when applying for an actual position. Still others will be follow-up letters, thanking people for their time in networking appointments or interviews or trying to clinch the deal when you're in the running for a particular job.

Each letter needs to be customized to the particular situation and target reader, so you will not have one approach letter and one cover letter in your toolkit. What you can have, though, is a template form of each letter—a basic form letter that you can tailor, customize, and personalize as needed. Having this template will save you many headaches and hassles as you get into the thick of your search and have to start churning out letter after letter or email after email, often under tight time pressure. With the templates, you won't have to reinvent the wheel each time.

Portfolio

To wow a prospective employer or networking contact, you might want to develop and use a portfolio. Portfolios are collections of documents that advertise what you have to offer. Put together in a loose-leaf binder, two-pocket folder, or bound inexpensively, portfolios may contain: your résumé; letters of recommendation from bosses; letters of praise from clients or coworkers; writing samples (if relevant); other project/work samples; copies of diplomas, licenses, or certificates; press clippings featuring you or your work; and anything else that would market you well for the type of jobs you are trying to land.

All of the self-marketing tools described here are discussed in more detail, including tips for developing them, in the online Bonus Chapter 3.

#12 Have a self-marketing sound bite

The self-marketing sound bite is a brief pitch that gives a quick overview of your background and qualifications. It can be a written version that becomes one of the building blocks of your résumé and job search correspondence, or a spoken version—something you say as a way of introducing yourself on a cold call, in networking meetings, or to answer that dreaded interview question, "Tell me about yourself." When spoken, the sound bite can take anywhere from 15 to 90 seconds to say, depending on what is appropriate for the situation.

A self-marketing sound bite is an absolutely essential item in your job search toolkit, but most job seekers don't have one. Every time they pick up the phone to introduce themselves to someone with whom they would like to network, they have to think of what to say about themselves in the first 15 to 20 seconds of the call. Every time an employer asks them to open the interview by telling a little about themselves, they ramble on circuitously for five minutes or more. By scripting and practicing a self-marketing sound bite from Day One of your search, you'll save yourself lots of time and worry after your search is underway and will communicate much more effectively than those who try to wing it.

#13 Communicate effectively

All the best tools in the world are worthless if you don't know how to use them. The self-marketing sound bite is one critical element of your communication, but there's more to effective job search communication than simply scripting and memorizing a brief personal pitch. Successful job seekers know that communicating well, both orally and in writing, is key.

If you don't speak and write clearly with proper grammar and syntax, and in a coherent, articulate manner, no one will

Bright Idea

If seeking jobs in a career field or industry in which you've never worked, try to speak the "language" of the new field rather than using jargon unique to your old field. You'll sound like more of an insider.

pay attention to what you're saying because they'll be too distracted by how you're saying it. This particular problem is a tough one to deal with, not because the solutions to it are difficult, but because most people don't even realize they have a problem. If you are a poor writer or an inarticulate speaker, chances are no one has had the nerve to tell you so. You must take it upon yourself to determine whether there is a problem—and then to fix it. Online Bonus Chapter 2, "Honing Your Communication Skills and Tools," discusses how to find out whether your communication techniques and style are holding you back and how to improve them. Also, don't forget that much of communication is nonverbal, so having the right image from attire and grooming to body language is critical.

Successful job seekers have a strategy

I have seen even certified project managers, chief administrative officers, and top-notch executive assistants, to name only a few, approach a job search in an alarmingly haphazard way. They throw together a résumé, apply for a few jobs online, and phone some people they know and call it networking. The next day they might do a little research, send out a résumé or two, and call a couple more people. These job seekers are the same people who, when on the job, map out detailed project plans and schedules, assemble major resources and tools before starting a project, and use careful tracking and record-keeping methodologies. So, what happens when they conduct their job searches? They don't equate looking for a job with coordinating or managing a large professional project, but that's what a job search is. It's a major, complex project that requires planning, organizing, and strategy. Successful job seekers know this and know that having a careful strategy works.

#14 Don't try to go it alone

Job searching can be a very solitary activity. You don't take your best friend, spouse, or mother into an interview. (And, if you were thinking of doing so, think again. If someone has to drive you to an interview, have them wait in the car or walk around the block!) You don't always have someone holding your hand when you make a cold call to someone whose name you've been given as a possible networking contact. You don't have a career coach looking over your shoulder helping you through tough salary negotiations in a prospective employer's office. It's just you against all the potential employers out there. As a result, the job search process can be lonely, frustrating, and, at times, confusing. The good news is you're not on your own to get through it.

By turning to your network of friends, family, and professional colleagues, as well as experts with whom you might consult, your job search success will be greatly enhanced. Plus, the process will be more manageable and even enjoyable as members of your network can provide emotional support and encouragement throughout your search.

As you prepare to market yourself, members of your network can help you take stock of your skills and strengths as you prepare asset statements (as described in Chapter 4). Some people need an objective third party to point out their positive qualities or to recognize their achievements, so consulting people who know you well is key.

Networking is also useful in the research stage, whether you speak to people to help you make career choices, explore a particular field or industry, or identify job leads. Also, as you'll see in Chapter 11, "Preparing for Interviews," interview preparation requires more than reading a company's annual report and glancing at their Web site. You have to talk to people who know anything about your target employers. Getting the inside scoop on your target employers is just one benefit of networking. You might also find that someone you know—or can get to know— knows someone at the place where you'll be interviewing. Being able to drop a relevant, respected name during an interview is a sure way to jump to the head of the class of appli- cants (as long as the name- dropping is not done in a pompous manner).

> 66 I use not only all the brains I have but all I can borrow. 99
>
> —Woodrow Wilson

Your network can also serve as a useful sounding board during the job search. Invariably, at times you will have questions about your overall technique and strategy. Having input from others can help you make good decisions and avoid taking wrong turns.

#15 Work hard and persist

Good ol' hard work is a key element of your strategy. Most job seekers whose searches drag on for too long are not putting in enough time and effort. Landing a job is hard work. It takes a lot of hours per week, along with much concentrated effort and focus. There's no magic to this secret of successful job seekers: just think back to times when you've had to work really hard to reach a goal and operate the same way with your search.

In addition to your hard work, be sure to be persistent. A common problem of less successful job seekers is that they give up too easily. You don't want to be a pest or pushy, but assertively following through, staying in touch, and otherwise communi- cating with people in your network and prospective employers is not just appropriate, it's critical. I cannot count the number of times—thousands at least—that I have witnessed job seekers reluctant to call an employer they had expected to hear from already or to loop back with a networking contact who may have forgotten about them. Out of sight is out of mind, and there are also countless examples of job seekers who land the job because they happen to be the ones who call or email to remind the employer of their interest and check on the status of a hiring decision. Given two equally qualified candidates, the job offer often goes to the one who follows up.

#16 Do sweat the small stuff

By sweating the small stuff, I don't mean you should agonize over matters beyond your control or work yourself into a frenzy because you messed up on something insignificant. I do mean, however, that you need to be detail-oriented, organized, and just generally have your act together during your job search.

Your behavior during every aspect of your search, with every person you encounter, is a reflection of how you might conduct yourself on the job. Besides your résumé, references, and account of your accomplishments, recruiters and employers must rely on observations of your behavior as an indicator of how you'll act on the job. So, you'd better have your act together during all encounters no matter how insignificant some of them might seem.

Some of the ways to convey that you have your act together include being organized and punctual, following instructions, and living up to your commitments. Getting your foot in the door to a prospective employer, completing the interview process, and negotiating the terms of employment are like any business transaction. Documents are faxed and mailed, emails are sent, voice mail messages are left, appointments are set, instructions are given, and loose ends must be attended to. For example, you may have an initial screening interview by phone and promise to email a résumé after that conversation. Or you might have an on-site interview and have to follow up with additional information such as a college or graduate school transcript, phone numbers of your references, or a sample of your work. You might apply for a position online and find that there are specific instructions for how to send your résumé electronically and what information to include in a cover letter. If you are late in doing any of these things, if you do them incorrectly, or if you don't do them at all, you seriously jeopardize your candidacy.

Not having your act together is not only inconvenient and annoying for the prospective employer, it also has implications for how you would handle the job in question. Many workplaces these days are busier than ever, requiring employees to handle multiple tasks and put out fires while also engaging in long-range planning. If you can't handle the relatively simple challenges of the job search, what message are you sending employers about your ability to handle the job itself?

#17 The danger of passive search methods

The best job search strategy is one that involves getting out and about, to see and be seen, while communicating with human beings. Unsuccessful job seekers tend to rely more on the passive methods, spending long hours at the computer applying for jobs online or licking hundreds of envelopes hoping that a job will come from a mailing of unsolicited résumés to a list of randomly targeted employers. Although online job hunting and even direct mail campaigns have a place in a good job search (if done strategically), most jobs are found through some form of personal contact. A friend or neighbor puts you in touch with someone who's hiring. You attend a professional association meeting and develop a whole new network of contacts who lead you to positions. Or you get active in an online networking forum where people from all around the country (or the world) point you in the right direction. However you define it, it's networking, and it works. In Chapter 9, you'll find a more in-depth discussion of how to network actively as a key element in your job search.

#18 Creative and resourceful thinking

In addition to getting up off your duff to go out among people who can help you land a job, another important element of your job search strategy is to call upon every creative and resourceful bone in your body—or synapse in your brain. Instead of seeing dead ends, see possibilities. There is always a way to get to the information, people, and places you need to reach. Let's say, for example, that you want to break into a particular company but don't know anybody there and don't know anybody who knows anybody there. Instead of crossing that item off your wish list, be creative and resourceful. Look up the officers of the company on their Web site, then do a keyword search to find out anything you can about those people. Find out what boards they sit on and which nonprofits are their pet community projects. Find out what they've written and where they speak publicly. Find out everything you can about them! Then, go back to your network and see whether anyone you know has any connection with the people and places with which your target is connected. Still reaching a dead-end? Then find something the target person has written and published in print or online. Or find something written about him or her, such as an announcement in the press about a promotion or special project. Read it and write to the person with congratulations about the promotion or a comment about their article or project. Then ask for a few minutes of their time to seek advice about your search and to get their insights into their profession or industry. Don't ask them for a job (at least not yet)! Follow up with a phone call or email until you get an answer. May sound like a stretch, but it works. All it takes is some willingness to go out on a creative limb.

#19 Don't sell yourself, consult

If there is one phrase I'd like to banish from the vocabulary of all job seekers, it's "sell myself." Too many job seekers think that the candidates who land the jobs are the ones who sell themselves the hardest. They see selling themselves as being the most convincing or most persuasive, or being the ones who shout the loudest or use the best gimmicks. Not true. Have you ever considered buying a product only to be turned off by a pushy salesperson who just tried to sell, sell, sell, without ever asking what you want? That's why selling yourself in a job search is not the strategy to use.

Bright Idea

If you find yourself saying, "I'm going to be interviewed for a job," switch that to, "I'm going to speak to some people about how I might be able to help them reach their goals." You go from being the powerless job seeker at the mercy of the prospective employer to being like a consultant who has valuable expertise and knowledge to offer.

Instead, you need to put a consultant's hat on. What do consultants do? They go into a situation where there are problems and challenges, assess the needs and desires of the client, and develop solutions to fix the problems and overcome the challenges. That's what a job search is all about. Employers have needs, and you have the knowledge, expertise, and skill to meet those needs. It's as simple as that.

#20 Prepare, practice, and practice some more

At times it can seem that communicating with prospective employers or with network contacts is like speaking a foreign language. You will find yourself talking about your experience, strengths, and goals in ways that you probably don't do in the course of a routine day. The only way to speak a new language effortlessly is to practice it. Winging it usually doesn't cut it.

To be a successful job seeker, you must do your homework before every networking meeting and interview. And, you must not only prepare what you are going to say and how you'll conduct yourself while saying it, but you also need to practice. Whether you simply practice your replies out loud (perhaps in front of a mirror) or formally in a videotaped mock interview, you must simulate the networking meetings and interview process in some way before they actually take place.

It is important, however, that you not go overboard with your practice and become over-rehearsed. Practicing means that you are getting used to some of the communication and behavior that might be called for in your search. Over-rehearsed means that you have a script to memorize and an act to perform. Remember that an interview is not a theatrical production. Be yourself. If you write scripts for your replies to anticipated questions or for your self-marketing sound bite, get to the point where you're so comfortable with the script that you can ad-lib casually to sound more natural and unrehearsed.

Twenty secrets summed up

Qualifications, timing, and luck often play less of a role in landing a job than you might have thought. What really makes the difference between you and the competition is attitude, focus, tools, and strategy. Within those four categories of differentiators, the 20 secrets are as follows:

- Positive in the face of adversity
- I've got the power
- Doin' what comes naturally
- Honesty is the only policy
- I'd like to thank the Academy...
- Realistic expectations are great expectations
- Know what you want
- Stand out from the pack
- Build a case with asset statements
- Make your résumé a marketing document
- Assemble a complete self-marketing package
- Have a self-marketing sound bite
- Communicate effectively
- Don't try to go it alone
- Work hard and persist
- Do sweat the small stuff
- The danger of passive search methods

- Creative and resourceful thinking
- Don't sell yourself, consult
- Prepare, practice, and practice some more

No matter what sort of job you're hoping to land in any industry or market sector, and whether you're entry-level or a chief officer, being clued in to these secrets of successful job seekers will dramatically improve your chances of success.

Just the facts

- Having a positive outlook, including feeling powerful and confident, as well as being yourself and always being honest, can make the difference between you and an equally well-qualified candidate.

- Distinguish yourself from the competition by taking stock of what you want and what you have to offer and being prepared to convey your marketable qualities with asset statements.

- Don't stop at the résumé when preparing the tools of your search; be sure to include a full range of self-marketing items in your job search toolkit.

- Assemble a solid network and support team to help you through your search rather than trying to go it alone.

- Employ a strategy that is carefully thought out, detail-oriented, proactive, and creative.

GET THE SCOOP ON...
The qualifications all employers want you to have
▪ How to be seen as a value-added candidate ▪
What employers mean when they say you're "not
the right fit" ▪ The six styles of decision-making
in hiring and what they mean for you

How Employers Think

If ever there was a time when the ability to read minds would come in handy, it's during a job search. Knowing what's on the mind of any given employer would certainly make the process a whole lot easier. Assuming that you won't be waking up suddenly in possession of telepathic powers tomorrow morning, this chapter is your best bet for understanding how employers think. Of course, there are individual differences in what any given employer is looking for, but the experiences of scores of job seekers who've gone before you have proven that there are plenty of common threads on which you can base your strategy when dealing with prospective employers. It basically boils down to understanding the criteria on which most selection processes are based and how hiring decisions are made.

What employers are looking for

Although the specific requirements for any given position will obviously vary, most anyone trying to fill an opening is essentially seeking a satisfactory answer to the following three basic questions:

- **Will you add value?** Employers want to know that you have much more than the basic qualifications to do the job. They want to know that you will make a real difference— a contribution that adds value above and beyond simply carrying out your everyday duties and responsibilities.

- **Will you fit in?** Can you be one of us? Can you get along with your colleagues, work in harmony with the organization's values, and present the image we want in our employees? Along with these issues of cultural and personality fit, employers also want to know whether you will fit into the organizational structure and into the budget allocated for compensation.

- **Will you make the commitment?** Employers want to know that you are coming to them with your eyes wide open— that you know what you're getting into. They want to discern whether this is the job you really want or whether you're just talking with them to get interviewing practice. They want to know that you will commit to being with them long enough to make their investment in you pay off (yes, hiring an employee is an investment) and that you'll be focused enough while there to get the job done.

To find answers to these questions, employers and recruiters take a variety of approaches. Rarely would they ask these three questions point-blank. They're more likely to gather clues from your résumé, approach letters, the interview process, and all other oral and written communication you have with them. Forget Big Brother—employers watch you every step of the way in the hiring process to determine whether you will add value, fit in, and make the commitment.

Will you add value?

Employers don't hire people to warm seats. They hire people who can jump into the hot seat and be producers and contributors. That means having the skills, experience, and potential not only to handle the basic job responsibilities but also to add value that will help the employer solve problems, improve the bottom line, gain or retain a competitive advantage, and reach goals.

The value that you bring to a prospective employer can be broken down into several factors: content knowledge, transferable skills, personal qualities, and experience. Let's look at these factors in more detail and examine the rationale for why employers care about them.

Content knowledge

The content knowledge that you bring to a job consists of the subjects that you know something about and in which you have some expertise. If you're applying for a pharmaceutical sales job, for example, then the relevant content knowledge you have to offer might be an academic background in chemistry or work experience as a nurse. Sales experience, if any, would be your transferable skill (discussed in greater detail in the next section). Similarly, if you are seeking a job with a public relations firm that specializes in promoting clients in the securities industry, then the employer would be pleased to learn that you understand the difference between a bond and an option and that you can converse intelligently about finance in general. In that case, your content knowledge lies in finance, and your transferable skills might be such functions as writing and media relations.

Technical skills are also a part of content knowledge. Knowing how to build a spreadsheet in Microsoft Excel, manage a database in DB2, or design a Web site in HTML are all examples of content knowledge (the knowledge being Excel, DB2, and HTML). The transferable skills that go hand-in-hand with the content knowledge are general software proficiency, database management, and Web design.

At a minimum, possessing knowledge of certain content areas assures an employer that you know enough to do the job in question. More important, however, is that your knowledge can help you make a real contribution to the organization above and beyond your basic job duties. Your knowledge base might enable you to bring innovation and insight to your new

Watch Out!

Don't assume that if you have all the required qualifications for a job, you have a very good shot at landing it. There may be hundreds of candidates who are just as qualified. To make it to the short list, you have to show how you can add value.

employer, two benefits highly valued as organizations try to thrive in an increasingly competitive marketplace. Chapter 3, "Marketing You, the Product," helps you identify your own content knowledge areas.

Transferable skills

It probably comes as no surprise that the changing structure of organizations over the past several years has brought about a need for employees with diverse, flexible skill sets. In addition to having specialized knowledge (as described in the previous section), you must have skills that are versatile enough to be of value in—or transferable to—a variety of roles and situations.

The transferable skills can be thought of as the skills that you might preface with the phrase "I can..." Chapter 3 offers many examples of transferable skills and details how to identify yours. The following are just a few examples.

- I can manage projects.
- I can coordinate an event.
- I can improve processes.
- I can write software code.

Transferable skills aren't as industry-specific or role-specific as content knowledge. Note that the previous example doesn't refer to programming which software, or managing any particular type of project, coordinating a particular type of event, or improving a certain type of process. Transferable skills show your versatility—an important trait for work environments and industries in which the pace of change is rapid.

Moneysaver

If you're concerned about lacking particular skills or knowledge, avoid the temptation to sign up for expensive courses or training programs until you've done enough research to know that the skills and knowledge you would acquire are an absolute prerequisite for the job you want.

Transferable skills are especially important if you are changing career fields or industries. In such cases, your content knowledge is likely to be less relevant because it may be too closely linked to your old field. Transferable skills are also useful when you have interviews or networking appointments that are exploratory in nature—that is, when you are not discussing a specific job opening but are meeting with someone to see where you might fit within a given organization.

Personal qualities

Personal qualities are the characteristics that describe you. They might be personality traits, aptitudes, preferences, passions, motivators, drivers, work style—anything that makes you uniquely you. Your personal qualities often are expressed in statements beginning with "I am..." Some examples include the following:

- I am detail-oriented.
- I am a leadership type.
- I am creative.
- I am calm in the face of chaos.
- I am outgoing.
- I am sensitive to others' needs.
- I am physically strong and agile.

As you can see, the personal qualities are not exactly skills; they are the characteristics that enable you to acquire particular skills. This is an important point because many employers want to know that you not only have the skills needed for the immediate job but that you also have the potential to handle the next step in a job—or a future incarnation of it. Your personal qualities are what enable you to adapt to the changing needs of the organization.

As with content knowledge and transferable skills, you'll find more details on assessing your personal qualities in Chapter 3. The objective here is simply for you to be aware of what constitutes the general question of "Will You Add Value?"

Table 2.1 describes more personal qualities, as well as transferable skills, that employers are seeking as a result of trends in today's workplace.

Table 2.1. Workplace Realities and Skills Needed

Trend	Transferable Skills Needed	Personal Qualities Needed
Lean operational and managerial processes	Budgeting, managing people and projects efficiently, systematizing, estimating costs, cutting costs, organizing, doing more with less, streamlining, trouble-shooting, hiring and firing	Resourceful, disciplined, detail-oriented, organized, efficient, effective, quantitative
Interdisciplinary work teams	Communicating effectively, negotiating, resolving conflicts, managing time, prioritizing, project management, leadership, subject matter expertise, training others	Team-oriented, flexible, adaptable, versatile, knowledgeable
Shifting business directions	Business development, sales, making presentations, account management, client development, relationship building, planning	Creative, innovative, resourceful, nimble, agile, seasoned, visionary, innovating, problem-solving, strategic

Trend	Transferable Skills Needed	Personal Qualities Needed
Commitment to diversity	Communicating, negotiating, managing or resolving conflicts, understanding other cultures, supporting others	Open-minded, diplomatic, tactful, patient, flexible, sensitive, tolerant, global in orientation
Less supervision	Managing one's own career development, taking initiative, following through, implementing plans	Independent, self-starter, disciplined
Service and quality	Quality assurance and control, overseeing production, process improvement, customer relations, oral communication, problem-solving	Conscientious, detail-oriented, communicative, articulate, dedicated, ethical

Experience

Employers also make hiring decisions based on your past performance. After all, it's easy to say that you possess a certain skill or personal quality; it's another thing to provide evidence. Your achievements from your work history (and, where relevant, your educational and avocational experiences) provide the proof that you can add value to your next employer.

When discussing your experience with prospective employers, avoid the common pitfall of focusing only on the responsibilities of your current or past jobs. Instead, you must spell out for the employer the skills and strengths you demonstrated in doing that work and the results that came of your actions. In other words, you have to show how you've made contributions in the past and build a case for how you can do it again. In Chapter 4, "Your Marketing Plan's Secret Weapon," you'll find more details on how to build your case with asset statements. For now, just keep in mind that as you begin to market yourself

in your search, you must take stock of your assets and achievements. In the mind of an employer, it is your past patterns of
success and aptitude for future success, not a laundry list of your
past job duties, that make you a safe bet.

Will you fit in?

In an employer's ideal world, all positions would be filled
through personal referral. People like to hire people they know.
Doing so eliminates much of the guesswork involved, making it
easier to predict what the new hire will be like as a person, not
just as a set of skills and experience on a résumé.

You may already be aware that the issue of *fit* is a significant
one when employers are looking for the best candidate for the
job. But, if you are defining "fit" as having the right personality
or as some vague notion of chemistry—as many job seekers do—
then you're overlooking some critical elements of the concept.

Fit means more than just getting along well with the people
you meet during the interview process. It's also more than wearing the right cut of suit or the same color tie as everyone at your
target organization. Personality and appearance are a part of fit,
but you also must have values and a work style that are congruent with the place where you want to work. Plus, you need to
meet some fairly objective criteria such as "Can we afford you?"
and "Do we have a place for you?"

This idea of fit is one of the more subjective variables to
enter into the hiring equation, but it is nonetheless possible to
make those variables more tangible, and therefore, more controllable. When I first began career counseling some years ago,
I worried that there was not much I could do to help clients
address this issue when preparing for interviews. They either
had it—whatever *it* was—or they didn't. The more I spoke with
people on the other side of the hiring desk, however, the more
I realized that there were certain tangible factors within the concept of fit that my clients could address. This seemingly elusive
criterion actually may be broken down into factors that you can
partially control: values, work style, image, and personality.

Values

Just as with individuals, organizations operate from a fundamental set of values that drive their objectives, aspirations, and daily behavior. In your own career, you may value such things as making a certain amount of money, helping society, or being creative. You may place the utmost importance on customer service, innovative problem solving, or producing top-quality products.

Organizations, too, place importance on some actions or results more than others. You might interview one day with a corporation that is obsessed with customer service and the next with a company focused solely on cutting costs. Some organizations' values are clearly stated in their published mission statements or orientation manuals. (Chapter 11, "Preparing for Interviews," discusses ways to research organizations to ascertain their values, among other things.) Be aware, however, that organizations' missions fluctuate and that the "value of the week" is not necessarily reflected in the company literature. You may have to speak to people familiar with the organization, or, ideally, with people who work there. Some values are common to most organizations these days, several of which are listed in Table 2.1 earlier in this chapter.

Work style

A second important element within the concept of fit is the issue of work style. Everything from the hours you expect to work, to whether you keep your office door open (assuming you have an office), to how team-oriented or competitive you are must be consistent with the policies and practices of your target employer. If an employer senses that you expect to leave at five

 Watch Out!

When considering how you fit with an organization's culture, don't forget to take into account the values and style of any outside people and organizations with whom you would be working, such as clients, vendors, consultants, and collaborators.

o'clock most days, but the job calls for significant overtime, then a big red flag has obviously been raised. Consider the following work style issues on which you may or may not be in sync with your target employers.

- **Work ethic**   How seriously do you take your job, and how strong of an allegiance are you willing to make to your employer?

- **Schedule**   What kind of hours do you expect to keep? Are you a clock-watcher ready to leave at the stroke of five, or are you willing to sacrifice nights and weekends for your job?

- **Formality**   Do you fit best into a staid, conservative, and serious office climate, or one in which cartoons adorn cubicles and jokes circulate through email?

- **Team orientation**   Do you believe that more is merrier when tackling a project, or do you prefer to go it alone? Are you collaborative or competitive?

Those are only a few examples of the many factors that can constitute work style. During interviews, be on the lookout for questions or directions in the conversation that indicate the interviewer is trying to discern your work style. Be aware, however, that the best approach to interviewing or any encounter with an employer is to be yourself, and this issue of work style is no exception. If you try to conform to an environment that conflicts too much with your preferred way of working, then you are not likely to be satisfied or successful—even if you *do* land the job.

Image

Work style refers to the way you do your actual work; image is defined as the way you look and the impression you give while doing your work. Employers aren't necessarily looking to hire clones of themselves and their colleagues, but they do usually want to hire people who have a similar air about them. So, one important element that determines whether you seem like you will fit in is that of your image.

Bright Idea

Want to improve your image in one simple step? Smile! As lyrics from *Annie Get Your Gun* advise, "It's what you wear from ear to ear and not from head to toe" that makes the best impression.

Social psychologists have found that the impression you make in about the first seven seconds of an interaction is the lasting one. The way you speak and the way you carry yourself, as well as what you wear, are critical to that first impression. Your accent, speech patterns, tone of voice, and volume of speech are reflections of you—for good or bad. Your comportment—including your posture, pace of walking, and air of confidence (or lack thereof)—also figure into an interviewer's decision about whether you will fit in.

Personality

Related to work style and image is the issue of your personality. The employer has to feel confident that you will get along well with your bosses, subordinates, co-workers, clients, and anyone else connected to the job. Of all the elements within the concept of fit, personality may be the most hit-or-miss. Instead of having to come across as a pleasant and reasonable person, you must convey the particular personality type needed to deal with specific people in that job. Once again, beware of altering your personality to fit the mold that you think a job requires. Your best bet is always to be yourself.

Fitting into the organizational and salary structure

When purchasing a product, you probably make the decision to do so based on both subjective and objective criteria—does this item appeal to me and can I afford it? Employers do the same thing when considering hiring you. They have to know that the salary and related compensation you are seeking—bonuses, benefits, and other perks—are both within the budget they have allocated for the position and in line with the compensation

The Importance of Being Earnestly You

Lydia was in the final round of interviews for a position as Director of Special Projects in the development office of a major nonprofit organization. She knew that the position required her to be extremely assertive to boost the ailing fundraising efforts of the organization. She needed to be politically astute, well-connected, and a tough manager. Lydia not only possessed those qualities, she also was able to present evidence of them in her past career accomplishments.

After three interviews, the pool of candidates was narrowed to Lydia and one other person. When she ended up not being the one selected, she was surprised and disappointed. To determine what went wrong, Lydia asked a colleague who knew people in that organization to do some checking. Much to her dismay, she found out that the person hired actually had less relevant experience and less of a proven track record.

So what made the difference? It was personality. Lydia learned that the hiring authorities felt she had too strong a personality and that she might be difficult to work with. Although Lydia was actually a very flexible, easy-going person, she had over-played her assertive side in the interview, assuming that was what they were seeking. After that experience, she knew never to make assumptions again about the personality characteristics sought in the ideal candidate and just to be herself.

packages of the employees who would be your peers. They also need to know that the level of responsibility you seek and the title you would require fit with the needs of a given department, group, or functional area within the organization. If your requirements do not match what they can offer, you may not be able to reach an agreement and will have to look elsewhere. Fortunately, however, there is usually some leeway when it comes to these matters, and with effective negotiating tactics, you can make yourself fit. (Negotiating the terms of a job offer, including salary, are discussed in Chapter 15, "Clinching the Deal.")

Will you make the commitment?

Of all the criteria on which employers base hiring decisions, the issue of whether you really want the job and will commit to doing it to your fullest is the one that most job seekers completely overlook. You might feel that you always express your interest in a position and show enthusiasm before, during, and after interviews. Well, those efforts are appropriate and useful, but they are far from being strategic moves that will make or break your success.

Most of your competitors will be expressing interest and saying that they want the job. What they won't necessarily be doing, however, is ensuring the employer that they know what they're getting into. Employers want to hire people who are going to stick around long enough to make their investment worthwhile. They don't want you to come on board only to discover two weeks or two months into the job that it's not what you expected or that it doesn't fit with your long-term career goals. They also want to know that not only do you plan to stay in the job but that you have the "sticktoitiveness" to keep your eye on the ball and not drop it even when the things

> 66 Organizations face unpredictable changes in many domains—technological, economic, regulatory, social, and political. They need employees who not only cope but respond to change in an innovative fashion. Employers want candidates who will flourish, not wilt, under stress. 99
>
> —Professor Lori Rosenkopf, Wharton School of Business

you're asked to do were not part of the original job description. Employers these days need agile workers whose commitment will not waver no matter how rough the waters get.

The only way someone will have complete confidence in the statement, "I want this job," is if you can say something to the effect of, "I know everything there is to know about this role, this organization, and this industry, and I have given careful thought to how my own goals will be met and my skills utilized." Then you need to take that one step further by demonstrating your commitment, agility, and focus in past positions.

There is also an element of ego-massaging at work with this hiring criterion. Employers want to know that you targeted them because of something unique they have to offer and that you haven't chosen them as part of a random sampling of prospective employers. The research techniques suggested in Chapter 7, "Where Will You Find Your Job," can help you identify aspects of the target organization and position that you can mention in the interview as being particularly attractive to you. These, of course, should be organizational qualities that do genuinely have some meaning for you.

Behind closed doors with the decision-makers

In many organizations—particularly medium-sized to large corporations and nonprofits—recruiting, interviewing, and hiring procedures are more complex and sophisticated than ever. As discussed in the introduction of this book, employers have become much more conscious of every dollar expended on their human resources. Each person hired must not just occupy a desk but must work to occupy a role in that company's success.

As a result, many employers have revamped their hiring procedures to ensure that everyone brought on board can contribute to bottom-line profits in the short term and help the organization reach its goals in the long term. This means that you, the job seeker, actually may benefit from a decision-making process that is systematic, careful, deliberate, and, therefore, more likely to be fair and efficient.

Of course, such model systems are not universal. You may still come up against a hiring process that is slow, random, disorganized, and not entirely fair, especially in smaller or start-up organizations. Larger, progressive organizations with established human resources departments are more likely to use strategic staffing methods. A large percentage of today's employment opportunities exist in smaller organizations, however, so you might encounter hiring practices that are all across the board. In some small businesses, you are likely to find that an office manager or the president of the organization does the recruiting and may not have any formal knowledge or training in interviewing and hiring.

Regardless of the methods used, all employers must do three basic things: collect data on candidates, review the data, and make a decision.

How data is collected on candidates

Some people land jobs without ever having a résumé or a formal interview. Through personal referral, they get in to talk with a hiring manager, have one casual conversation about the job and their qualifications, and get an offer on the spot. At the other extreme are those situations where the employer puts candidates through a grueling process of résumé screening, a preliminary telephone interview with human resources, multiple on-site interviews with all personnel involved in the hiring decision, and a battery of assessment tools (a.k.a. "tests"), all followed by a long waiting period while candidates' references are checked and credentials evaluated. The way information is collected about you and what will be done with it will vary from place to place, but you can be sure that the data will most likely be gathered in any of four basic ways: résumés and other written documents; interviews; observation of behavior; and formal assessment (testing).

Résumés and related written self-marketing materials

Some employers rely heavily on basic credentials on paper when hiring. They pay close attention to the content and presentation of your résumé, to what you say in your cover letter, and possibly to work samples and other documents in your portfolio. (You'll find more information on these documents in Part III: "Preparing Your Self-Marketing Tools"). Some employers might even want to view copies of your school transcripts and standardized test scores, particularly for entry-level positions.

Interviews

An interview is certainly the most common way to collect information about an applicant. Interviews take a variety of forms, from one-on-one, to group meetings with multiple candidates and one or more interviewers, to panel interviews with one candidate and multiple interviewers. You may be screened by an inexperienced human resources assistant or a seasoned human resources manager. You might meet with the person who would be your boss, or the people who would be your subordinates or team members. Interviews can be conversational and friendly or stressful and intimidating. In some, the interviewers ask easy, general questions, while others challenge you with behavior-based questions that require you to think of specific examples in which your past behavior demonstrates your qualifications and achievements.

All of these interviewing scenarios can take place at a variety of venues, including college campuses, the employer's offices, or conferences and conventions, and they may be conducted in person or via telephone, video-conferencing, or over the Internet. The various types of interviews are described more in Chapter 12, "Types of Interviews and How to Handle Them"; typical questions and discussion topics are addressed in Chapter 13, "Typical and Not-so-Typical Interview Questions," and Chapter 14, "Interview Curve Balls."

Observation of behavior

Instead of merely asking about who you are and what you're capable of, some employers want you to show them who you are and what you can do. Much of the observation is informal and unofficial—you're simply being judged throughout all of your interaction with a prospective employer or recruiter. The level of professionalism, courtesy, and efficiency with which you conduct yourself throughout your search is as important as how you conduct yourself when you're officially "on," as in during an interview.

Observing you more formally in situations that simulate the workplace is also an excellent way for employers to assess issues of skill, fit, and personal character. Some observation may take place in an interview, particularly in a group interview in which the group may be given a task to accomplish and everyone is observed while working on that task together. Or you may be asked to make a presentation of some sort, particularly for sales, training, or consulting jobs. You might even be invited to come on board for a trial period to do the actual job with the understanding that your performance will be assessed and, if satisfactory, you will be hired formally. An indirect way that recruiters can observe your behavior is to ask your former employers about their observations of you. Reference checking, including the limitations on what past employers can reveal about you, is discussed in Chapter 5, "Résumés."

Assessment

The use of tests as a way to evaluate candidates has been on the increase in the past several years as employers become increasingly careful about who they hire. Assessment is most often used when hiring senior management and executives, but some companies routinely do some degree of formal assessment with almost everyone they are seriously considering hiring. Many large companies send candidates to an in-house or external assessment center to be interviewed by a psychologist or to sit through tests of personality, psychological makeup, intelligence, integrity, aptitudes, and/or specific job-related skills. The results are compiled and reviewed by psychologists and other qualified professionals and are reported to the hiring authorities for use in their final decision. Assessment is discussed in more detail in the online Bonus Chapter 6.

Six styles of decision making

After the information about you is collected and the interviewing process is complete, the hiring authorities turn to the task of reviewing the data and making a decision about which candidate should receive an offer. As with everything connected with hiring, the methods for review and decision making vary widely. Although you may feel at the mercy of the system at this point, it helps to know that there are six basic types of decision-makers when it comes to hiring and you can watch for clues to which type you might be dealing with.

> 66 Hiring mistakes are costly and result in lost productivity, dissatisfied customers, and more. Companies that hire strategically strive to choose the right person as much as a job seeker strives to be the one hired. 99
>
> —Louise Kursmark, co-author, "How to Choose the Right Person for the Right Job Every Time," McGraw-Hill, 2004.

Model decision-makers

Model decision-makers use a process that is so balanced and fair it seems straight out of a human resources textbook. They begin with a clear idea of their hiring criteria. Then they carefully evaluate all the applicant data from a variety of sources— behavior-based interviews conducted by multiple interviewers, candidates' credentials on paper, assessment results, references, and formal and informal observation—and make a carefully thought-out decision. They are likely to make decision making both a quantitative and qualitative process, relying on numerical ratings of each candidate as well as more subjective reactions. They also make the process a team effort so that no one person's opinion weighs too heavily, and they are swift and expedient in coming to a conclusion and notifying the candidate of an offer. If only they could all be this way!

Quantitative decision-makers

These decision-makers can't make a move until the test results are in. Instead of using formal assessment only as a complement to data gathered in interviews, they rely heavily—often too heavily—on what the tests tell them. This type also has a tendency to be a keen student of research showing correlations between various applicant characteristics and future job performance or retention. For entry-level positions, they are likely to look closely at grade-point-averages and standardized test scores.

Gut-feel decision-makers

At the opposite end of the spectrum are the gut-feel decision-makers. They reject most hard data and prefer instead to rely on their intuition. They prefer a subjective, go-with-what-my-instinct-tells-me approach over a more methodical evaluation of objective data. This approach is common among managers and business leaders with extensive experience, as well as anyone who has the utmost confidence in his or her ability to judge people. Sometimes this random process works, and sometimes it doesn't.

What's-your-pedigree decision-makers

Some employers are overly concerned with whom you are on paper, usually wanting to hire people who meet some elitist standard of an ideal employee. They might want to hire only someone who attended an Ivy League college, who has an M.B.A. from a Top Ten school, or who has worked for only the most prestigious firms. They might even care about your social status or whether you belong to the right country club. Not only does this practice venture dangerously close to the edge of employment discrimination, it is at the least simply frustrating for job seekers. There is very little you can do to sway someone who has such rigid criteria.

Who-do-you-know decision-makers

These decision-makers only want to hire through personal referral. If you don't know someone in the company or have a mutual acquaintance, then you may not have much of a chance. If you think you're dealing with this kind of employer, then you need to pay special attention to the strategies recommended in Chapter 9 on networking.

Just-get-me-a-warm-body decision-makers

Some employers need to fill a position so quickly that they throw all traditional hiring methods out the window and take the first warm body that comes along and reasonably fits the bill. This type of decision-maker may at first seem to be a job seeker's dream come true, but savvy job seekers know it's a trap. If you get an offer that seems to come too quickly or to be based on insufficient information about you as a candidate, think twice before accepting. The offer may very well be something fantastic, but an offer made prematurely can cause problems down the road.

Such a cavalier approach to staffing may reflect a lack of professionalism in the people with whom you would be working or throughout the organization in general. If very little thought goes into a hiring decision, then what does that say about how the organization conducts the rest of its business? An indiscriminate choice may also mean that after you get started with the company, they may find that you are not exactly what they were looking for and send you back pounding the pavement. Those who hire in haste are likely to fire in haste as well.

Wildcard variables that affect hiring decisions

Unless you are lucky enough to get the first job for which you interview, it is inevitable that at some point in your search

Bright Idea

Want to know what employers are really thinking? Read the books they read on how to recruit, interview, and hire the best people. Several of these are listed in the Recruiting and Staffing section of the online Bonus Appendix 2, "Recommended Reading List." Find it at www.wiley.com/go/michelletullier.

you will come up against some insurmountable—or seemingly insurmountable—obstacles. I'm not talking about relatively minor objections employers might have to your candidacy, such as a lack of a particular skill or an unexplained time gap on your résumé. These can be dealt with. Instead, I am referring to forces that tax the limits of even the most confident job seeker. Much of the time, these are beyond your control, but there are occasional times when you can regain some control. Following are several of the most common wildcard variables.

Hiring internally

Some companies have a policy of posting open positions internally to give current employees a first crack at them before advertising to the public. In cases of companies that don't have such a policy formally in place, most do advertise positions both internally and externally, so either way you might end up competing with other candidates who already have a toe hold in that organization. They know the ropes, whether that's the nature of the business, corporate culture, or key players, and the key players know them, or at least can find out about them easily. You, however, are an unknown commodity, an outsider. Although some employers want the fresh ideas, new perspectives, and innovation that can come from hiring from the outside, others want to go with people they know. So, if you think you have a particular job in the bag only to find out that you didn't get it, the reason may be that the employer hired internally. They may have even planned to do so all along and were only going through the motions of interviewing others just to widen their pool of applicants before settling on someone from the inside. If an organization has a commitment to promoting from within, or simply feels more comfortable going with a known quantity, there's not much you can do to surpass the internal competition other than to emphasize the fresh perspectives you would bring.

Nepotism

Similar to the issue of hiring internally is that of nepotism. I use this term loosely in that I do not necessarily mean only the hiring of a relative. In fact, many companies have policies that prohibit relatives from working for the same organization. In its looser sense, nepotism here describes a situation in which one person at a given organization has enough power to persuade all the decision-makers that his or her friend or colleague must be hired. Sometimes upper-level managers owe favors, and as a result, need to offer jobs to friends' sons, daughters, spouses, or the like. Or, sometimes a manager comes on board at a new company and wants to bring his or her former colleagues along. Regardless of who is involved, the point is that someone who has the power to override others' opinions—and who has a pet candidate—might interfere with your ability to get hired.

Opting for a temporary employee or outsourcing

A major development of the past several years has been the dramatic growth in the temporary staffing, contracting, and outsourcing industries. According to the American Staffing Association, nearly 2.25 million people per day were working in temporary and contract positions in the United States in 2003.

 Watch Out!

If you're very unlikely to get a particular job, do what you can to overcome the barriers and be persistent following up with the employer, but at some point cut your losses and move on. It's easy to waste precious time pursuing an offer that isn't going to materialize.

Employers find the use of temporary employees, contract workers, or outsourcing providers—for many functions from clerical to bookkeeping, to customer service, to managerial and technical—to be an efficient way to allocate resources. If an organization needs more people to handle a temporary increase in workload, hiring permanent employees leaves the company carrying a heavy payroll burden after the work is done and the employees are no longer needed. Hiring temporary employees or outsourcing the workload as needed is often an attractive solution.

This phenomenon affects your job search in that you may come across an employer who is very interested in you but can't justify the expense of bringing you on permanently. In that case, you might need to work extra hard at proving how you could make a contribution in the long run, not just with the immediate needs of the organization, so that you—not a temporary employee—will be chosen.

Also, you need to be prepared for some employers who try to get you on board in a temporary or consulting capacity instead of in a permanent staff position. If you agree to those terms, make a careful assessment of the probability that the temp route will turn into permanent employment. Although federal laws regulate the use of temporary employees, enforcement of the rules is sloppy; many employers get away with using temps on a long-term basis, never having to make a particular position permanent. Or, if that's not so much of a concern to you, make sure that taking the contract position would not cut into your job search time too much. If you're collecting unemployment benefits find out whether taking temporary work will cut those off and what the financial trade-off is.

Whether you're dealing with the wildcard variables or a model decision-maker, and whether the employer cares more about skills or fit, it helps to be aware of how you are being judged and how the final decision is made. You'll find a further discussion of hiring decisions in Chapter 15, "Clinching the Deal," which offers advice on follow-up techniques that can sway the decision in your favor.

Of course, this chapter would not be complete without mentioning that most elusive of all factors: luck. Your job search success will no doubt be affected by a little luck—being in the right place at the right time. There's nothing like a good strategy and some hard work, however, to get the luck pouring in your direction.

Just the facts

- Most employers are concerned with three key issues: Will you add value? Will you fit in? Will you make the commitment?

- Hiring decisions are based in part on an assessment of what you know, what you can do, what you have accomplished, and what you have the potential to do.

- How you will fit into an organization is determined by subjective factors such as your values, work style, image, and personality, as well as by tangible criteria such as your desired compensation and title.

- Time, effort, and money go into hiring and training a new employee, so employers must have confidence in your commitment to them before they'll make a commitment to you.

- Hiring decisions are based on methods that range from sophisticated and systematic to random and subjective. Recognizing each type of decision making style will help you better cope with the process.

GET THE SCOOP ON...
Identifying your most marketable skills and
qualities ▪ The importance of a job search wish
list ▪ Making tough decisions about your career
direction ▪ Finding your market niche

Marketing You, the Product

Chapter 3

Y ou don't have to be a marketing expert to
know that there's more to moving a box of
cereal off a grocery store shelf than plopping
it down there and hoping someone buys it. There's a
strategy behind the name of the cereal, the packag-
ing design, which geographic and socioeconomic
markets it's sold in, and just about everything else
that could influence whether the consumer will take
it from shelf to check-out line. Plus, there's market
research that precedes that strategy. Manufacturers
have to find out what consumers want, how they
think, what the competition is up to, and other marketplace intelligence that helps them position the
product in the best way to optimize sales potential.

As you've probably surmised by now, landing a
job is not all that much different a process from the
marketing of a product. In this case, you are the
product. You have to know what you have to offer
and what the market needs, and you must be able to
communicate that what you offer best meets those

needs. Throughout that process you also have to know what it is *you* want and make sure that you not only meet the needs of the market but also your own.

This chapter helps you zero in on specifically what you have to offer prospective employers and guides you in developing a job search wish list to ensure that your own needs and priorities don't get lost in the shuffle. You'll go through the three steps to marketing yourself for a job.

1. Assess what you have to offer an employer.

2. Decide what you want and need in your next job.

3. Determine who needs what you offer and offers what you need.

The sections that follow explore each of these steps in detail. By the way, this is a working chapter. Where appropriate, I have provided space for you to complete exercises directly in this book, but you may choose to do your work on separate paper or on a computer. Whichever way you do it, the important thing is that you get something down. Too many job seekers think they have such a good handle on their strengths and skills that they don't need to write them down—or that doing so is too elementary. If that happens to be your attitude, then consider whether you would approach a bank or venture capitalist for money to start a business without a written business plan. The same principle is at work when trying to land a job. You need to get your plan out of your head and onto paper to be sure that you're building the strongest case possible for why you are the best candidate.

 Watch Out!

If you happen to be a marketing or sales professional, don't assume that you won't need to learn how to market yourself. Many marketing and sales experts find it's a whole different ball game when the product is themselves. Take yourself through Chapters 3 and 5 to ensure you'll do it right.

Assessing what you have to offer

There's an old guiding principle in the field of advertising that says, "sell the benefits, not the features." It means that people buy a product because they see the potential benefit of that product—what it will do for them, rather than basing their purchase solely on the features, for example, the fine print describing the product's ingredients or components, how it's made, and so forth. Employers are the same. They select the candidate who can bring about the benefits they need—candidates who offer the right package of relevant skills, personality qualities, experience, and demonstrated ability to get results. To persuade employers that you're the best candidate for the position, you must communicate how you will add value, how you'll fit in, and how committed you will be. In order to do that, however, you have to know yourself first. You must have a clear picture of your skills, capabilities, areas of expertise, and personal qualities as they relate to your target jobs and must give hard evidence of how you've used those qualifications to add value and to fit in. That's the only way you'll be able to get an edge over the competition.

In the sections that follow, you'll have the opportunity to take inventory of what you have to offer, using informal checklists and worksheets to structure the process. Informal assessment is one effective way to assess what you have to offer, but be aware that you may need to go beyond the exercises in this chapter. You might benefit from some formal assessment, such as interest inventories, skills measures, personality assessments, and other tools that career development professionals use.

For now, I recommend getting started with some informal self-assessment by completing the exercises in the sections that follow. The assessment will involve three simple steps:

1. Take stock of your content knowledge.

2. Identify your transferable skills.

3. Assess your positive personal qualities.

The Inside Scoop on Career Assessment

If you're struggling with defining your career focus or want to be extra thorough in taking stock of your marketable qualities, consider formal testing offered by a career consultant in private practice or through outplacement firms, colleges and universities, and some community-based career centers or libraries. Hundreds of assessment tools are on the market, so it can be tricky to know whether the ones offered to you are the best ones for you. Take a sneak peak at some of the more popular tools by viewing them at the same sites career professionals visit:

- Campbell Interest and Skill Survey (www.cpp.com)
- Career Anchors (www.pfeiffer.com)
- Holland's Self-Directed Search (www.self-directed-search.com)
- Myers-Briggs Type Indicator (www.cpp.com)
- Strong Interest Inventory (www.cpp.com)

Reading about the tests you might take will make you better informed before plunking down a sizeable chunk of money to have a career consultant administer them.

Even if you already know what sort of jobs you're going after, this self-assessment is a critical step in your self-marketing strategy, so taking the time to complete the exercises will definitely be worth your while.

Taking stock of your content knowledge

As defined in Chapter 2, your content knowledge consists of the subjects and topics with which you are familiar, as well as your

Bright Idea

A fun way to identify your content knowledge is to imagine that you've been invited to take a year off and travel on a world cruise for free. The only catch is that you have to lead a shipboard seminar or discussion group once a week. What topics would you choose?

areas of expertise or specializations. Your content knowledge not only enables you to do your job, but it also brings an added bonus to your employer.

Consider the case of Fran, a corporate attorney who wished to make a career change into investment banking. Although she had not worked directly in that field, she had worked on financial transactions from the legal perspective. The fact that she could discuss subjects such as commercial lending, corporate restructuring, and bankruptcy in her interviews made her seem less like a career-changer and more like someone who could hit the ground running. In addition, Fran had lived in Spain for a year and had worked in Central and South America. Her knowledge of Latin American culture and business would be an added bonus to prospective employers involved in financial markets in those areas.

Some of your content knowledge areas will be obvious, especially those that relate to your job. A real estate broker, for example, might know something about financing, mortgage banking, property development, urban/community planning, interior design, landscaping, architecture, or engineering. A social worker might be familiar with public policy, psychiatry, and nursing. Other content knowledge evolves out of your hobbies, personal interests, and academic background. Examples of content knowledge are endless and vary widely from person to person. To identify yours, take a look at Worksheet 3.1 and see whether any of the questions reveal your areas of expertise.

Worksheet 3.1. Content Knowledge

To jog your thinking about your own content knowledge, ask yourself the following questions:

1. Consider your current employment (or most recent, if not currently employed). What do you have to know to do your job, or what have you learned as a result of doing your job?

2. Now do the same for past jobs you have held.

3. Think about any hobbies or activities you are involved in outside of work. What do you know about as a result of those involvements?

4. What topics do you discuss with friends or family, read about in books or magazines, or follow on the Internet?

5. In which subjects are you conversant or proficient as a result of your academic background—whether from a full degree program or just a course or two?

Identifying your transferable skills

The next step in taking stock of your assets is to identify your transferable skills. Unlike content knowledge, which consists of subjects, topics, or areas of specialization, transferable skills are things that you actually do. You can think of them as functions, actions, or behaviors. These skills are also not linked to any one job, project, or employer—they're generic enough to be of interest to most anyone.

That attorney interested in working in investment banking, for example, did not go into interviews using legal jargon and focusing on skills unique to the law, such as drafting and filing motions, analyzing appellate briefs, or conducting hearings. Instead, she spoke about her ability to analyze financial data,

 Moneysaver

If you're concerned about lacking particular skills, avoid the temptation to sign up for expensive courses or training programs until you're certain that the skills you would learn are an absolute prerequisite for the job you want.

Watch Out!

Beware of aptitude testing centers offering expensive, lengthy test batteries. Although they may do a good job of measuring general aptitudes such as spatial relations, verbal reasoning, and musical ability, most job seekers need to identify their more tangible, specific, job-related skills with the help of a career counselor.

solve problems, work in teams, structure deals, negotiate, write reports, and maintain relationships with clients.

To identify your own transferable skills, review Checklists 3.1 through 3.10 and put a check next to any skills you possess. When you've gone through all the lists, go back and circle (or highlight in whichever way you prefer) the 10 to 15 skills that are likely to be most marketable and relevant to your target job or employer.

Checklist 3.1. Business & Management Skills

Appraise value	____
Assess/oversee quality control	____
Bargain	____
Barter	____
Compete	____
Conduct meetings	____
Consult	____
Delegate	____
Develop a business plan	____
Direct	____
Estimate costs	____
Fund-raise	____
Handle office politics	____
Improvise	____

continued

Checklist 3.1. *(continued)*

Interview candidates   ____

Make decisions   ____

Make presentations   ____

Manage people   ____

Manage projects   ____

Negotiate   ____

Plan strategy   ____

Process improvement   ____

Reprimand   ____

Set goals   ____

Supervise   ____

Train employees   ____

Troubleshoot   ____

Checklist 3.2. Cognitive Skills

Analyze situations/facts/data   ____

Assess needs   ____

Concentrate for long periods of time   ____

Conceptualize   ____

Develop theories/hypothesize   ____

Employ logic   ____

Extrapolate   ____

Memorize/recall information   ____

Observe   ____

Read carefully and critically   ____

Research   ____

See the big picture   ____

Synthesize/integrate ideas or information   ____

Checklist 3.3. Creative Skills

Brainstorm _____

Create works of art _____

Design programs or procedures _____

Develop marketing campaigns _____

Invent products or services _____

Make spaces/objects aesthetically pleasing _____

Perform _____

Use imagination _____

Visualize _____

Checklist 3.4. Interpersonal Skills

Advise _____

Advocate _____

Build teams _____

Coach _____

Collaborate _____

Console _____

Counsel _____

Educate _____

Empathize _____

Entertain _____

Facilitate others' development _____

Facilitate groups _____

Guide _____

Host _____

Influence people _____

Interact effectively cross-culturally _____

continued

Checklist 3.4. *(continued)*

Listen attentively ____

Mediate conflicts/disputes ____

Mentor ____

Motivate others ____

Network/keep in touch with people ____

Nurture ____

Orient newcomers ____

Persuade ____

Provide constructive criticism/critique work ____

Serve/assist customers or clients ____

Teach ____

Checklist 3.5. Oral Communication Skills

Be humorous ____

Debate ____

Explain things to others ____

Interpret ____

Interview others for information ____

Lead seminars or workshops ____

Learn/speak foreign language(s) ____

Make conversation ____

Mediate disputes/conflicts ____

Moderate a panel of speakers ____

Speak in public ____

Checklist 3.6. Organizational Skills

Coordinate projects or events   _____

Coordinate schedules   _____

Handle details   _____

Handle multiple tasks simultaneously   _____

Implement plans/follow through   _____

Monitor the flow of a project   _____

Oversee a production effort   _____

Process documents   _____

Reorganize systems/procedures   _____

Set up and maintain record-keeping systems   _____

Checklist 3.7. Quantitative Skills

Administer accounts payable   _____

Administer accounts receivable   _____

Analyze data   _____

Calculate/tally numbers   _____

Conduct statistical analyses   _____

Cut costs   _____

Generate financial reports   _____

Handle collections   _____

Plan and work with budgets   _____

Solve complex mathematical problems   _____

Bright Idea

To identify more of your transferable skills, check the written job description for your current or past positions (usually available from Human Resources if you don't already have a copy).

Checklist 3.8. Sales Skills

Close sales _____

Conduct sales presentations _____

Convince _____

Develop new markets _____

Identify prospects _____

Make sales calls in person _____

Maintain client/customer accounts _____

Negotiate _____

Persuade _____

Telemarketing _____

Checklist 3.9. Technical Skills

Build/construct things _____

Fix/repair things _____

Make installations _____

Operate machinery or equipment _____

Troubleshoot malfunctions _____

Use physical strength _____

Use tools _____

Checklist 3.10. Written Communication Skills

Copy write	____
Edit	____
Proofread	____
Translate	____
Write for business	____
Write creatively	____
Write grants	____
Write journalistically	____

Uncovering additional skills

Reviewing these checklists is just one way to identify your transferable skills. You also need to tackle the problem from the opposite perspective—thinking about your experiences and accomplishments and pulling skills from those.

Take the case of Leon, a former client of mine who had been a high school English teacher for five years since completing a master's degree in English literature after college. Leon decided that he wanted to make a career transition and enter a management training program with a major insurance company. When he first reviewed skills checklists similar to those on the preceding pages, he was concerned that he had little to offer a corporate employer.

 Bright Idea

Reading your performance reviews from past jobs is a great way to identify some of your most marketable assets.

When he carefully analyzed his background by breaking down his job as a teacher and his avocational activities into generic functional areas, however, he was relieved to find that he possessed more transferable skills than he had imagined. He had demonstrated management and teamwork skills while supervising student clubs and participating on faculty committees; used his quantitative abilities as treasurer of his condominium building's board; and obviously used presentation, public speaking, listening, and analytical skills as a teacher and graduate student.

Think about your work, academic, and personal experiences and the skills that you have demonstrated throughout them. If you find any skills not already checked off on the lists provided previously, add them.

Assessing your personal qualities

The final step in taking stock of your assets is to assess the positive personal qualities that may be of value to your target employer. Read through Checklist 3.11 and place a check next to any characteristics that you think describe you. Then go back and circle the five to seven characteristics that best describe you out of all the ones checked.

Checklist 3.11. Personal Qualities	
Adaptable	____
Aggressive	____
Artistic	____
Assertive	____
Athletic	____
Calm	____
Communicative	____
Conscientious	____
Considerate	____

Creative   _____

Dependable   _____

Detail-oriented   _____

Diplomatic   _____

Disciplined   _____

Discreet   _____

Driven   _____

Effective   _____

Efficient   _____

Energetic   _____

Enterprising   _____

Enthusiastic   _____

Ethical   _____

Expressive   _____

Faithful   _____

Flexible   _____

Funny   _____

Gregarious   _____

Honest   _____

Independent   _____

Loyal   _____

Mathematically inclined   _____

Mechanically inclined   _____

Musically inclined   _____

Observant   _____

Open-minded   _____

Optimistic   _____

Organized   _____

continued

Checklist 3.11. *(continued)*

Patient   _____

Perceptive   _____

Persevering   _____

Persuasive   _____

Poised   _____

Practical   _____

Punctual   _____

Quiet   _____

Reserved   _____

Resourceful   _____

Responsible   _____

Scholarly   _____

Self-aware   _____

Self-confident   _____

Self-disciplined   _____

Sensitive   _____

Serious   _____

Sincere   _____

Tactful   _____

Technically inclined   _____

Thoughtful   _____

Visionary   _____

 Bright Idea

Make copies of the Personal Qualities checklist for at least three friends, colleagues, or family members before you complete it. Have them check off the qualities that they see in you, then compare all the results to see how the perspectives vary.

Deciding what you want

Although identifying the marketable skills and knowledge that others will want is the most critical step in marketing yourself for employment, you also owe it to yourself to go after what will make you happy. What's the point of landing a job that you won't enjoy and won't satisfy your needs?

Knowing what interests, motivates, and satisfies you not only does you a world of good, it also makes you sound more focused to employers. In networking appointments and interviews, you'll find that the questions asked of you don't all center on what you have to offer. Many people will ask what you're looking for, that is, what you want your next employer to offer *you.*

As you learned in Chapter 1, "Twenty Secrets of Successful Job Seekers," one secret is to have a clear focus, and that focus doesn't always mean being able to put a precise label on exactly the kind of job you're looking for. Having a focus means that you can describe the qualities of an ideal position, work environment, and type of employer. You can paint a picture that is clear enough for others to be able to see where you might fit, but just blurry enough that you don't paint yourself in a corner if you want to leave your options open for various types of positions and environments.

The process of defining a career focus and targeting particular types of jobs can be confusing and overwhelming, but it need not be. Basically, it boils down to these five steps:

1. **Discover what makes you tick:** Define the types of work-related activities and environments you prefer, the sorts of people with whom you want to work, the skills you want to use and prefer not to use, and the values and priorities that you need satisfied.

2. **Explore your options:** Conduct research on various occupations, professions, industries, and market sectors by talking to people, reading print and online resources, and even trying out various options in a hands-on way.

3. **Examine the pros and cons of a career change:** Consider whether making a complete career change to a new role in a new industry or sector, or making a moderate career shift (such as new industry but same old role) makes more sense than staying with the work you've always done.

4. **Expand your horizons with alternate paths:** Consider self-employment, free agency, or temporary work as an alternative to finding traditional employment.

5. **Make a decision:** Based on all these steps and using tried-and-true decision-making methodologies, select a career direction in which to head.

Worksheet 3.2. Job Search Wish List

This worksheet is a place to pull together all the factors you've identified throughout this chapter as being what you have to offer prospective employers and what you are most looking for in your next position. Use this form or create your own to have more space. Either way, be sure to compile some sort of wish list along these lines as a way of summarizing in one convenient place all the key data that forms your self-marketing plan.

What I Have to Offer	What I Need/Want
Content Knowledge	Activities/Responsibilities
Transferable Skills	Motivated Skills

What I Have to Offer	What I Need/Want
Personal Qualities	Work environment
Additional Expertise	Values/Needs

Explore your options

After you've painted a picture of your ideal next job using the exercises in earlier sections of this chapter and culminating in the Job Search Wish List, it's time to see which career options might match that picture. Researching occupations, professions, and industries enables you to identify career options you hadn't thought of before and to further investigate options you've already been considering. You can do this in three simple ways: read, talk, and try it out.

Explore your options: read

The Internet, public and career center libraries, and bookstores are all sources of books, directories, and periodicals that give insight into various career options. Keep in mind that you are not reading to find job openings or to research specific organizations or companies at this point. For now, you want to read about various types of work and industries to start identifying those that you want to target—the ones that match your preferences and assets. An enormous amount of information is out there, but all you really need to know is that it all boils down to two types of information you are seeking: (1) basic occupational and industry data; and (2) specific career and industry data. It ain't rocket science when you know what you're looking for! Here's how to find the two types of data:

Basic occupational and industry data

Gives an overview of the nature of the work, types of positions, typical work settings, training and qualifications required, employment outlook, and salaries. The best starting point for this sort of information is the *Occupational Outlook Handbook* (known to career industry insiders as the *OOH*), a publication of the U.S. Department of Labor, available in the reference section of libraries and online at www.bls.gov/oco/home. The *OOH* describes hundreds of occupations grouped into broad functional categories such as: Executive, Administrative, and Managerial; Professional and Technical; Sales; Service; Administrative Support; Production; and more. Note that the *Occupational Outlook Quarterly*, accessible from the BLS home page (www.bls.gov), is also useful for more up-to-date salary and employment data. A companion directory, the *Career Guide to Industries* at www.bls.gov/oco/cg/home is also very useful. It lists all the types of jobs available within various industries. A helpful tip for using this guide is to realize that the industry tabs you'll see along the left side of the page are only a sampling of the industries that the guide covers. To see all industries, click on the letter A at the top of the screen where you'll see an A–Z index.

Specific career and industry data

After getting a basic overview of various occupations and industries through sources like the *OOH* and *Career Guide to Industries*, you'll probably want some more detailed information. At that point, it's a good idea to turn to books you'll find in bookstores and libraries. . There are hundreds of titles on the market that take a particular industry, profession, or subject area and outline all the types of jobs within the category. Books such as *Careers for Computer Buffs and Other Technological Types, Career*

Opportunities in Education, or *Guide to America's Federal Jobs* are just a few examples. In addition to basic information about work settings, typical qualifications required, salary ranges, and the like, these books often include case studies of people working in those fields and detailed resources for finding work in that area. You'll find additional books and directories listed in the "Researching Occupations and Industries" section of the online Bonus Appendix 2.

Additional sources for more specific career or industry information include popular newspapers and magazines as well as professional association Web sites and publications. To find an association for the field that interests you, check the online Bonus Appendix 3, "Professional and Trade Associations."

Explore your options: talk

Reading about your career options will only get you so far. To make a fully informed decision about your own career direction, you need to talk to people who are familiar with the fields you're considering. They can give you information that may be more up-to-date and real-world than that found in published sources. You can talk with people by phone or in person in formal appointments or informal encounters. In Chapter 9, where networking is discussed in detail, you'll see ideas for how to find people to talk to for information and suggested protocols for conducting such meetings.

Explore your options: try it out

The most direct way to get a feeling for what a particular career or industry is like is to work in it. If you're a student or someone with no financial concerns and lots of time to spend exploring, then you've got it made. You can have an internship or apprenticeship in an area you're considering or can do short-term observations (part of a day, a day, a week) in various workplaces, often called "shadowing." If you're a more senior professional beyond the internship stage and need to get a career focus and find a job quickly, don't despair. There are other options. Doing

Watch Out!

Avoid the temptation to choose a career direction just because some article has touted it as the latest "hot job" or fastest growing industry. Although such projections are valuable, make sure that the field is a good match for your interests, skills, and values. If you don't fit in, it will do you no good that it's a "hot" field.

volunteer work, contract or project work, temporary assignments, or moonlighting in a part-time job are all ways to explore new fields before fully committing to them.

Examine the pros and cons of a career change

As you review your Job Search Wish List, you might find that you are unlikely to find a job in your current field that will satisfy your needs and utilize your talents to their fullest. You might find that you need to change your functional role, that is the specific types of positions, job titles, or departments that a position would be a part of. A sales manager may find that he no longer wants to manage a sales force, even though he has the skill to do it, and instead wants to return to a hands-on sales rep role. He doesn't need to go to a new industry selling a new type of product or service; he just needs to change his role.

For others, an industry change is what is needed. That salesperson might be tired of selling food products and want to start selling technology. After all, his sales skills are highly transferable, and if he can sell cases of canned corn to school cafeterias, why couldn't he sell point-of-sale (a.k.a. cash register) systems to school cafeterias?

Or, what if that salesperson has had a personal epiphany in which he is now more motivated by being of service to his community than by the commissions he can earn? He might consider a transition to a whole new sector, from private sector (that is, corporate world) to the nonprofit sector or government. He might find a way to transition his sales and management skills to a charitable organization where he can help with fundraising or managing teams of volunteers. Or, he could forget the sales experience and take his content knowledge of food products and management skills to find a position with a government agency or program involved with feeding the needy.

As you can see from those examples, career changes come in a variety of combinations. It's all a matter of determining what is most important to you. Do you want to keep using particular skills but do so in a new arena or to get away from skills you've been using? Do you have content knowledge or subject matter expertise that you want to continue building a career around, or are you tired of it and want to learn about something new? What about academia? You might find that a move from the corporate world to teaching children or adults would be satisfying at this stage of your career. Have your values changed? Maybe you want to move to the nonprofit sector where salaries tend to be a bit lower, but the intrinsic rewards are often higher. Or, do you desire the security and stability that could come with a government position? Table 3.1 shows all the possible combinations you can choose from when deciding to make a career change, and Table 3.2 shows an example of how those combinations might play out.

Table 3.1. Career Change Options

Same role	Same role	Same role
Same industry	Different industry	Same industry
Same sector	Same sector	Different sector
(No change.)		
Different role	Different role	Different role
Same industry	Different industry	Same industry
Same sector	Same sector	Different sector

Table 3.2. Sample Career Changes

Operations manager	Operations manager	Operations manager
Manufacturing	Technology	Manufacturing
Private sector	Private sector	Government sector
Training specialist	Training specialist	Training specialist
Manufacturing	Technology	Technology
Private sector	Private sector	Nonprofit sector

Four Biggest Mistakes Career-Changers Make

If you decide that one of the career change or career shift options described in Table 3.1 is right for you, be aware of some common pitfalls that would-be career-changers slip into.

Not having a strategy

A sound career change strategy needs to be well thought out and realistic. You need to conduct extensive self-assessment and research, network heavily, and retool your usual job search methods to fit the new field. You also have to learn to speak the language of the new field and might need to identify interim steps to get your foot in the door, such as moonlighting or taking courses before you can get a full-time job in it. You also need to have enough money to finance your transition because you're likely to be out of work longer than if you were job searching in your old field and may have to pay for some retraining.

Running out of steam

Career transitions take a long time. Exactly how long varies widely, but on average, a major career change (involving a new functional role, industry, or sector) will take at least six to nine months, with more than a year being not uncommon. Most career-changers start out with high hopes and enthusiasm and

Moneysaver

Changing careers can be expensive, and, if you make the wrong choice, the decision is even more costly. I highly recommend the book *Career Change* by David Helfand as the best way to know what you're getting into, how to make the right decision, and how to transition most efficiently.

do fine the first few weeks or months. But then they run out of steam. They get tired of the time and effort that goes into breaking into a new field and give up.

Having tunnel vision

Making a career change requires that you see a connection between your past work experience and skill sets and the new field. It also requires that you be creative about how to make the transition. Connecting the dots from point A to point B is often difficult for many people to envision, but to make a successful career change, you have to be able to deal with ambiguity and think outside the box to blaze a path—probably a circuitous one—from point A to B.

Not being fully committed to the idea

Some people say they want to go into a new line of work, but in their heads they're not fully convinced of it. No matter how bored or miserable they may be in the current role and environment, some people worry that they'll be labeled as flaky or a job hopper. Others feel guilty about losing the time, money, and effort they've invested in their current career or job. These views are natural but unfortunate. Changing careers and jobs is so much the norm these days that there is no stigma surrounding wanting to make a fresh start in your career. As for the guilt factor, which is worse: staying in a career long term that you are unhappy with, or cutting your losses and making a clean break?

Who needs what you offer and offers what you need?

When you've chosen the direction in which to head, this in turn dictates the types of jobs you'll be seeking. You need to start zeroing in on the types of employers and even specific employers—actual companies or organizations by name—that will match your wish list. Your goal is to find out which employers need what you have to offer—the knowledge, skills, personal qualities, and experience that you now are so aware of—and which ones offer what you need—the preferred activities and work environments and the values and needs you have. You can use the same three-part methodology that you used for exploring career options: read, talk, and try it out. All the same sources, people in your network, print and online resources, and, when feasible, short-term work experience can help you focus in on the specific organizations or types of organizations that fit the bill for you. In Chapter 8, "Landing a Job through the Formal Marketplace," you'll find much more detailed information on how to conduct research on specific employers to develop a "hit list" of places and people to target in your search. For now, take satisfaction in knowing that if you've gone through the exercises in this chapter, you're off to an excellent start in the process of marketing yourself, and as a result, have given yourself a huge leg-up on the competition.

Your self-marketing sound bite

As I mentioned in Chapter 1, "Twenty Secrets of Successful Job Seekers," one secret is to develop and use a brief statement that hits the highlights of who you are and what your situation is. Now that you've determined what you have to offer employers and what your career focus is, it's time to develop this statement, called a self-marketing sound bite. The self-marketing sound bite can be in written form to be used in your résumé and job search correspondence or in spoken form—something you say as a way of introducing yourself on a cold call, in networking meetings, or to answer that dreaded interview question, "Tell me about yourself." When spoken, the sound bite can take anywhere from fifteen seconds to two minutes to say, depending on what is appropriate for the situation. You'll use the shorter sound bite (usually about 15 to 30 seconds) when time is short, such as when leaving voice mail or introducing yourself to someone at a networking event. You'll use the longer version, speaking for up to a minute-and-a-half to two minutes when someone asks you to tell them about yourself, such as during a networking meeting or interview.

Having a self-marketing sound bite keeps you from having to reinvent the wheel every time you approach someone, though you do tailor it slightly to fit each situation. By scripting and practicing a self-marketing sound bite from Day One of your search, you'll save yourself lots of time and worry after the search is underway. You'll also communicate much more effectively than those who try to wing it and end up rambling or getting tongue-tied.

The three parts of a self-marketing sound bite

You can say so many things to introduce yourself to someone and to present yourself in a positive light that it can be difficult to know what to include and what to leave out. The way to choose the best information for your pitch is to think of what is relevant to the person you're communicating with, your goals, and the situation at hand. It's unlikely that the other person wants you to start with the day of your birth and recount every life event since that day. Instead, think of the sound bite as a very brief marketing pitch—often called an elevator speech—that hits the highlights of your background and your situation. You need to develop one standard sound bite and then tailor it as needed for various situations and audiences. No matter what the unique circumstances are, your sound bite almost always has three main components:

Summary of qualifications

First, put yourself on the map by briefly summarizing your professional experience and credentials. The summary often starts with stating the overall number of years of experience you have in a given industry, functional role, or profession and then follows with a few examples of specific areas of expertise, credentials, education, and assets. You don't have to mention everything just listed. For example, if you want to be open to jobs in a variety of industries, don't mention your own industry background right away. If you are trying to move up to a higher level, don't state your previous titles; refer instead to your functional role more generally. If your education is not particularly relevant or noteworthy, don't feel that you have to mention it.

Summary of Qualifications example: "As an accomplished marketing manager with 18 years of experience, I offer special expertise in partnering with senior management to grow businesses in ways that are innovative and aggressive yet fit within the organization's financial constraints and strategic plans. For example, I helped [last company name] generate a 22 percent increase in revenue by forming key strategic alliances."

Reason for looking/situation

After establishing who you are with your summary of qualifications, you next need to explain what your situation is, such as why you're out on the job market. This is called your Reason for Looking statement. It's a concise explanation of why you left your last job (or were asked to leave) or why you want to leave the job you're currently in. Always conclude with a positive comment about how you're looking forward to new challenges. If you are making a career change, or just seeking career advice, this is also the place where you would state that.

Reason for Looking/Situation examples:

"My company decided to centralize the human resources function by moving my department to the East Coast. I chose not to relocate my family and so am seeking new opportunities here in Southern California."

————

"As you may know, the banking industry has been undergoing major reorganization in recent years, and [bank name] is no exception. Due to our restructuring, my position, along with hundreds of others, was eliminated and I am now using this opportunity to apply my customer service skills in a new industry."

————

"I've been very happy at [current company name] and am proud of the contributions I've made there over the past several years, but it's time for new challenges so I'm exploring opportunities outside of [current company name] where I can make similar contributions."

Personal

A small portion (usually about one-quarter or less of the overall time) in your self-marketing sound bite would be devoted to a few comments about yourself personally. Keep in mind that you should not reveal too much personal information, such as marital status or number of children, early on in a job search, if ever. And, you would almost never discuss personal information related to religious affiliation or political beliefs. (I say "almost never" because there are cases where this information would be relevant to the job and discussing it would be necessary.) For your self-marketing sound bite, stick with topics like your geographic background, community activities you're involved with, or hobbies and interests you have. If you prefer not to mention anything personal, that's fine; this is an optional component of your sound bite, particularly when using the shorter version.

- "Originally from Portland, Maine, I've now been in Tampa for 10 years and am very involved in the community here, including volunteer work for a hospital and a lot of coaching for my son's neighborhood sports teams."

Examples of self-marketing sound bites

The following samples of self-marketing sound bites give you an idea of how they can, well, sound when the three elements are put together. Remember that the self-marketing sound bite is only part of an overall conversation or piece of written communication. The information you see here would go along with formalities like a greeting, stating your name, mentioning how you were referred to the person, discussing next steps, and so on.

- "I'm an experienced operations manager with most of my career in manufacturing, including the past five years at a chemicals manufacturer. Our company was recently acquired, and hundreds of positions, including mine, were eliminated. I am now looking to bring my expertise to a smaller start-up company in any industry where I can initiate new business practices focusing on cost reductions through process improvement measures. Throughout my career, I've always been commended for my ability to streamline processes, motivate teams, and cut costs. For example, at my current company, I've cut our division's operating costs by 15 percent over the past year by building and overseeing teams implementing continuous process improvement. I've also recently begun working on an executive MBA, which is strengthening my knowledge of cutting-edge business practices."

- "In a few months, I will be graduating from Boston University where I've done extensive community service and majored in anthropology. I would like to pursue a career in program or project management within the nonprofit field. Last year, I founded an organization on campus to help the homeless in our community and have grown it to more than 200 student members. I'm originally from Pittsburgh but am open to working in any location."

■ "For the past 15 years I've developed a strong track record in sales and sales management, consistently busting my own quotas and building teams that beat theirs. I've become known as "the turnaround guy"—the person who wins back lost accounts, saves troubled accounts, and brings businesses back to profitability. I began my career with [company name #1] where I was an outside sales rep for three years before a promotion to management. After two years in sales management there, I was recruited by [company name #2] to build up their professional services division. We were recently bought out by [acquiring company name], and my position was eliminated. I'm now excited about bringing my track record to a new employer who needs someone to hit the ground running and make an impact on the sales organization."

Constructing your self-marketing sound bite

Now that you've seen how the three components of a self-marketing sound bite can sound when put together, try developing your own sound bite. Remember that you'll start with a basic one that can be altered as needed to fit various situations. The template that follows uses a fill-in-the-blank method to walk you through developing your self-marketing sound bite. Keep in mind, however, that after you get a basic draft put together

---

 Watch Out!

Age discrimination is all too real in hiring. If you need to downplay how much experience you have so as not to appear overqualified, don't mention a specific number of years in your self-marketing sound bite.

using this template, you should go back over it, reordering sections as needed to present the most relevant and positive information first or to make it sound more interesting.

Step one: summary of qualifications

I have __ years of experience as a (functional role/title(s) goes here). The majority of my career has been in the _____ industry, although I have also worked in _____ and _____. My past employers have included _____, _____, and _____.

Within (overall functional area, for example, marketing, administrative work, human resources) I have special expertise in _____ and _____.

Throughout my career I've gained a reputation for (skills and personal qualities, that is, assets). For example, I recently (asset statement goes here).

My work experience is complemented by (educational degree or relevant training).

Step two: reason for looking/situation

If not currently employed: As you know, the _____ industry has been undergoing major changes and (former company name) is no exception. Due to (state succinctly what happened such as a reorganization, relocation, facility/ division closing, and so on), my position, along with (number) others was eliminated, or I chose not to relocate, or I chose to take early retirement. I am proud of my contributions to (former company name) and look forward to new challenges.

If currently employed: I am proud of my accomplishments at (current company name) and have enjoyed my (number) years there, but I am ready to pursue new challenges and grow in my career.

Step three: personal

I am originally from _____ and have lived in _____ for
years. When not working, I volunteer my time at _____
and enjoy (hobbies or interests) _____.

After going through the three steps in the preceding template, read back through what you have and see where you need
to smooth out the parts that don't sound right to you. You might
find that you don't want to mention something that the template
included, such as names of specific organizations you've worked
for, or a reference to your education. You might even want to
leave out the personal section entirely; in fact in your short (15-
to 30-second) sound bite for voice mail, phone calls, and brief

---

Trimming the Fat instead of Chewing It

When marketing themselves and communicating who they
are, people too often include unnecessary information
that clutters their self-marketing sound bite. Extraneous
detail or information that can be seen as negative should
always be left out. If you're making a transition to a field
you've never worked in but have transferable skills for, talk
about those skills before getting into details of your work
history. If you're a recent grad applying for jobs that are
not related to your major, for example, don't mention
your major, at least not right off the bat. In other words,
be strategic. Information that is not directly relevant to
your goals should not be offered until after you've stated
the more positive, relevant aspects of your qualifications
and experience. Then when the less relevant points are
raised, de-emphasize them as much as possible. To make
sure that you're putting your best—and most relevant—
foot forward, write out a script of your sound bite, and
then edit, edit, and edit some more.

introductions, you would just about always leave the personal information out unless it's a major selling point for you.

Also, look at how you might want to reorder the content in the three steps. Some people like to start with the personal information and work backward. Others might want to start off with a bang, saying their asset statement first like a news headline and then filling in the rest of the story with their work history. Get creative with it, and above all, make sure that you are comfortable with your statement and feel that it is something you would naturally say or write. The wording given in the template is very boilerplate, particularly phrases like "look forward to new challenges." Fee free to change the language to something that you would actually say. The template language is provided only as a jumping off point for you.

Just the facts

- The most critical step in marketing yourself to employers is to identify the assets you offer—your content knowledge, skills, and relevant personal qualities.

- Don't forget to consider what *you* want out of a job and an employer—which types of activities, work environments, and colleagues you prefer and which values and priorities you need met.

- When you know what you have to offer and what you're looking for, conduct thorough market research to target the types of employers who need what you offer and offer what you need.

- A self-marketing sound bite is critical for conveying who you are and what you are looking for.

GET THE SCOOP ON...
Gaining a competitive edge by showcasing your
potential ▪ Developing asset statements that
prove you can get results ▪ Overcoming common
problems when discussing your achievements

Your Marketing Plan's Secret Weapon

Chapter 4

A s with personal assets like stocks and bonds, real estate, and a bank balance, your professional assets—content knowledge, skills, and personal qualities—have value in the eyes of others. Most wise investors wouldn't purchase property without seeing it, and they wouldn't buy stock in a company they know nothing about. They need proof that an investment has a certain value or value potential, often based on past performance. The same holds true in the hiring process. For a prospective employer to see value in you and want to invest in you, you must provide evidence of your worth.

Anyone can make claims about having the necessary qualifications for a job. Not everyone can, or will think to, back up those claims with evidence. Most anyone who gets past the initial screening process and into an interview will have met the basic requirements for the job. The way to distinguish yourself from the competition at that point is to instill confidence in the employer by showing, not just saying, that you have what it takes to make a difference. This is particularly relevant at higher levels, where it's a given that you have the basic skills and experience to do the job. What's not so obvious, however, are the results of what you've accomplished in the past and exactly how those past achievements could help you meet an employer's current and future needs.

In this chapter you'll learn how to provide evidence of your assets with asset statements—brief "stories" that demonstrate how you've used your strengths and talents to make a contribution to past employers. These asset statements will form the foundation for your résumé, networking conversations, and, most important, your replies to questions in behavior-based interviews.

Building your case with asset statements

As the secret weapon in your self-marketing plan, asset statements consist of three basic elements: context, action, and outcome. Context refers to a situation you faced or responsibility you were given; action is how you handled or approached that situation; and outcome is the result of your action. When combined, these three elements form a vignette from your past experience that demonstrates what you could do in the future for your next employer.

Here's an example to illustrate this context-action-outcome (CAO) formula: Phil is a plant manager for a chemicals manufacturer. The situation he faced when he started in this job was that employee morale in the plant was very low, and turnover was high. Employees were not satisfied with their working conditions, they were tired of constant changes in policies and processes, and they were leaving for better opportunities with competitors. Phil implemented several innovative programs to improve morale and productivity and coached managers and supervisors to improve their effectiveness and build a stronger

Bright Idea

Asset statements aren't just for résumés and interviews. Using them while networking helps your contacts have more confidence in recommending you to others and gives them a clearer picture of what you can do and which organizations you might be of benefit to.

team. His actions brought about a reduction in turnover by 64 percent in his first 18 months on the job.

See the CAO in this example? The context is that he came into a challenging situation where employee turnover was too high. The action he took was to make some significant changes that brought about the positive outcome of a reduction in turnover rate. On his résumé, Phil would give only brief highlights of this story—just enough to whet the reader's appetite. In a networking meeting or interview, he could then get into more specifics about his actions, such as details of the programs or his coaching and team-building abilities and tell more about the results and their impact on the organization.

If Phil listed only basic duties on his résumé, such as "developed and implemented new programs and policies" or "coached supervisors" or made only general claims in interviews, "Sure, I can reduce your turnover; that's one of my skills," he would be doing nothing to distinguish himself from other candidates. The reader or listener is left saying, "So, what?" But, if you tell them what was significant about what you've done, then you're really setting yourself apart from the pack. You would be amazed how few job seekers prepare and use asset statements, so if you make the effort to do so, you will be miles ahead of your competition.

Before developing your asset statements, it's important to think about which aspects of your background will be most relevant for the types of employers and jobs you are targeting. For each targeted job objective or for a particular employer you are approaching or preparing to interview with, ask yourself the following questions:

1. What does the employer need or the job require?
2. What assets do I have that enable me to meet those needs?
3. How would I use those assets to the employer's benefit?
4. How have I proven in the past that I can do what I claim to be capable of, that is, from which experiences should I develop asset statements?

The sections that follow provide more detail on what each of these questions, or steps, entails, and space is provided after each step for you to write down some thoughts to begin building your own asset statements.

Step one: identify the employer's needs

In the "Workplace Realities and Skills Needed" table in Chapter 2, you saw some universal skills and personal qualities that many employers are looking for. In Chapter 3, you learned research techniques that help you find out what is required of people who work in various career fields, and in Chapter 7, "Where Will You Find Your Job?" you'll read more about researching employers and positions. Through all of that, plus your own knowledge of what an employer needs, along with clues you may find in the official job requirements stated for advertised job openings, you should have, or will have, a good sense of what your targeted employers are looking for. Using that knowledge, you need to make sure that the asset statements you prepare are relevant and timely. You should develop asset statements that show you have solved the same or similar problems and met the same or similar goals.

Example: Frank is applying for a position in human resources management with a major commercial bank to handle IT staffing. Through his networking and research, he has identified some of the bank's primary needs as investigating the pros and cons of outsourcing some IT functions overseas, cutting IT personnel costs, and improving retention of high potential "keeper" employees.

Think about the needs of the employers you are targeting and jot down some notes in the space that follows about the needs of one specific employer you're approaching or job you're targeting, or more general notes about the typical needs of most employers and jobs you're likely to target.

Step two: identify which of your assets can meet the employer's needs

For each problem to be solved, growth area to contribute to, or other need of the employer, identify one or more of your assets that enable you to meet that need. Whether it's a skill, content knowledge, or personal quality, the asset should be relevant and beneficial to the job and the organization.

Example: Frank first chooses to focus on the bank's cost-cutting challenge. He thinks about his quantitative skills, problem-solving abilities, and knowledge of outsourcing.

Identify two or three of your assets that would be relevant to the employer needs you cited previously. Remember that the results of your self-assessment exercises in Chapter 3 can help you pinpoint some of your assets, whether transferable skills, content knowledge, or personal qualities.

Step three: state the benefit of your assets to the prospective employer

The next step is to think of how your strengths can be of direct benefit to the employer, either immediately or in the near future. Instead of offering vague promises, be sure to specify and quantify what you can do.

Example: Frank could tell prospective employers during interviews that he estimates he could cut costs by certain percentages within the first year and in subsequent years, based on his preliminary understanding of the problem and past experience.

Of course, you don't want to make promises you can't keep, but by being as specific as possible using your best judgment, you get employers excited about what you could do for them. Think about what sorts of results you would feel comfortable claiming you could achieve for your targeted employers, and write those in the following space.

Step four: give an example of a past accomplishment

Here's the meat of the process. This is where you craft asset statements to illustrate how you could meet the employer's needs. These statements help you back up the claims made in Step 3 with hard evidence, that is, past accomplishments. Examples of how you've solved problems in the past, met challenges, overcome obstacles, reached goals, and otherwise achieved success give credence to your claims. By showing that you have accomplished something similar in the past, you are not making empty promises, but are demonstrating solid evidence of your capabilities.

Plus, you're telling a story of sorts, which adds color to your discussion and makes the employer's encounters with you more memorable. Whenever possible and appropriate, to make it even more memorable, enhance your story with props that further illustrate the past incident or accomplishment you are describing. Letters of praise or thanks for work done well, formal commendations or awards, reports, photos, or other relevant documents from your portfolio can be powerful evidence of your achievements. (Portfolios and their contents are discussed more in the online Bonus Chapter 3, "More Self-Marketing Tools.")

Developing your asset statements

Now you should have a foundation for developing your asset statements (the foundation being what your targeted employers need and which of your assets and accomplishments are most relevant to meeting those needs). So, the next step is to start developing some asset statements. It's important to do this before getting too far into your job search as you'll need them during the early stages when writing your résumé and networking to explore options and generate leads. You'll then continue to need asset statements after you get into the thick of marketing yourself—speaking with prospective employers or recruiters to get your foot in the door and then closing the deal through the interviewing process and follow-up. To develop asset statements demonstrating your relevant past accomplishments, first you need to determine which accomplishments you want to feature and then script some asset statements that showcase those accomplishments.

Digging deep for asset statements

Thinking of achievements may be a cinch for you. You might be able to come up with several off the top of your head. You might even be the organized sort who has kept an ongoing written record of your achievements as part of your own career management strategy. What if you just can't think of anything you've accomplished? This is particularly common in people who've done work that doesn't have an obvious direct impact on an employer's bottom line in a dollars-and-cents sort of way, such as technicians or support personnel who do important work but don't always see the impact they have on their organizations. "I just did my job and did it well," they often say. Or perhaps you've been a stay-at-home parent who feels your biggest achievement has been raising healthy, happy kids, but you don't know how to turn that into an achievement story for the business world. Don't despair—everyone has achievements that are worthy of asset statements. To find them, try asking yourself the following questions:

- Is there something I am particularly proud of (whether it was formally recognized or not)?
- Was I able to do more with less?
- Have I done something in a new way? Been more creative, innovative, or efficient?
- Did I save my organization money by cutting costs or through other measures?
- Did I bring money into my organization? (Even if you weren't in a direct revenue-generation role, did you work

on projects or provide support to business development efforts that yielded a certain amount of revenue?)

- What makes you different from the people you've worked with? Are you known for a particular skill or talent? Known for doing something better, smarter, faster? Relied upon as the go-to person for something?

- Did you receive rewards or special recognition for anything?

- Did you get special mention in a performance review for something you did?

- Did you do your job well despite very challenging conditions or hurdles to overcome?

- Did you take the initiative to do something worthwhile that was not part of your regular job?

- Did you develop or design something significant?

- Did you manage people or projects effectively?

- Did you hire, train, or supervise people? How many?

- Did you improve productivity or reduce downtime?

- Did you successfully manage budgets or projects that had a budget?

Accomplishments come in all shapes and sizes. They might contain impressive dollar amounts or major awards or honors. They may have taken place during exceptionally challenging times, or they may simply be things you did well under fairly routine circumstances. As long as it is something you are proud of, that brought about positive results, and that you think

---

 Bright Idea

If you've ever had what is called a 360-degree review in which your peers, subordinates, and others you work with—not just bosses—rate your performance, you have valuable data to use in asset statements to distinguish yourself from the competition.

showcases your skills and distinguishes you from the competition, it's a worthy achievement.

Scripting an asset statement

Now think about an achievement you can discuss in your search and use the space that follows to develop an asset statement describing that achievement in the CAO formula.

Context

What was the context of your achievement? Was it a particularly challenging situation? Was there a problem to solve? Costs to cut? Business to develop? A troubled account to turn around? Productivity to improve? Systems to streamline? You might use phrases such as "during a period of major organizational restructuring," "despite challenging market conditions," "within exceptionally tight deadlines," or "accomplished as additional responsibilities while successfully maintaining regular workload." Give enough detail to set the context, but not so much detail that the story becomes too long.

Those are only a few examples of situations that can form the context of your asset statement. Describe the context of your asset statement here:

Action(s)

Next, list the actions you took to meet the challenge you described in the "Context" section. You don't need to record every detail of a project or incident. Simple jot down key phrases or short sentences to describe the specific actions you took in the situation. Use direct, action verbs as much as possible, such as "Identified unnecessary departmental expenses," rather than "Unnecessary department expenses were identified." You (or your team) is who did it, so say that!

Outcome

Briefly describe the results that came from your actions. Whenever possible, quantify the results by citing dollar amounts, quantities, or percentages, such as revenue generated, costs reduced, productivity rates improved, number of safety incidents decreased, or amount of time saved in hours, weeks, and so on. If the outcomes cannot be expressed in numbers because the nature of the situation simply did not involve anything quantifiable, that's fine; just be as precise as possible, presenting the results in as tangible, measurable a manner as you can.

Watch Out!

Personal pronouns (such as I, we, our) don't go in résumés. You may use them here to make it easier to start writing your asset statements and of course use them when you speak about your accomplishments, but remember you'll have to take them out when you put the asset statements in your résumé.

Now that you have the components of your asset statement under the Context, Action(s), and Outcome sections, you have the makings of a good asset statement, but it probably sounds quite disjointed. It's time now to make it flow together.

When Blowing Your Own Horn Feels Like Blowing Hot Air

If you're reluctant to tout your accomplishments because you don't like "blowing your own horn," that's understandable but a big mistake. The competition will be talking about theirs so you'd better do the same! Consider these ways to overcome common objections and get more comfortable with using asset statements:

"But it was a team effort. I don't want to take all the credit." Sure it was a team effort, but you were an integral member of the team and deserve some credit.

"It wasn't a big deal. It's just my job." If it wasn't a big deal, then why should a prospective employer bother to read your résumé or listen to what you have to say? If you accomplished something positive, it was a big deal, even if it was just all in a day's work to you.

"I don't want to sound like I'm bragging or have a big ego." As long as you state the facts in a nonboastful tone and intersperse your conversations with "We did it," not just "I did it," you won't sound like you're boasting.

Making it flow

Asset statements that will appear in résumés need to be quite brief, usually no more than about three to four lines of text on a typical résumé page—typical being a page set with left and right margins of one-inch each and a font size of about ten to twelve points. (More specifics of résumé layout are discussed in Chapter 5.) There are no hard and fast rules for length, but most readers will start to lose interest or overlook key details when an asset statement goes on for more than a few lines.

> 66 With competition more intense than ever, companies can no longer ... carry on their payrolls excessive numbers of employees who do not make a measurable contribution to the competitive effort. 99
>
> —Max Messmer in *The Fast Forward MBA in Hiring*, New York: John Wiley & Sons, 1998

Asset statements that you'll be speaking out loud when networking or interviewing can be a bit longer. You can flesh out the details by saying more about the context, actions, and/or outcome. Even then, however, avoid talking for more than about 90 seconds to 2 minutes, or you risk losing the listener's attention. You can hit the highlights in a minute or two, wait for the other person to comment or ask a follow-up question, and then continue with more details of your story if the other person seems interested in knowing more.

Whether written or spoken, asset statements need to be scripted so that you know all the pieces flow well together. Don't try to memorize your asset statements word-for-word, however. Script them only to be sure you have the stories fleshed out coherently and concisely and then practice speaking them in a way that flows naturally without reading from the script. (You might want to list key points from your script in bulleted format to help you remember what to say.)

Repeat this process until you have at least eight to ten asset statements prepared, pulling accomplishments from various times in your work history, with most of them coming from your more recent positions. You won't necessarily talk about all of the accomplishments in any given networking meeting or interview, and you might not need to include all of them in your résumé, but having several prepared will enable you to select the ones that are most appropriate for each situation. The examples in the next section will help you see how yours might sound.

Examples of asset statements

To further help you get comfortable developing your own asset statements, I've provided the examples that follow to give you an idea of how asset statements can sound. You'll see that the order of context, action, and outcome varies, with some statements opening with the outcome or result, and others opening with the context or action then ending with the outcome. All of these are written as they would be for a résumé. When speaking about these assets and accomplishments, the statements would be fleshed out to give more detail and have less of a brief, formal tone.

Asset statements with quantified outcomes

Notice how these assets statements make use of numbers to document the results that were achieved. The numbers can be dollar amounts, percentages, time frames, or quantities. If you quantify your asset statements, make sure you can back up the numbers either with formal documentation or by describing a logical thought process that led you to come up with the figures.

- Defined and drove 30 percent cost reduction measures through assets management and process improvements.

- Increased sales by more than 300 percent through innovative direct mail campaigns and client presentations during first 1-1/2 years with the organization.

- Consolidated two call centers, which increased customer responsiveness 40 percent and reduced expenses by 60 percent.

- Organized and led a team of two managers who supported 400 customers, built a pipeline of $10 million in services opportunities, and closed $4 million in services opportunities in nine months.

- Created and presented workshops and proposals on implementation plans to hundreds of customers, resulting in millions of dollars in new business.

- As president of a homeowners' association, envisioned and spearheaded improvements that led to equity increase of $6.4 million among 245 homes, a much faster rate of increase than that of surrounding subdivisions.

- Realized synergy and saved $500 thousand per year for two years by establishing a profitable working relationship between two departments.

- Established and grew a company over a three-year period. Identified new products and services that leveraged location and size. Sales increased from $800 thousand to more than $2 million from Year Two to Three.

- Defined and delivered marketing strategies and marketing programs across all product areas to achieve a Number Two market share position.

- Under exceptionally challenging market conditions, transformed region from least profitable in the company to company average in two years through focus on controllable expenses and elimination of nonperforming units.

- Produced the best two-year shrink reduction performance in the company, with savings exceeding $600,000.

- In business analyst role, identified $2000 per month in unnecessary project management expenses.

Watch Out!

Even though it strengthens your résumé considerably to include quantified asset statements, never make the mistake of making up numbers just to have numbers on your résumé. You must be able to explain where the numbers came from. Do not lie!

- Exceeded annual key business indicator quotas consistently by an average of 15 percent for two years by initiating new products and services to assigned accounts.

- Introduced 10 new accounts by conducting personal sales calls, exhibiting at trade shows, and developing key contacts via email and phone.

- Ensured corporate, departmental, and client needs were met in a timely manner, by maintaining a training compliance at or above 99.8 percent for the district's 700 employees.

- Eliminated a staff position and restructured operation of phone system to reduce annual costs by $60,000.

- Developed supplier base and logistic processes to support lean manufacturing objectives. Targeted supplier cost reduced 3 percent annually with 45 percent reduction in defective materials.

- Led two high-profile projects totaling more than 8,000 hours. Met aggressive target dates while satisfying high-quality standards and ensured timely communication with project stakeholders at all levels in the organization.

- Raised more than $10,000 for local high school fund-raiser by revamping solicitation system and better organizing parent volunteers.

Asset statements with non-quantified outcomes

The asset statements below are strong and effective despite the fact that no numbers are mentioned. There are times when results you have achieved just cannot be quantified. That's fine as long as each asset statement passes the "So, what?" test. Make sure that each statement is fleshed out sufficiently to tell the reader what is significant about the actions you took.

- Identified the need for, and developed under a tight time line, Web-based customer care tools to provide more effective and user-friendly online self-help.

- Consistently exceeded sales goals for assigned territory, including maintaining ongoing contracts and relationships with the company's largest healthcare customers.

- Promoted to Assistant Vice President within two years as a result of dedication and ability to learn all aspects of the company.

- Personally visited or contacted top 100 customers soliciting input regarding support expectations and then shifted the service organization from a reactive to a proactive philosophy that anticipated customer needs and offered immediate solutions for major accounts.

- Developed and implemented measurable objectives for two regional call centers, improving performance for maintenance and order entry.

- Prepared correspondence, including complex mail merges, involving sensitive information with no breaches in confidentiality.

- Took the initiative to create a special project team to handle escalations and work large projects to meet customers' needs in a more timely manner. Success of this method led to company-wide adoption.

- Mentored peers on human resource policies, as well as interviewing and hiring practices, resulting in employees better matched to their jobs and less turn over.

- Received the *[Company name] Excellence Award* for developing business improvement processes.

- Received recognition from senior management for successful improvement of the budget process by creating detailed, user-friendly financial templates, conducting budget training, and implementing control procedures to ensure accuracy.

- Revamped divisional policies and procedures manual issued internally and externally to third-party property managers, resulting in minimized problems related to third-party reporting practices.

- Successfully implemented new online marketing initiatives and product launches under tight timelines with limited resources.

- As an integral player in the organization's turnaround efforts, drove the rebuilding of region district manager team by focusing on performance and team-building skills.

- Initiated a productivity improvement plan and training initiative that resulted in increased store sales productivity and reduced selling cost.

- Planned and completed an office move, relocating employees, furniture, and equipment to new office space within budget and without loss of productivity.

- Initiated activities involving employees in community service programs, improving morale.

- Offered new technology training at all employee levels, which improved the billing process and enhanced productivity for the Southeast district.

 Bright Idea

As much as your schedule allows, participate in community service, *pro bono* professional projects, and other purposeful activities during your job search so that you have current examples of accomplishments to discuss during interviews.

- Readily took on the extra assignment of training both new hires and continuing employees while performing regular duties.

- Acted as a liaison between the operations support and customer service departments, improving relationships between the two groups.

- Participated in an internal Web site committee to steer the creation and direction of an intranet site to benefit the department by making information more accessible.

Asset statement FAQs

If you've been in sales, it will probably be easy to develop asset statements for your résumé and to speak about them in interviews. You've had to keep close track of when and by how much you've met or exceeded sales quotas, how much revenue you've generated, and other achievements. Similarly, if you've been a manager responsible for saving money, making money, improving productivity, quality, or processes, or any of a host of bottom line objectives, you won't have much trouble coming up with asset statements either. Many of them can probably be quantified, too.

What if it's not so easy to come up with asset statements? Perhaps you've not been in a role that had an obvious, direct impact on the organization. You had a job to do, and you did it, but were far removed from the bottom line. Or, maybe you haven't worked in paid, full-time employment in a long time (or ever) and haven't racked up a long list of professional achievements. These are among the many common situations that trip up job seekers when trying to develop asset statements. Many of these issues are addressed in the frequently asked questions sections that follow.

I can't quantify my achievements? Do I have to?

Do make an effort to quantify whenever possible. If dollar amounts or percentages aren't relevant to your accomplishments, or you just don't have the data, you can refer to other numbers such as numbers of people you managed or supervised, number of clients or accounts you served, or hours involved in a project. As you saw from the previous examples, many good asset statements contain such numbers or do not contain any numbers at all. If quantifying just doesn't make sense, then at least describe the positive impact of your actions. If you weren't in a position to have much impact at all, such as in internships or some entry-level or short-term positions, emphasize the skills you developed or demonstrated and the things you learned.

I can't think of any challenging situations I've been in

Asset statements don't always have to be built around an all-out challenge. If you did face challenging situations, great. If not, it's not a problem. Speaking about the positive outcome of carrying out your routine tasks well is often just as powerful.

Do all of my asset statements have to be from work-related experiences?

As often as possible, you should pull examples from professional experiences because those will undoubtedly be more relevant for the interviewer. Remember that these experiences can include not just current or past jobs but also involvement in trade and professional associations, as well as community business activities such as boards of trustees, Chambers of Commerce, leadership in Junior Achievement, or related groups. There are times, however, when you do not have a work-related example with which to demonstrate a particular asset, especially if you have limited paid work experience outside the home or school, so you must draw from your personal or academic life. Doing so is acceptable if the example is relevant—point out how your participation in a sport shows leadership skills, or tell how you've gained knowledge of a particular subject through a personal hobby. You saw some examples in the previous section, such as an accomplishment from a school fundraising effort, and one emphasizing leadership in a homeowners' association. If the example is especially strong and relevant, you might even be better off using it rather than a professional one.

How old is too old when choosing examples?

Generally speaking, the more recent the example, the better. This is certainly true if the accomplishment you are describing relates to an industry, product, or type of job that has changed significantly since the event took place. However, if you want to use an older example that is much more powerful or relevant than anything you've done in the past few years, then by all means use it.

I held a job for a short time and don't have any results to report, what can I do?

This has been a common problem during times of economic downturn and labor market unrest when organizations often have to lay people off shortly after they've come on board. The first thing to do in this case is to contact people still at the organization to see whether any actions you took while there brought about some results after you left. If so, feel free to speak about them, stating that something you developed or began to implement while there was later fully implemented, resulted in a certain amount of revenue, or had some other positive result. If nothing like that has occurred, then focus on what you did do while there, fleshing out basic responsibilities in a bit more detail to distract from the lack of results. As long as you have some outcomes, or results, elsewhere on your résumé, this won't be a problem.

> ❝ I've never been much of a self-promoter, but when I started talking about my strengths in terms of tangible results my efforts led to, I no longer felt like I was bragging. I was just stating a fact. ❞
>
> —*Marilyn, management consultant*

What if I know I possess a particular asset but can't think of any example that demonstrates it?

This is a common dilemma that I find most people can get past if they just put some thought into it. It's often difficult to think of great examples off the top of your head, so don't worry if nothing comes to mind right away. You may need to jog your memory a bit by walking yourself through your résumé to recall incidents worth talking about in an interview. You can also enlist the help of others, particularly current or past coworkers who may remember your successes better than you do. Don't forget about the "Digging Deep for Asset Statements" section earlier in this chapter that offered lots of suggestions for how to think of your accomplishments.

What if I have more than one example that demonstrates an asset?

Great! You will most likely have more than one accomplishment in your past that provides evidence of a particular asset. You will end up with a repertoire of sorts from which you can pull the best example for each occasion. By the way, the reverse can happen as well—you have one example that demonstrates more than one asset. This is especially common because we invariably use multiple skills, personal qualities, and knowledge bases to accomplish any one task.

What if I can't discern the organization's needs despite a concerted research effort?

If you simply cannot get the inside scoop on a particular organization, don't despair. You can always prepare asset statements for the needs that are universal to most employers. Also, you'll learn in Chapter 13, "Typical and Not-So-Typical Interview Questions," about ways to determine an employer's needs after you get into the interview, so you can pull from your repertoire of asset statements as needed.

Just the facts

- To build a case for why you're the best candidate, you must use asset statements to provide evidence of past accomplishments, problems solved, and results obtained.

- Employers are more interested in the skills, knowledge, and character you demonstrated on past jobs and on the positive results those qualities brought about, than on a basic description of the jobs themselves.

- An asset statement is a very concise story demonstrating a situation (Context) in which you took particular actions (Action) that brought about positive results (Outcome). Use the Context-Action-Outcome, or CAO formula when creating asset statements.

- Asset statements are critical elements of your résumé, networking conversations, and replies to questions in interviews, especially in behavior-based interviews.

- Asset statements must be relevant to the reader or listener.

Gaining the Competitive Edge—How to Market Yourself

PART II

Résumés

Put Al Franken, Rush Limbaugh, and Bill O'Reilly in a room, let them loose on the most controversial topic of the day, and they're more likely to reach consensus than would a room full of people trying to agree about how to write a résumé. What makes a résumé effective is highly debatable. Everybody's got an opinion. Everybody's an expert. Everybody knows what they like to see in a résumé, and as often happens with that funny little thing called personal opinion, the next person's going to want to see something different than what the last one wanted.

You may have heard all sorts of so-called absolutes about résumés. Résumés must be only one page long! No, a résumé shorter than two pages makes you look inexperienced and weak! Only go back 10 years in your professional experience. No, list every professional job you've held. Never list graduation dates on your résumé! No, list all graduation dates no matter when they were. Those are only a few of the résumé topics on which you'll hear conflicting advice. It's enough to drive a job seeker crazy.

So, how do you cut through the chaos? Well, you don't. I don't mean that you can't put a great résumé together. You can. What I mean is that you don't try to find the absolute right and wrong answers. There aren't any. Instead, you educate yourself about the pros and cons of various approaches and then factor in your career goals, who your audience is, and what your own personal style is. You create a résumé that fits what *most* people are looking for, while tailoring it to your own situation and preferences. That's what I'm going to help you do in this chapter.

Do I even need a résumé?

You might have heard about some of the trends that pop up from time to time in the world of job hunting advice that tell you to toss your résumé and forget about even using one. Although it's true that a résumé has serious limitations for what it can do in your search (because just sending out a piece of paper is no substitute for getting out and talking to people directly), it's not true that you don't need one. If a résumé is prepared as a marketing document, highlighting your assets in a way that is relevant to the reader, then the résumé plays an enormously important role in your job search.

Your résumé serves as an introduction of who you are and what you have to offer, and when you have a clear career objective in mind, it conveys what you're looking for as well. Your résumé tells prospective employers and recruiters two things. First, it tells them what you could do for them. By including not just a list of your past jobs and credentials but also your accomplishments (those asset statements you developed in Chapter 4), you show how you've made a difference for past employers, and thus, how you could contribute to your next employer. This first task of your résumé is the door-opening function. It piques enough interest to get people talking to you and interviewing you. The second thing your résumé does is to document what you've done and what you know. After someone gets interested in you after reading the highlights of your background and

Traditional Résumés versus Electronic Résumés

The focus of this chapter is on traditional résumés—résumés created as a document in a word processing application like Microsoft Word or WordPerfect. Traditional résumés look nice. They use styling features such as bold and italic, centering or right justifying some text, and perhaps borders, tables, and columns. Use your traditional résumé when you need hard copy to hand to someone or send through regular mail. Also use it when you know someone will open it as an attachment to an email. Fax it when you know the recipient will read it rather than having it scanned electronically. Your electronic résumé—eRésumé as I call it—is used when uploading the résumé to a Web site, sending within the body of an email message rather than attached, or faxing into an electronic system where it will be scanned. Your eRésumé doesn't look pretty; it has no fancy styling or graphic design, but it's readable when transmitted electronically. More about the differences between the two types of résumés and detailed instructions on how to create an eRésumé are discussed in Chapter 10, "Online Job Hunting." For now, concentrate on your traditional résumé to get the résumé content ironed out; then it will be easier to convert the format to an eRésumé.

accomplishments, the résumé then documents the details of your background. You don't include every detail, or the résumé will become too long and boring, but you give sufficient detail to show what you were doing during certain time periods, who you have worked for, what titles you've held, what degrees you hold, if any, and so forth.

Is it possible to secure interviews without anyone seeing your résumé? Sure, it happens. Through networking you speak to people who are willing to bring you in for an interview based on nothing more than your self-marketing sound bite. Is it possible to land a job without anyone ever having seen your résumé? Yes, that happens too, although it's rare. In most cases, you're going to be asked for a résumé, so you'd better have a strong one at the ready.

Avoiding the biggest résumé mistakes

I review and edit thousands of résumés every year in my role as a career counselor. I have also been in a position to read résumés of job seekers and to speak with countless employers and recruiters about what they find right and wrong with résumés. We all tend to see the same mistakes over and over. The most common mistakes are as follows.

Too long

How long is too long? Keep in mind that most résumés are read in about 10 to 30 seconds. If someone wants to know more, he or she might spend an additional minute or two reading it more carefully. Because of that, your résumé needs to be a length that can be quickly skimmed to pick up on the key points and highlights. This usually means that your résumé should be no longer than two pages. A one-page résumé is fine for job seekers with less experience, or when the background and credentials can be presented so succinctly that they fit onto one page without leaving anything important out. The two-page length usually works better for those with at least several years of experience or those who have had a lot of different employers and positions, or with experience that is somewhat complicated, such as project-based work or lots of consulting work in which there is simply more information to list than with other jobs.

A résumé is not a detailed account of everything you've ever done. It is a marketing document that hits the highlights of what you've done and what you have to offer in the future.

Bright Idea

If you have more to say than fits on two pages, consider adding a page or two of addendum to give details that would make your main résumé too cluttered. More on addendums in "Résumé writing section by section" later in this chapter.

When you buy a packaged good in a store, you probably don't read every bit of fine print on the box—at least not until you're pretty sure that you are likely to buy the product and want to know more. Instead, your preliminary buying decision is probably based on the most eye-catching, brief buzzwords that tell you about the product and its benefit to you. Résumés are much the same. You whet the reader's appetite with buzzwords, power phrases, and just enough detail, all laid out in an easy-to-read format. Don't describe every responsibility and task or every special project on every past job. Be selective, including only relevant information that gives a quick overview of what you did and how well you did it. The concise, marketing-oriented résumé gets you noticed and gets your foot in the door; then you provide the details after you're on the other side of the door.

Too short

If you find that all your résumé information fits easily onto one page with plenty of room to spare, then you're probably not saying enough. This is common with students and recent graduates or others with limited work experience, as well as with those whose job responsibilities were not very complex or high level. Although brevity is nice because it means your résumé can be read quickly, don't be too brief. Make sure that you have fully fleshed out job descriptions and asset statements. Also be sure to include all résumé sections relevant to the types of jobs you're seeking. These are described in "Résumé writing section by section" later in this chapter.

Laundry lists of duties

Read the list of bullet points that follows and see whether you can answer the question: "How would this candidate add value to our organization?"

- Responsible for generating new accounts.
- Negotiated contracts.
- Hired and trained new sales associates.
- Assisted marketing department with special projects.

A list of basic duties and responsibilities does nothing to distinguish you from the competition. Sure, you need to mention what you were responsible for, but that should be a minimal part of each job entry on your résumé. (Later, you'll learn how to group the duties together into one brief paragraph, a "Job Context Snapshot" under each job title.) The focus instead should be on your achievements—how you made a difference and brought about positive results while carrying out those duties. Look at the difference when we turn those points into asset statements:

- Successfully met the challenge of generating new accounts for a stagnant product line. Trained sales force in creative lead generation techniques, resulting in the acquisition of five new key accounts and a 15% sales revenue increase over previous year.
- Used relationship-building talents and collaborative negotiating strategies to secure three national contracts representing more than $12 million in revenue.
- Hired and trained more than 20 new sales associates, including mentoring 3 associates who were promoted to management positions within 18 months.
- Used technical product knowledge and presentation skills to collaborate with marketing department on a new national trade show exhibition strategy that directly yielded several new customers.

By turning the statements of basic duties into asset statements, the marketing power of this résumé increases dramatically.

No clear objective

If you have a clearly defined job target, then you might want to include an actual objective statement at the top of your résumé. Example: "A position in sales management leveraging expertise in team-building, training, and marketing strategy to expand markets and increase revenue." But, if you are open to a variety of types of opportunities, you'll probably be leaving the optional objective statement off of your résumé. Doing so is fine as long as your résumé makes it clear to the reader what sorts of skills and strengths you bring to the table and as long as your résumé text has a coherent theme. Be sure not to include any irrelevant information that distracts the reader from your focus. For example, I recently read the résumé of an insurance claims adjustor applying for positions in that field. When I got to the education section, I saw that the candidate had very recently completed a paralegal studies certificate program. This immediately raises a red flag, as it tells me that the job seeker might be looking for jobs in insurance only out of necessity but is really trying to become a paralegal. If you're working toward a career change, keep it to yourself and don't advertise it on your résumé if the résumé is for jobs in your old or current field.

Not customized

If you are targeting one narrowly defined type of job in one narrowly defined industry, you can probably get away with a one-size-fits-all résumé. But, if you are keeping your options open for a variety of roles in various settings, then you might need to have more than one résumé. Make sure that every word, every job description, every asset statement, and every educational or professional credential included on your résumé is tailored as much as possible to your job target. If you've held jobs that don't directly relate, don't worry. I don't mean that you should omit them, but do look for ways to downplay them or to describe them in terms that are relevant to the target job at hand.

Poorly worded

If writing is not your thing, find a friend or colleague who writes well to help you with the wording of your résumé or hire a professional résumé writer. You need not use fancy language and overly sophisticated vocabulary—in fact, simpler words are much better for a résumé because they're quicker and easier to read—but you do need to be sure that you've used words properly. Clunky wording not only slows down the reader and makes it likely that they won't have time to finish reading your résumé, it also reflects poorly on you as a professional. So, make sure to have lots of people read your résumé and give you some honest feedback on where language improvements could be made.

Typos and errors

I can't even count the number of times I've heard hiring professionals and headhunters say that if they spot a typo or error of spelling or grammar in a résumé, they toss it out without reading any further. No excuse can be offered for sloppiness on a résumé. It's easy for mistakes to happen, however. I know full well how tired you get reading your own résumé over and over. There's a simple and obvious solution: have plenty of other pairs of eyes take a fresh look at your résumé.

Crowded or hard to follow visually

The layout and overall look of your résumé plays a surprisingly big part in how your text will be read. Not only should your résumé look nice to project a polished, professional image, your résumé's visual presentation needs to make it easy for the eyes to zero-in on key data and understand what text goes with what. Avoid crowding the résumé with too much information. A text-heavy résumé doesn't invite the reader to want to read; it looks like it will be too much trouble to read. If your résumé looks crowded, go on to a second page if it's currently on only one

---

Wordly Wise

Avoid these all-too-common vocabulary snafus on your résumé:

- The past tense of the verb to lead is *led,* not lead.

- You *ensure* quality standards are met; you don't insure them unless you are writing an insurance policy.

- When you train people, you don't orientate them, you *orient* them.

- You *effect* change, not affect it.

- You monitor procedures to determine *whether* they were in compliance, not *if* they were.

- *Irregardless* is not a word. Use *regardless.*

---

page. If it's already a two-pager, go through it with a fine-tooth comb to edit out any nonessential information.

The sample résumés provided in the Appendix, "Action Verbs and Sample Résumés," show you some effective layouts and styles for résumés that are easy to read.

Writing style/editing

It doesn't matter if you earned straight As in English class or can write a best-selling novel, résumé writing is its own beast to tackle. Use the following guidelines to learn the language of résumé writing and ensure that your résumé can be read quickly and understood easily.

No personal pronouns

Omit I, my, we, and our from your résumé. It's assumed you're talking about yourself and the organizations you've worked for, so you don't need the pronouns to specify who you're talking about.

Direct action verbs

Instead of saying something like "Management of the quality control process," or "The quality control process was managed," say "Managed the quality control process." The simple process of converting a passive verb or verb phrase ("was managed") or a gerund (a verb acting like a noun) into an action verb makes a world of difference in the strength of your résumé. In the Appendix, you'll find a helpful list of action verbs to give you some ideas.

Short sentences

Until you get used to hearing or reading it, résumé language sounds unusually succinct and even choppy. It requires writing incomplete, short sentences that would seem to break all the usual rules of sentence structure. For example, instead of "I wrote a new training manual that helped all of our employees learn new technology to increase their productivity," you would say "Created technology training manual that increased employees' productivity." Leaving the subject "I" out of the phrase, as well as articles such as "a" or "the" and pronouns like "our" keeps the statement brief and helps the résumé be a quicker read overall.

> 66 I've been in this business [recruiting] 32 years, and I've never read a résumé. I scan, peruse, look for buzzwords, but I don't read every word. I want to hear the details directly from the candidate. 99
>
> —Dutch Earle, Managing Principal, Executive Strategies, Inc.

Short blocks of text

In addition to keeping sentences short, you need to keep paragraphs or other blocks of text as short as possible. Although there are no magic numbers here, a résumé that has blocks of text longer than about four or five lines is less inviting to the reader. Dense paragraphs and long blocks of text cause you to run the risk that important information will be glossed over when the résumé is skimmed quickly. Try to break up text into bullet points whenever it makes sense to do so.

Universal language

Avoid using too much industry- or role-specific jargon or acronyms and abbreviations unless you are certain that your résumé will be only in the hands of people who would not only understand that jargon but expect to see it as a way to determine your level of knowledge in your field. If you're trying to appear versatile for various types of jobs or industries or are making a career change, convert jargon to more universal terms whenever possible.

Résumé writing section by section

Okay, folks, it's show time. Let's go through the typical sections of a résumé to get you started on creating a new résumé or revising an old one. If starting from scratch, open up a plain document in your word processing application or write the résumé by hand and have someone else type it. If using a computer, start with one-inch margins all around and a font size of 11 point in Times New Roman or Arial. You can always change the margins and font after you see what amount of text you're dealing with.

Name and contact information

This section of your résumé might not seem like rocket science, but you actually need to watch out for a few important things when putting together the header of your résumé.

 Watch Out!

Don't try to write your résumé without having done some self-assessment to identify your assets and career objective. Revisit Chapters 3 and 4 if you need to do some more work in those areas.

Name

List both your first and last name. Middle initial (or first initial if you go by your middle name as I do) is optional. If you go by a nickname, you would typically err on the side of formality and list your full name, saving the nickname for when you start speaking with employers. Some people feel strongly about including their nickname, however, and if you're one of those, then it's your choice. You can list your full first name with your nickname in parentheses right after it.

If you hold an advanced degree or professional designation, you might want to include the acronym after your name. This is usually advisable for those who hold a master's or doctoral degree that is relevant to the job sought. Exceptions to this are the M.B.A. and J.D., which are typically not listed after one's name unless there is some reason you particularly want or need to highlight this credential. Usually, you just list these in the education section of the résumé. If you hold a professional designation such as a P.M.P. (a project management credential) or any designation relevant to your job target, then it can be advantageous to list it after your name.

As for where all this goes, start with a simple header where your name is centered at the top of the page and all contact information is centered below it. Later, you might want to make a snazzier header with the name and contact information left or right justified. No matter where you put it, though, make sure the size of your name is not overly large, say no more than about 14- to 16-point bold font. Nothing says egotist like a name in 26-point font!

Street address

You have a couple of options here. To list complete contact information, you would include street address, apartment number if any, city, state, and ZIP code on two lines centered below your name. For security reasons, however, you might prefer to omit your street address and list only city, state, and ZIP code.

To be even more secure, you can omit any address information and list only email address and phone number, or just your email address because addresses can sometimes be traced from a phone number. If you're using your résumé primarily to network with people you know or know of through colleagues, or to apply for positions with companies where you know who will be reading your résumé, such precautions may not be necessary. For wider searches and certainly online job hunting, you might feel more comfortable leaving off any identifying information other than name and email address. And, to take the security one step further, if your name is somewhat rare, you might want to list only first initial with your last name so that your contact information could not be traced as easily from your name. The bottom line is to take reasonable measures for personal security without being overly paranoid. Use your own judgment and take my advice as only general guidelines. This topic of security and your résumé is discussed in more detail in Chapter 10.

Email address

You must include an email address on your résumé as many employers will want to contact you by email. With all the free services out there (such as Yahoo and Hotmail), there's no excuse for not having one. Even if you don't have a computer with Internet access, have a reliable friend check your email and/or use computers at the public library until you can get your own. Also, make sure that your email address sounds professional rather than overly personal or cutesy and is easy to type.

Phone numbers

All an employer needs is one good phone number at which to reach you. Some job seekers list home, work, home-office, mobile, and any other number where they can sometimes be reached. This is overkill. List one or two numbers where you know you are most likely to be reached or to be diligent about checking messages.

Moneysaver

Never print too many copies of your résumé at one time. You're likely to make changes from time to time as you use your résumé, so print only the number you need on hand at any one time and make more as needed.

Fax Number

It is optional to include a fax number, and usually not necessary. Most employers or recruiters will call or email you after reading your résumé and might need to fax you something only after that initial contact, such as to send an application. Don't waste space on the résumé with a fax number; you can always provide it later when requested.

Objective

An objective is a brief (usually one- to two-line) statement of the type of position you're looking for. Of all the debatable aspects of résumés, the issue of whether or not to include an objective statement at the top of the résumé is one of the most controversial. Some people say always include an objective, and others say you should never do so. I'll let you in on the inside scoop here: It depends.

Do include an objective if...

- The experience listed on your résumé does not make it obvious that you are seeking a particular type of job, such as when you are changing careers. In that case, the objective helps clarify your job target for the reader when the rest of your résumé would not clearly point to that target.

- You are a recent graduate or anyone seeking a position at entry-level where your work experience is limited and educational degree or major may not directly speak to your target.

- You are applying to a particular job opening and can tailor the objective statement to that job's specfications, or you are sending the résumé to someone whose interests you know, so you can tailor the objective to that targeted reader.

Do not include an objective if...

- You want to keep your options open in terms of the type of positions or industry in which you're aiming to work.

- You are a senior-level professional or executive. It is customary to open with an "Executive Profile" (see the "Qualifications Summary" section later in this chapter) rather than an objective.

- Your résumé includes a qualifications summary that helps the reader "put you on the map"—that is, see what sorts of roles you might be right for. An objective might be redundant with a summary.

In general, objective statements are very optional. Only include one if you feel it would greatly help your case, such as when you are a recent grad or career-changer. If you do choose to use an objective, make sure that it is concise and substantive. Too many objectives are far too vague: "Seeking a challenging and rewarding position with advancement opportunities utilizing extensive skills and experience." What do we learn about the candidate from that? Nothing, except that he or she wants what most people want. We don't know anything about this person's desired role, level, or industry; the types of skills and experience he or she wants to use; or any contribution he or she can make.

Sample résumé objectives

The sample objectives that follow illustrate these components of an objective statement (as well as a few very brief ones stating only the type of position desired with skills, experience, and contribution not mentioned).

- Sales management position that utilizes strengths in leadership, team development, and relationship building to contribute to solid growth and client allegiance.

- An accounting position in which strengths in leadership, problem solving, and communication will be used to improve operational efficiencies and meet corporate goals.

- A contract position as a Java programmer.

- Technical position in network systems utilizing five years of experience installing, supporting, and troubleshooting servers in a WAN environment.

- A part-time technical support position utilizing coding and debugging skills.

- A management position in sales and marketing utilizing strong leadership skills with a focus on introducing new value-added products to the market to help solve customers' problems.

- Seeking employment as a Senior Software Test Engineer utilizing breadth and depth of experience in a wide range of software systems.

- An operations management position with emphasis on team building, creative problem solving, and use of technology to support growth and profitability.

- An executive-level IT position capitalizing on extensive experience, passion, and talent for managing and leading people, processes, and technology to decrease company costs and increase shareholder value.

- A senior management or consulting position in healthcare leveraging expertise in strategic planning, process improvement, and workflow analysis to increase shareholder value and create strategic advantage.

- Management position in which strengths in project management, marketing communications, and problem solving will be utilized to increase market share, strengthen customer loyalty, and achieve the organization's strategic goals.

- An administrative position utilizing strengths in organization, oral and written communication, attention to detail, and customer service to contribute to the progress of a dynamic organization.
- An entry-level position in advertising account management.

Note that the preceding objectives rarely go beyond two lines, so keep your objective as short as possible. Also note that you don't see the words "I" or "my" in these samples. Personal pronouns are unnecessary in the objective (and anywhere else on your résumé for that matter) because it's assumed that you are talking about yourself. Your résumé should be written in the third person as if someone else wrote it about you.

Qualifications summary

Almost every résumé can benefit from a summary section near the beginning of the résumé to give the reader a quick glimpse of who you are and what you have to offer. If you include an objective statement on your résumé, and if your work history is pretty straightforward and easy to decipher, then a summary may not be necessary, particularly if you're trying to keep the résumé to one page. But, in most cases, even if you did include an objective, the summary is a real asset to your résumé and important to make room for.

What to call your summary section

The summary section goes by any number of names. You might call it Qualifications Summary, Summary of Qualifications, Summary, Career Summary, Career Highlights, or Profile. If you are an executive or senior manager, the heading Executive Profile or Executive Summary is appropriate. You can also substitute a "tagline" for these generic headings. For example, you might say "Call Center Manager," "Software Engineer," or "Marketing Professional—Banking and Finance," "Administrative/Executive Assistant." Any sort of "tagline" that denotes your functional role, level, and/or industry affiliation is a nice alternative to the nonspecific heading. Be careful, however, as the tagline needs to be versatile enough to fit all possible types of opportunities for which you would want to be considered. Otherwise, you have to change the tagline to suit different situations. This can get time-consuming, so many people opt for one of the generic headings.

What goes in your summary section

The summary section is kind of a mini-version of your self-marketing sound bite (self-marketing sound bites are discussed in detail in Chapter 3). In fact, some job seekers write their résumé summary first and then develop their oral self-marketing sound bite from it. Or, if you've already composed your sound bite, you can modify it to form your résumé summary. Whichever way you do it, the résumé summary needs to tell the reader, very briefly, what you've done, what you know, and what your assets are. Specifically it includes any or all of the following (pick whichever elements are relevant to your job search and will present you in the best light):

1. Your number of years of experience. (Leave out if worried about age discrimination or if you have very limited experience.)

2. Your basic functional role (for example, sales, marketing, IT, human resources, general management, and so on).

3. Your level, such as entry-level, mid-level, or senior.

4. Your industry experience. (Leave this out if you're trying to appear versatile to cross over into a new industry.)

5. Your assets (skills, knowledge, and personal qualities).

This information can be presented in one brief paragraph or in a combination of a brief paragraph followed by bullet points. The samples that follow show how these five elements can look and sound in various combinations.

Sample résumé summaries

QUALIFICATIONS SUMMARY

Accomplished information technology professional with extensive experience in positions of increasing responsibility in project management, telecommunications, and mainframe computer operations. Known for developing strong implementation teams focused on improving customer productivity and increasing company profitability. Proven track record in the following areas:

Budgeting and Planning	P&L Responsibility
Vendor Management	Process re-engineering
Mentoring and Team Building	Delivering presentations

PROFILE

Legal/administrative assistant with more than twenty years of experience in corporations and law firms. Proven ability to handle sensitive information. Highly organized team player, skilled at building business relationships on all levels of an organization. Excellent interpersonal skills. Reliable and responsible.

SUMMARY

Project Management professional and business analyst with ten years' experience in the banking industry. Demonstrated exceptional flexibility in changing and fast-paced work environments. Strong multi-tasking and problem-solving skills. Certified Project Management Professional (PMP). Open to travel.

OPERATIONS MANAGER

Process Re-engineering · Cost Control · Team Building

Spearheaded 2 major turnarounds for global
Fortune 500 leader

Results-driven executive who quickly identifies operational issues and designs/executes solutions that improve across-the-board performance. Respected manager who thrives on challenge, leads by example, champions employees' development and inspires teams to top performance. Consistently improves productivity, quality, service, and profits.

EXECUTIVE PROFILE

Senior financial executive with broad international experience and significant contributions to key global initiatives. Creates and implements strategic solutions to resolve complex business problems. Synthesizes disparate data leading to sound business decisions and profitable growth. Excellent people development, collaborative, and decision-making skills.

SUMMARY OF QUALIFICATIONS

Conscientious professional who leverages strong analytical, organizational, interpersonal, and team-building skills to achieve business objectives. Recognized for achievements in:

Strategic Budgeting & Planning	Process Improvement
	Research
Project Management	Training & Presentation
Client Relations	

Professional experience

After the summary section, you'll typically go right into your work history. The names of this section vary, with choices including Professional Experience, Work History, Employment History, or Career Summary. Note that if your technical skills are highly relevant to your target jobs and are one of your primary assets, then your Technical Skills section (discussed later in this chapter) would come between the summary and work history.

Employer names and locations

Start your professional experience section by listing your most recent employer's name at the left margin under the heading "Professional Experience." (The heading should be centered on the page.) List the company or organization name, not an individual you worked for—individuals' names go only on your reference list. Write out the full, formal business name, except in rare cases where the organization is better known by its acronym, such as IBM. If the company name has changed due to mergers, acquisitions, or simply a name change, list the current name with the former name(s) following it in parentheses.

Repeat this process until you've gone back through your work history listing all employers worked for during the past 12 to 20 years. How far back to go in your employment history is highly debatable. Some experts advise going back only about 10 years. Others say go back at least 15. As with most résumé issues, it depends on your situation. Your experience over the past several years is what will be most relevant, but you do need to go back at least about 10 to 12 years (assuming you have that much experience or more) in order to document a substantial part of your work history. Go back as far as you need to demonstrate your most marketable experience and to fit within the space constraints you have. If recruiters or employers want to know more, they can ask.

Next to each employer name, list the city and state where the organization is located. There's no need to list street address and ZIP code; that information goes on your reference list. If you did not work in the headquarters' location, you have the option of not listing that location and instead listing where you were based next to each job title you held with that company. For example, The Coca-Cola Company is based in Atlanta, Georgia, but someone who worked for them in other cities and never worked in Atlanta could leave the city and state off of the line where Coca-Cola is listed and only list the cities next to each job title. Or, Atlanta could be listed next to Coke to show that it's the headquarters' location, but then the other cities and states would also be included next to each job title.

Job titles

Under each employer name list all job titles you held while at that company. If you had only one title, list just the one. List each title on its own line under the company name. If your job title has a very internal sound to it, meaning that it might not make sense to the outside world (for example, Service Implementer II), either change the title (with your employer's permission) or put a brief explanatory phrase next to it (for example, "equivalent to Customer Service Representative").

Dates

On the same line with the employer's name, put the dates you were employed at the right margin. Start with years only (for example, 1999–2005). Including months is optional and usually only necessary if you need to clarify a period of time you were employed somewhere. For example, Jan. 2003–Nov. 2004 is more effective than 2003–2004 as it shows that you were there for close to a year, whereas 2003–2004 could lead the reader to wonder whether it was a very short stint, say December, 2003, to January, 2004. Of course, if it was a short stint, listing only years works in your favor. If you're still employed, your current dates would end in "to present," as in "2004 to present."

If you held only one position with each employer, all you have to list is the overall employment dates. But, if you have more than one title under an employer, list those overall dates out at the right margin on the same line as the employer's name, plus dates that you held each position, listed right after each title. Example:

Wachovia Bank—Charlotte, NC   1995–2005

Head Teller, 2003–2005
Teller II, 2001–2003
Teller I, 1998–2001
Administrative Assistant, 1996–1998
Receptionist, 1995–1996

If you've held numerous positions in one organization, such as in the preceding example, you could list only the most recent one or two positions and summarize the others. Example:

Wachovia Bank—Charlotte, NC   1995–2005

Head Teller, 2003–2005
Teller II, 2001–2003
Various clerical and teller roles, 1995–2001

Do this if space is an issue or if you feel that the older, lower-level positions do not need to be a significant feature of your résumé.

Employer descriptor

If any organizations you've worked for are not exactly household names, or even if they are, you can help the reader better understand them by including a short (usually one line, maybe two) description of the organization. Example:

Wachovia Bank—Charlotte, NC   1995–2005

A diversified financial services company with a broad range of banking, asset management, wealth management, and corporate and investment banking products and services. Offices across the U.S. and abroad with more than 85,000 employees.

Head Teller, 2003–2005
Teller II, 2001–2003
Various clerical and teller roles, 1995–2001

Job context snapshot

Now that you have the basic data down, it's time to fill in the meat. First, start by giving an "in-a-nutshell" view of each position held. I call this the Job Context Snapshot. It puts your role in context and gives a snapshot view of the scope of your responsibilities. The Job Context Snapshot is a brief paragraph that appears immediately under your job title (no more than about four to five lines long, but as with all résumé matters, there's no magic number; just use your judgment to keep it brief).

The Job Context Snapshot should convey your level, scope of responsibilities, reporting relationships, geographic territories (if relevant), and budgets managed (if applicable). Example:

XYZ Insurance Company—Hartford, CT   2003–present
Underwriting Manager
Managed and supervised a multi-line commercial underwriting staff of 12 and diverse agents throughout New York, New Jersey, and Connecticut. Territory produced approximately $30 million in written premiums from an agency force of approximately 375 agents. Reported to the Commercial Business Manager.

Don't feel that you have to include every suggested element in your snapshot. If you didn't manage a budget, or it was smaller than the ones you aspire to manage, don't mention budget. If you had no direct reports, that's fine. If the position of the person you reported to would be assumed (such as an administrative assistant reporting to the office manager), no need to mention it. Include only what is relevant.

Asset statements

The final thing to add to your professional experience section is your list of achievements. Most of your basic responsibilities and duties should be covered in the Job Context Snapshot.

Now, all you have to do is follow that paragraph with bullet pointed statements that highlight your achievements. This is where you provide evidence of your most marketable achievements and skills—features that you probably mentioned in your summary section. Taking the time to craft strong asset statements and to select the most appropriate ones for your résumé is one of the easiest ways to distinguish yourself from the competition. If you haven't already worked on your asset statements, be sure to read Chapter 4 to learn more about the "secret weapons" in your marketing strategy and to be led step-by-step through developing them.

At the risk of sounding like a broken record, there is no magic number for how many asset statements you should list under each job context snapshot. Start by trying to write one asset statement for each year on the job for your jobs that stretch over the past 10 years. Then, you might need to pare down the list to only about four to six asset statements (with a minimum of two if you can't think of four to six) for your most recent job(s). As you get into older jobs, particularly if you have a long work history, you can cut back to one or two asset statements, or even no asset statements and just a brief job context snapshot for the oldest jobs.

Education and training

After your work history section, you'll usually follow with Education and Training. If you hold a degree or multiple degrees or attended college but did not earn a degree, this is where that information goes. If you have only job-related training, such as various seminars and courses or certification programs, you list only that information.

Begin this section by listing your most recent degree or educational experience. List the college or university name, the city and state (or country) where it's located, the degree you received, if any, and the date received or dates studied there if no degree (optional). Listing degree date is optional because dates of education can be obvious clues to your age. So, if your graduation date (or dates that you attended the school if no degree) would put you in a precarious position for age discrimination, you might prefer to leave the degree off. But, if the dates put you in your forties or younger, then you're better off including them, or it will look like you're hiding an older age.

If you have a bachelor's degree plus an advanced degree or two, list the highest degree first followed by the lower degrees. If you have two degrees at the same level, such as two bachelor's or two master's, list them either in reverse-chronological order (most recent on top) or list the more relevant degree first. If you earned an associate's degree before going on to complete a bachelor's, you do not need to list the associate's unless there is some special reason you would want readers to know about it. Note that if your degree (of any level) is from another country other than the one where you are applying for jobs, you might need to put in parentheses after the degree a brief statement explaining the comparable degree in the country of your job search.

If you did not earn a degree, you have the option of listing dates studied, or simply referring to the amount of time, such as "Two years of undergraduate business studies," or "Completed 40% of course work toward B.S. in Communication."

For additional training, such as employer-sponsored seminars or courses you attended on your own, list the exact names and who offered the courses if you have only a few to list, or if numerous, simply summarize them, as in "Attended more than 20 seminars and training programs on topics including communication, conflict resolution, time management, and supervisory

---

 Watch Out!

Avoid redundancy in your skills and training sections. If you are proficient in, say, Microsoft Excel because you took courses in it, list Excel in your Technical Skills section but don't list the Excel course in your Education and Training section.

skills." It is very optional to include the dates of such training. Give dates only if recent to show that the skills or knowledge you acquired is still reasonably current.

Technical skills

As mentioned earlier, your technical skills might be such an important part of what you offer an employer that you want to include the section earlier in the résumé, high up on the first page under the summary statement, or after the objective if you don't use a summary. If the technical skills are not that critical, such as listing programming languages on a résumé for someone who knows how to program but is seeking an IT project management job, the technical skills are relevant to show that the job seeker has that knowledge, but they don't need to be highlighted early in the résumé and can appear near the end.

Make sure that you don't go overboard listing every skill you've ever acquired. List only those that are up-to-date and at least somewhat relevant to the job you seek. If you have a lot of technical skills that fall into different categories, group them into subsections, such as Software, Operating Systems, Client Server Tools, or whatever is applicable to your set of skills. To save space, you can list the skills in paragraph form, separated by commas or semi-colons. Or, if you have plenty of space, list each on its own line.

Optional sections

After the work history, education, training, and skills, are covered, résumés start to vary widely. The following are optional sections that you may choose to include if you have relevant information in these categories, and if you have the space to do so.

Honors and awards

If you've received at least two or three professional awards or community/civic honors, you have enough to constitute an honors and awards section. (The section can be called Honors and Awards or just Honors or just Awards.) If you have only one, list it as an accomplishment under the job you held when you received it (or in the Community Affiliations section, if awarded for community work). You can also do this if you are hard-pressed to think of achievements on any of your past jobs; listing an award as an asset statement can help you beef up your asset statement list. Wherever they go, list the name of the honor, what it was awarded for, and by whom. Include the date unless you want to disguise the fact that it was an older award. Be consistent, however, giving either dates for all awards or for none. If the award was a cash bonus, don't list the amount, just refer to it as a cash award. If an award was an educational honor, it would usually best fit in the education section. Use the separate honors section only for professional, on-the-job sorts of honors.

Language skills

If you speak any languages other than your native language well enough to consider this one of your marketable skills, then you might want to include a language skills section. You can also mention language abilities in your qualifications summary as opposed to having a section devoted to them. This is a good space saver, or good for when the language skills will be a major selling point for the types of jobs you're seeking and so you want the reader to spot them early on in the résumé. Wherever you include them, give not only the language but some idea of your level of proficiency. Example: "Fluent in French; basic working knowledge of Spanish." If the language you know is one with a different alphabet in which someone might be conversational but not proficient in the written language, then specify your knowledge. Example: "Conversational Mandarin; moderate proficiency in written and spoken Arabic."

Certifications/licenses

If you hold licenses or certifications relevant to your target job, list them in their own section. If only one, or if you don't want to take up space with a whole section on this topic, simply list the license(s) or certification(s) either in your opening sum-mary section on the first page or as an accomplishment under the job you held when you earned it. Note that if you achieved certification after completing a training program, you probably don't need to list the training program in the Education and Training section. Listing only the certification avoids redun-dancy, and it's assumed that you underwent some training to earn the certification. Some certifications or licenses are signif-icant enough that you would want to list the acronym after your name in the main header of the résumé. And, some organiza-tions allow you to use a particular logo connected with their cer-tifications; if so, you may put that at the top of your résumé next to your name or in a corner.

Professional affiliations

If you are a member of a professional association or industry group, list it here. As with the other optional sections, you should have more than one to constitute a section, so if you have only one membership, find another place for it, such as in your summary or tacking it onto the Education and Training section. List the organization, your role (member or a leader-ship role), and the dates you've been a member or were a mem-ber (for example, "Career Masters Institute, member since 2000" or "Project Management Institute: member 1999–2004; IT Division Chair 2002–2003.") It's okay to list memberships that are no longer active as long as they were fairly recent.

Community affiliations

If you've done a good bit of community service—any sort of vol-unteer work, charitable work, or civic duty—feel free to list it on your résumé if you believe it strengthens your case by showing you as well-rounded or possessing certain skills you might have honed through that work. Community service is relevant for some positions and employers more than others, so use your judgment about how this information will be viewed. List each organization and your role (it's optional to list dates), or if

Watch Out!

Be careful when listing potentially controversial community service on a résumé, such as political or religious involvement. If you've done this sort of work, refer to it generically to avoid discrimination, not mentioning parties, candidates, or religious institutions by name.

you've done so much community service that the list would get too long, summarize it in a few lines.

Military

If you have military experience, this can be a beneficial piece of information to include on your résumé. If your experience was a significant part of your overall professional history, you may list the military positions within your work history section along with civilian jobs, if any. Otherwise, make it its own category near the end of the résumé, listing branch of service, location(s), rank, and positions held. Give a "job" description only if you have plenty of space to spare and if the description would demonstrate relevant skills and knowledge.

Hobbies and interests

The jury's still out on this one. I guarantee you that 10 people will tell you to include a section on hobbies and interests. ("It adds color, shows you as well rounded, and is a great conversation starter!" they'll say). Another 10 people will say not to include hobbies and interests—that it's just filler, doesn't add anything, and is not professional. I leave it up to you to decide.

I can tell you that I tend not to like to see these on résumés because that's information I can get after I speak to someone. The professional credentials are what's most critical for determining whether I would want to hire someone. Then, in the interview, I can get a feel for the whole person beyond those credentials. I can also tell you, however, that I do sometimes enjoy reading this section if it contains interesting, offbeat activities.

Wacky Hobbies and Interests

After nearly 20 years of reading and editing résumés, I have my personal hall of fame for résumé bloopers. My favorite two entries (from two different job seekers) in the Hobbies and Interests section are: "red jello" and "I have a twin brother." Let's deal with the twin brother matter first. Overlooking the problem of a personal pronoun on a résumé, think about why this is relevant to any sort of job being sought (other than as an actor in a Doublemint gum commercial). Sure, it's an interesting factoid, but I saw no relevance and suggested the candidate delete it. So, how about the red jello interest? Would you believe I let this one slide? It was on a college student's résumé, and she was seeking creative positions in the advertising industry. She had a solid résumé with excellent corporate internships, a diligent record of part-time work to support herself through school, and good grades. She came across as capable and qualified, and the red jello comment only added a pleasant bit of whimsy to a heavyweight résumé for a very creative type of job.

But, if your hobbies tend toward reading, sewing, and jogging, don't bother.

Addendum

As mentioned in the earlier discussion of résumé length, you might need to use an addendum to your résumé to cover details that had to be left out of the one- or two-page résumé. In most cases, an addendum is not necessary, so don't feel you have to have one. But, if you have done a great deal of project-based work or consulting assignments you might find it particularly challenging to construct brief job context snapshots and asset statement lists. Or, if you have a long work history and had to

Watch Out!

Don't include your reference list in the same electronic file as your résumé. You want to keep your references close to the vest and only give them out when they're requested so that you retain some control over when and how your references are being contacted.

leave older jobs off the résumé or summarized them only briefly on the résumé, an addendum can give you a place to go into more detail.

Create an addendum by putting your name and contact information at the top of a blank page in the same style and layout as on your résumé. Then, centered under that information, type the words "Résumé Addendum." Follow with whatever content you need to include, using headers such as "Employment Details," "Project Details," or any other heading that makes sense.

Don't send the addendum out routinely with your résumé as that defeats the purpose of not overwhelming the recipient with too much to read. Create it as a separate electronic file from your résumé and have it on hand as a follow-up to your résumé after you've established initial contact with a recruiter or prospective employer.

Résumé design and layout

After you have your résumé content finalized, it's time to polish up your résumé's layout and style. You might choose to get someone to help you with this process if you're not proficient in your word processing program or don't have a good eye for graphic design. But, before investing money in professional help or taxing a friendship or family relationship with requests for free résumé services, try following these simple instructions for the design of your résumé.

Margins

Try to keep all margins—top, bottom, left, and right—set at one inch. This will ensure that your résumé doesn't look crowded and that there's no danger of any text getting lost if the résumé is scanned. (Sometimes text that trails out to the edges of the paper won't get picked up in an electronic scanning system.) If you are struggling to make your text fit, read the résumé one more time to find words and phrases you can cut out to save space before shrinking the margins below one inch.

Font style and size

The most common font styles for résumés are simple, classic ones such as Arial and Times (a.k.a. Times New Roman). Palatino, Bookman, and New Century Schoolbook also work well. For a refined look, popular with bankers and lawyers, Garamond adds an elegant touch to a résumé. Choose whichever font style appeals to you. Whichever you pick, try to use the same font style throughout as that usually gives a cleaner look.

As for size, try to keep the font for the basic text of the résumé between 11 and 12 point. Headings of sections can be the same size, or a point or two larger than the text size. If you are struggling to keep your résumé fitting on one or two pages, 11 point can work well. Use 12 point if you have a bit more room to spare. Try not to go down to 10 point if you can avoid it as the smaller size can be hard on the eyes and make the résumé look too text heavy and crowded. Don't forget about the half sizes, too. These aren't a standard choice on the font pulldown menu on your toolbar but can be typed in wherever you change the font size in your word processing application. Using 11.5, or if pressed for space, 10.5, can be a visually attractive happy medium. Also be aware that some font styles are simply

 Bright Idea

Time yourself reading your résumé very quickly. If it takes you longer than about 20 to 30 seconds to skim the résumé and pick up on the key points, then you may need to shorten the résumé or modify the format so that high-lights stand out better.

bigger than others. For example, Arial 10 is a bit bigger than Times New Roman 10. So, you may need to play around with various style and size combinations that not only appeal to you aesthetically but also work for the spacing issues you have.

Bold, italic, and other styling

Judicious use of styling elements is important for drawing the reader's eye to the most important information on the page and for distinguishing one type of information from another. For example, you want to draw readers' eyes to the headings that separate your résumé sections, so you would usually bold them. You might want to draw them to the types of positions you've held but downplay your employer names (because you're trying to break into a new industry), so you could bold the job titles or put them in all capital letters while keeping the employer names more subtle in regular, nonbolded font. The résumé samples in the Appendix will give you ideas of how bolding, underlining, italic, borders, and capitalization can make a résumé not only look nice but be more readable. Don't forget that all this styling will have to be removed when you convert your résumé to an eRésumé!

Spacing

Be sure to spread text out well across each page of your résumé, making sure that it is balanced from top to bottom and side to side. Also be sure to separate each section with at least a double space so that the reader can easily tell where one section ends and another begins. If you have long lists of bullet points, you

---

 Watch Out!

Never include a photograph of yourself with your résumé (except for performing arts jobs). Employment laws to protect job candidates against discrimination prevent the recipient from knowing what you look like before inviting you to interview. Your résumé might even be tossed in the trash if it comes with a photo.

might also want to introduce some space between each statement rather than single-spacing the list. This makes the text look more inviting to the reader and not as much of a chore to read. Note how the sample résumés in the Appendix make good use of spacing.

Paper

The choice of paper to print your résumé can seem a bit overwhelming when faced with all the color, texture, and weight choices. One way to make it easy is to ask in a photocopy store or print shop what they recommend for résumé paper. You can also pick up reams of paper called "résumé paper" in office supply shops. This takes much of the guess work out of the process. When in doubt, however, follow these guidelines:

Size

Résumés for use in the United States should be printed on our standard 8.5 × 11-inch size of paper. For an international job search, consult the international career books listed in the online Bonus Appendix 2 for conventional sizes in other countries.

Weight

Your résumé should be printed on heavier paper than the flimsy paper typically used in photocopiers and printers. Anywhere in the range of 16- to 25-pound with a cotton fiber content of 25 percent or more is a good résumé paper weight. If you want to be extra fancy (and pay more), 32-pound paper with 100 percent cotton content is the way to go.

Texture

When you don't know whether your résumé will be scanned electronically from the hard copy, it's best to be on the safe side and go with paper that has a very smooth finish. Those interesting papers with a recycled look to them showing bits of "debris" in the paper as well as those with a mottled, marbled, or speckled look can be pleasing to the eye but don't scan well. Two classic textures that résumés have traditionally been printed on are laid and linen, where slight lines run through the page in a woven or vertical pattern. These shouldn't cause too much trouble when scanned or photocopied as the texture is very subtle, but when in doubt, go with the smooth finish.

Color

In 99.9 percent of job search cases, it's best to choose one of the conservative colors that résumés have traditionally been printed on. These are white as well as very pale shades of ivory or gray. What about that other one-tenth of the time? Those are cases where you are in a highly creative field and can get away with using a more unconventional color choice. Even then, don't go too wild, or you'll end up looking gimmicky and unprofessional. The content of your résumé should be strong enough to attract attention; you shouldn't have to rely on shocking pink to do it.

Printing and distributing

It's fine to have your résumé photocopied from a sharp, clean laser printed original or directly from disk or CD, rather than printing every copy from your own printer. Most print shops will do a good job of photocopying your résumé, but do ask to see a first test copy before the entire job is run to make sure that the copy quality is good.

Purchase envelopes that match your résumé paper. It's fine to fold your résumé into thirds to fit into regular business size envelopes (known officially as #10—the size that requires you fold the résumé into thirds). Be aware, however, that when sending your résumé to a large company that is likely to scan most

 Moneysaver

When printing large quantities of your résumé on good paper, use a photocopier rather than your laser printer. As long as the photocopy quality is good, no one will know the difference, and you'll save a lot of money on ink cartridges and printer wear-and-tear.

résumés into a résumé database, you should send it unfolded in a large envelope. This ensures that the résumé will scan properly and not have text obscured by the folds.

If you do find yourself sending some résumés through regular mail (as opposed to email, hand delivery, or faxing), regular first class postage for normal delivery is usually sufficient. Sending your résumé by overnight or second-day air, or by registered mail in which a return receipt is requested smacks of desperation and should be done only under unusual circumstances.

Résumé writing—variations on a theme

The previous pages helped you put together a good, basic résumé in what we call the chronological or reverse-chronological format. There are times, however, when you need to go beyond the basics to best showcase your assets. The following are two ways you might do that.

Functional résumés

Also known as combination functional-chronological or hybrid résumés, a functional résumé puts your content in a slightly different arrangement to downplay your employment history and play up your achievements and transferable skills. The main difference with a functional résumé is that instead of going from Qualifications Summary to Professional Experience, you include an achievements section. Then your job listings in the Professional Experience section include either nothing more than employer name, titles, and dates, or that basic information plus the Job Context Snapshot. You might also move the education section higher in the résumé if it helps build your case better than your work history.

Functional résumés work well when you are changing career fields, have a checkered work history with gaps in employment or short-term assignments, or have held basically the same jobs over a long period of time. You'll find two examples of functional résumés in the "Sample résumés" section of the Appendix.

Curriculum vitae ("C.V.")

The term C.V. is sometimes used interchangeably with the term résumé, so if someone asks you to send your C.V., they might mean a regular résumé. If in doubt, ask them, because the true definition of a C.V. is quite different from a résumé. If they are expecting an actual C.V., you'll need to send a much longer, more detailed, and less marketing-oriented document than your résumé.

C.V.s are typically used in academia but can be found in the business world for very senior-level positions or other specialized roles. A C.V. has the following features:

- Its tone and layout should be serious, formal, straightforward, and not marketing-oriented. You are simply documenting your history and achievements.

- It would be at least two pages long and more typically three to several pages.

- You would usually not include a summary or objective statement.

- Your education section would come before professional experience in most cases, except executives who would usually open with professional experience.

- The work history section would still include a Job Context Snapshot and asset statements bulleted.

- Most of the optional sections from a résumé would be suitable for a C.V.

- A C.V. would include additional sections, such as publications, presentations, patents, teaching experience, and anything else relevant to the work sought.

Some of the résumé books listed in the online Bonus Appendix 2 and the career advice sites in the online Bonus Appendix 1 include further guidance on developing a curriculum vitae, along with samples.

Résumé quality control checklists

Checklist 5.1. Content

_____ Does everything on the résumé relate to and support my career objective, or did I include unnecessary, distracting information?

_____ Are all the claims I make in my Qualifications Summary backed up with evidence elsewhere in the résumé?

_____ Is my Qualifications Summary succinct, touching on only the highlights of my functional role, industry background, areas of expertise, and key skills/personal qualities?

_____ In my Professional Experience or Employment History section, did I describe each job briefly in a Job Context Snapshot in paragraph form immediately under each job title?

_____ Do my lists of bullet points focus primarily on achievements (asset statements), much more than basic duties or responsibilities?

_____ To the extent possible and relevant, have I listed the context, actions, and results in my asset statements (not just results) and quantified the results?

_____ In my education section, did I remember to include all relevant continuing education and special training beyond degree studies?

_____ If I included additional sections to the résumé beyond experience and education, are they relevant to my objective and as concise as possible?

_____ Did I omit the personal information (such as marital status, age, height, weight, and so on) that should not be included?

_____ Do I convey all the most important information on the first page (if a two-page résumé) or early on the page if a one-page résumé?

_____ Can the most important information on my résumé be gleaned in 30 seconds or less?

_____ Is the résumé a true marketing document or just a chronicle of my work and educational history?

Checklist 5.2. Writing style

_____ Have several detail-oriented people who are good writers proof-read my résumé to check it for errors and proper language usage and grammar?

_____ Do I have too many details or repetitious information?

_____ Do most of my statements of experience and asset statements begin with an action verb?

_____ Did I not include personal pronouns? (There should be no personal pronouns, such as I or my.)

_____ Did I keep the wording very brief by omitting articles (the, a, an) in most places unless necessary for clarity of the text?

As a final check, know when to stop! No résumé will get you a job. The résumé can get your foot in the door, but you take it from there. After you know your résumé is in reasonably good shape and has passed muster with several colleagues and friends whose professional opinions you respect, then stop the tweaking and editing and adjusting and get out there to start using it.

Just the facts

- Opinions about résumés vary widely, so realize that you can never please all the people all the time, but you can put together a strong résumé that will work for most recruiters and employers.

- Make sure to do a sufficient assessment of your strengths before trying to write your résumé.

- Résumés are typically skimmed in only 10 to 30 seconds, so you must be brief.

- Follow the guidelines in this chapter for the best advice on each section of your résumé.

- Know when to stop editing and revising your résumé and put it into circulation. It will never be perfect, but it can be very good!

GET THE SCOOP ON...
Why cover letters and cover email messages are
a critical element in your marketing strategy ▪
Why many people *do* read them ▪ The two types
of cover letters and what they look like ▪ How
to make writing cover letters a painless process

Job Search Correspondence

Chapter 6

Cover letters and thank-you letters can feel like a royal pain in the neck to write, which is probably why so many job seekers do not bother to do them. Considering them optional, however, can be a major mistake. By taking the time to send an introductory letter along with your résumé or to craft a deal-clinching follow-up letter after an interview, you will set yourself apart from the competition. Chapter 15, "Clinching the Deal," discusses follow-up letters (commonly referred to as "thank-you letters"), and Chapter 9, "Networking," deals with written communication to introduce yourself in networking situations. This chapter focuses on cover letters and email messages that introduce you as a candidate for jobs, usually as an accompaniment to your résumé.

Does anyone even read cover letters?

Many job seekers don't bother to send cover letters because they assume they won't be read. It's true that some employers and recruiters prefer to go straight to the résumé and toss the cover letter, but you cannot assume that will always be the case. Many people who read résumés regularly find that a concise, well-written cover letter makes their jobs easier. When done correctly, a cover letter answers questions that are typically on the mind of someone who is about to read your résumé:

- Why is this person sending me a résumé?
- What is this person's background?
- What could this person do for me or someone I know?
- What action do I need to take?

A cover letter serves as a brief introduction to your résumé, letting the recipient know why you're sending your résumé (such as, that you are applying for a particular position or asking for an exploratory interview to discuss possible openings) and highlighting areas of your background that are most relevant and impressive. When crafted strategically, your cover letters are important marketing documents that start to sway the odds in your favor before your résumé even gets read.

So, if they can be so helpful to the recipient, why are they sometimes not read? Most cover letters are lousy. Simple as that. They are either so brief and vague as to be meaningless and useless or so long and packed with information that the recipient doesn't want to slog through them. Nevertheless, cover letters are certainly worth the effort because they do get read in many cases, and they can be a critical element in your overall self-marketing strategy.

 Watch Out!

When sending your résumé as an attached file to an email, don't attach a cover letter file as well. This is an unnecessary inconvenience for the recipient. Instead, type a cover message in the body of the email, saying the same things you would say in a traditional cover letter.

Two categories of cover letters

It's very easy to get a handle on the two categories of cover letters. There are letters sent when you know of a definite job opening and letters sent when no opening has been advertised. Basically, you are either using a letter (and often a résumé as well) to apply for a job or to explore the possibility of a job opportunity. Within each of these categories are a few variations:

Letters for definite openings

When a job opportunity has been announced formally through a posting online or classified ad, or when you've heard about an opportunity through the grapevine, it is important not to fire off your résumé by itself. You wouldn't send a birthday present in the mail without a card, so don't send your résumé without some introductory email message or letter. The ways you might do this include:

- Cover letter to a recruiter with résumé
- Cover letter to an employer with résumé
- Email cover message to a recruiter with résumé
- Email cover message to an employer with résumé
- Résumé substitute letter or email (a letter or email sent without a résumé accompanying it)

You'll find samples of these types of letters later in this chapter.

Letters when no definite opening is known

When approaching a recruiter or employer to explore possible opportunities, a cover letter is critical. The recipient is not expecting to hear from you because no position has been announced, so emailing, mailing, or faxing a résumé with no explanation as to why you're sending it would be ludicrous. Over the years, I have from time to time received a résumé by fax or email with no cover message or letter explaining why it has been sent. What am I supposed to do with the résumé? I usually send it straight to the trash, and that's what would likely happen if you were to approach someone cold with no introduction to your résumé.

Whether you are approaching someone whose name you've been given through networking or are conducting a large mailing to organizations you've targeted (direct mail campaigns are explained in more detail in Chapter 8, "Landing a Job through the Formal Marketplace"), the quality of your letter can determine whether you get your foot in the door for a networking appointment or interview. The types of letters you are likely to write in this category include the following:

- Direct mail campaign letter to a recruiter with résumé
- Direct mail campaign letter to an employer with résumé
- Email cover message to a recruiter with résumé
- Email cover message to an employer with résumé
- Résumé substitute letter or email (a letter or email sent without a résumé accompanying it)

As with the letters for definite openings, you'll find samples of these types of letters later in this chapter.

Crafting cover letters— a step-by-step guide

You've read about a job opening that sounds perfect for you or have the name of someone who could be a key contact in your search, but the minutes tick away like hours as you stare at the computer screen or paper trying to write a cover letter to express your interest. There's so much you could say that you don't know where to begin, or maybe you've always written such short, general cover letters, that now you don't feel you have enough to say. Writing a cover letter need not be a painful

A Why-Bother Cover Letter

A why-bother cover letter is one that isn't worth your time to write and send and does not do the recipient any good. A why-bother cover letter is too short, too vague, and does nothing to make the employer's or recruiter's job easier or to distinguish you from the competition. Here's a typical example:

> To Whom It May Concern:
>
> Enclosed is my résumé for the position you advertised in the *Boston Globe.* I am sure that my skills and experience are a good match for the position. I look forward to hearing from you.
>
> Sincerely,
> Ivan Tajob

This letter does not specify which position is being applied for—the employer may have advertised for many jobs in that newspaper on several recent dates. It also does not give the reader a quick synopsis of the applicant's background and specific skills that relate to the position. And, it leaves follow-up in the hands of the employer rather than stating that the job seeker will take the initiative to follow up.

process. Knowing some basic ground rules to get you started, along with taking it section by section, is all you need to do to turn out job search letters like a pro.

Begin with the end in sight

Consider the following tips as ground rules before putting finger to keyboard or pen to paper:

Know how you will transmit it

Decide whether you will send your cover letter as an actual letter by mail or fax or as an email message. This will determine how much you can write. Email communications need to be shorter because people tend to be less willing to read and pay attention to longer content when viewed electronically. Make your email able to be read without scrolling down more than once or twice.

If sending the cover message as an actual letter, not as an email, keep the length to within one page. A cover letter's purpose is merely to introduce yourself and why you're writing and to point out highlights of your qualifications. You do not have to summarize your entire background.

Make it a marketing document

Imagine that you've already sent your letter and have landed an interview. Picture yourself sitting across from the interviewer and think about what you would say to give a synopsis of your qualifications and to express your interest. Try saying this out loud before you begin writing your letter. Doing so will put you in the mindset of marketing yourself directly to a prospective employer.

Be real

Remember that you are writing to a fellow human being. Although written communication tends to be somewhat more formal than spoken communication, you don't want to sound overly formal or use awkward sentence structures. Let the writing flow naturally, as if you were speaking directly to another person.

Edit out the editor in you

Don't edit yourself prematurely. You will drive yourself crazy if you try to make every sentence and paragraph perfect as you write your cover letter. Just jot down your thoughts in a reasonably coherent fashion and then clean it up when you have all the content down.

Leave formatting to the end

Don't worry about the format as you begin to write. If you'll be sending it as a hard copy letter or fax, you can set the letter up in proper business format later. If sending as an email, all you have to worry about now is keeping the message concise and fairly short, with no special styling such as italic, underlining, or bolding that may not transmit well electronically.

Writing your letter: the beginning

The simplest way to write a cover letter is to break it down into a beginning, middle, and end and tackle one section at a time. The beginning includes the salutation and the introductory remarks.

Salutation

Always try to have an actual name of a person to whom you're writing. When you do have a name, address your letter to "Dear Mr. or Ms. [last name]." Of course, if you know that "Dr." or "Mrs." is appropriate for the recipient, then use those courtesy titles. If you know the person well and know that they would not mind you taking a familiar tone with them, you may call them by first name after the "Dear."

At times you might not know or cannot find the name of a person to address in your letter. In those cases, you might say

Bright Idea

If you are considering relocation, try to sound more committed to the new location by declaring that you plan to move there (rather than that you are just thinking about it). Also, try to have a local address (local to the new location) on your letterhead or omit the address and use only a cell phone number and/or email address that won't reveal where you are presently living.

"Dear Hiring Manager," "Dear Recruiter," "Dear Human Resources," or "Dear Search Committee." Avoid at all costs using "To Whom It May Concern."

Introduction

The introduction of your letter is usually a paragraph of no more than two to three sentences in length. State why you are writing and give a brief preview to your qualifications. It is also optional to mention why you are searching for employment. Your "reason for looking" statement as described in the online Bonus Chapter 2, "Honing Your Communication Skills and Tools," is what you might use here. Examples of introductory paragraphs follow:

> As a registered nurse with excellent communication skills and natural sales ability, I am interested in discussing entry-level pharmaceutical sales positions with your organization.

> Having recently completed my bachelor's degree in criminal justice, I am pleased to submit my credentials for the Security Coordinator position announced in the University of Florida *Bulletin.*

> Your January 17th advertisement in the *Milwaukee Journal Sentinel* for a Call Center Manager is an ideal match for my skills and experience.

> I enjoyed your speech at last week s Eastern Consulting Society conference. As a proven leader in logistics and supply chain management with more than 20 years of international consulting experience, please accept my candidacy for the Senior Consultant role you mentioned at the conference.

> Our mutual acquaintance, Edward Carlson, suggested I contact you to explore potential opportunities at ORC Corp. Ed is aware of my contributions in leadership roles with Vista, Inc., and thought you and I would benefit from speaking with each other. After Vista's acquisition by Horizon, my position was eliminated as they retained their senior management team.

After establishing why you are writing and precluding a discussion of your qualifications, you're ready to move into the main portion of your letter.

Writing your letter: the middle

The middle portion of your letter is really the meat of it. This is where you turn a hum-drum letter of introduction into a marketing tool. How you handle the middle section depends on the purpose of the letter, whether replying to an announced position opening or requesting an exploratory meeting. No matter what the situation, the middle of your letter must showcase your assets and let the reader see why you would be a good fit for a particular organization or role.

You might begin the middle section of your letter either with the assets showcase or a statement of fit. I happen to describe the assets section first, but you might prefer to begin with fit.

Showcase your assets

In the introductory paragraph you gave a sneak preview of your qualifications by mentioning your background in general terms, perhaps citing the number of years of experience, functional expertise, industry background, or specific skills. Now, as you move into the middle of your letter, you need to elaborate on your qualifications to expand on that preview. Do not go overboard, however. The cover letter is not a summary of your entire résumé. The idea of showcasing your assets is that you review your résumé and select the assets and achievement statements that are most likely to be relevant to the job at hand or the person to whom you're writing.

The easiest way to put this section together is to take your self-marketing sound bite (discussed in Chapter 3) and adapt it for your cover letter by making it briefer and including only relevant elements of it. You might find that the summary section of your résumé is also a good place to draw from for your letter. Of course, you should not repeat your entire résumé summary in your letter, but an abbreviated version of it can be effective.

After opening the middle of the letter with a couple of sentences from your sound bite or résumé summary, follow with some bullet points that highlight relevant achievements. These may be taken almost verbatim from your résumé, although you should try to alter them somewhat to relate them to the job for which you're applying or to the organization where you want to explore opportunities. Note that if you are applying to a specific job ad, a particularly effective technique is to state many or all of the job requirements listed in the ad and show how you qualify. The "Cover Letter to an Employer: Response to a Newspaper Ad" section later in this chapter provides a good example of this.

Explain the fit

Think about junk mail you receive that calls you by name as if the letter and marketing enclosures are being sent only to you or sent to you by someone you know. You usually see through this ploy, right? You know the piece of mail is probably part of a huge mass mailing that has used technology to generate your name. If you take this same approach to your job search correspondence, your letters and résumés may end up being seen as nothing more than junk mail.

When applying for definite openings, you have to say something about why you see a fit between you and the employing organization or the position. Do your homework to learn something about the employer beyond what's mentioned in the job posting. Pick some aspect of the organization or the division or department in which you would be working and relate that to your own experience and talents. Even if replying to a blind ad, you can at least speak to the position being a good fit. Many job seekers fire off hundreds of letters and résumés indiscriminately for any job that sounds remotely like a fit. If you can show that you are not just cranking out letters randomly but have carefully selected a particular job announcement as being of interest to you, the employer or recruiter is more likely to take you seriously.

When sending a letter where no definite opening exists, it's even more important that you relate yourself to the organization or to a potential position. Employers and headhunters can always tell when a letter is one of hundreds generated by a job seeker's mail-merge program where a company name is plugged into the letter, but nothing else about the letter is customized. Employers and recruiters want to know that you have a good reason for approaching them, so you must mention something specific about the organization and show that it is relevant to your background.

Writing your letter: the end

Wrap up your letter as concisely as possible. Too many job seekers get long-winded at the end of their cover letters. It's as if they have finally gotten on a roll with the writing and don't want the letter to end! Keep in mind that your letter is likely to be read very quickly—usually just a quick skim—so you need to be succinct. Simply reiterate your interest, state what the next steps are, and thank the reader.

Interest, next steps, and thanks

Restating your interest in an advertised position or in speaking with someone to explore possible opportunities can often be presented in conjunction with a statement of next steps. Examples of this include the following:

> I'm very interested in contributing to the profitability of XYZ Corp. through effective call center management and will call you within the next several days to see whether we might arrange to meet.

> I am excited about the opportunity to join your organization's leadership team during this critical period of growth and expansion and look forward to hearing from you.

The Salary Issue—to Reveal or Not to Reveal

If writing to a headhunter, either to explore possible openings or to apply for an advertised position, you do need to state an approximate salary range you are seeking or general figures representing your recent salary history. Headhunters need to know this information before they start working with you.

If writing to someone in a case where no definite opening exists, such as when you're simply requesting an exploratory interview, do not state any salary history or requirements.

If replying to an ad or online posting in which you're instructed to reply directly to the employer (as opposed to a headhunter) and to state your salary history or requirements, you have a choice. You may ignore the request and not mention salary at all—a tactic that usually does not hurt your chances—or to mention salary in very broad ranges rather than specific figures. This choice is discussed in more detail in "The Salary Issue" section of Chapter 8, "Landing a Job through the Formal Marketplace."

If an online application requires that you select a salary range from a drop-down menu, try to trick the system by typing in $1.00 or "flexible." If you are forced to choose a legitimate range, select the salary range that is the most "middle-of-the-road" and is in line with salary research you have conducted.

Note that in the first example, where the job seeker has initiated the contact, the follow-up stated that the job seeker will take responsibility for follow-up. In the second example, the job seeker has replied to a blind ad where the employer is not identified. In that case, the job seeker usually has no choice but to sit back and wait to be contacted.

After restating your interest and addressing follow-up, conclude with an expression of appreciation. A basic "thank you for your time and consideration" will usually suffice.

Signature

If sending a hard copy or faxed letter, don't forget to sign your letter with both first and last name. If the recipient knows you well, you may sign only your first name, but be sure that your full name appears on the page, either typed under your signature or in the printed letterhead. Precede your signature with the closing of your choice, such as "Sincerely," "Sincerely Yours," "Best Regards," or "Regards."

If sending your message by email, be sure to include a signature block at the end of the email, including your full name and contact information.

Letter samples

The sample cover letters and email messages that follow demonstrate different forms, lengths, and styles, yet all of these communications follow the guidelines discussed in the previous section of this chapter for crafting a cover letter step-by-step. All of these letters or messages let the readers know why the sender is contacting them, what the sender's background is, where the potential fit is, and what the next steps are. Feel free to borrow heavily from these samples, but make sure that your letters and email messages are tailored specifically to you and your targets.

Cover letter to an employer—response to a newspaper ad

Clarence Webb
4455 Shady Drive • Fairburn, GA. 33333 • 222.999.3333 • cwebb@fauxmail.net

---

September 14, 20XX

Mid-State Shipping Corp.
200 Interstate Parkway
LaGrange, GA. 33333

RE: Warehouse Supervisor ad #013694, *Atlanta Journal & Constitution,* September 12th.

Dear Human Resources Committee:

With more than 10 years of experience in industrial manufacturing, including the past three as a warehouse Assistant Supervisor for Harold-Smith, Inc., I am confident that I offer what you need in a Warehouse Supervisor.

I have proven my ability to handle daily services and maintenance, receiving and distribution, and all other functions of warehousing. I have also operated and maintained a license to drive many different types of equipment. Specifically, I have the following qualifications that meet your requirements:

- **Personnel Management.** I was promoted to Assistant Supervisor at Harold-Smith after only one year as Distribution Coordinator. The Head Supervisor relied on me to help manage 43 warehouse employees, including contract maintenance personnel, on the second shift.
- **Excellent Communication Skills.** In my current position, I communicate by phone on a daily basis with buyers, managers, and suppliers. My boss often travels to other sites and is comfortable leaving me in charge of all daily critical communications.
- **High School or GED. College Degree Preferred.** I am a high school graduate and will complete my associate's degree in business management in May of 20XX.

Throughout my career, my performance reviews have shown me to be loyal, hard working and always striving to perform my job tasks more efficiently. I am a team player, willing to do whatever it takes to get the job done correctly. I am aware of the rapid growth Mid-State Shipping is undergoing, and I would like to contribute to that growth, while growing into a higher level management role in my own career.

After you have had a chance to review the enclosed resume, I look forward to meeting to discuss how I might make a difference at Mid-State Shipping. I appreciate your consideration and look forward to talking with you soon.

Sincerely,

Clarence Webb

Cover email message to a recruiter—response to an online posting

```
Mr. Vince Bondurant
Senior Consultant
Brasch, Williams, Harris
v.bondurant@bwh.com

Dear Mr. Bondurant:

In response to your posting on Monster.com for Senior Project Manager
position 012398, I applied online on 4/8/XX. I am taking this additional
opportunity to alert you to my qualifications as they appear to be a very
strong match for your client's needs:

* 8+ years of project and program management experience, including the
past three years managing numerous high-risk, complex global projects
simultaneously for BCD Consulting.

* Recognized by the sales team and partners of BCD for my ability to
contribute valuable input to sales strategies and for strong presentation
skills. Played a significant role in several major multi-million dollar
wins for the organization.

* BS and MBA degrees.

* PMI Certified.

* Compensation history in the $105-130 range.

I will contact you soon to discuss how my qualifications are aligned with
the criteria of your search. Thank you in advance for your time and
consideration.

Best regards,

J. Scott Forsythe

Mobile:  111-404-4444
Email:   JSFMBA@fauxmail.net
```

Direct mail campaign letter

Note that this letter is set up for use with a word processing software's mail-merge function. Actual names and addresses would be inserted where you see space for them indicated by the double arrows.

BENJAMIN L. JONES

1212 River Road
Albany, NC 22222

(444) 333-9999
bjonesalbany@email.com

April 20, 20XX

«Sal» «Full_Name»
«Title»
«Company_Name»
«Street_Address»
«City», «State» «Zip»

Dear «Sal» «Last_Name»:

As an experienced leader in the facilities management arena, I am interested in learning about the challenges and goals «Short_Company_Name» is currently facing and discussing how I might meet your needs.

My background includes operations and sales of facilities management to healthcare, education, and industrial markets. I have overseen housekeeping, plant operations, clinical equipment, materials management, pharmacy management, and food service. My major accomplishments include

- Developed and implemented a national program for a major hospital chain with 106 sites in 32 states.
- Attained $8 million gross profit over five years through actual shared cost savings.
- Generated direct sales to colleges and hospitals in excess of $5 million.
- Initiated sales effort for the eastern U.S. in a joint venture.
- Implemented cost reductions exceeding $3 million for a regional hospital chain.
- Directed sales force of nine reps, increasing productivity by 60%.

I was with FacilService for the past seven years, including the past three years as SVP of the southeast region. Due to the acquisition of FacilService by Arrow, Inc., my position was eliminated. I now aim to contribute to the growth of an organization by utilizing my experience with customer relations and management in a multisite environment. I am open to relocation, depending upon the opportunity.

My resume is attached for your review. I would appreciate the opportunity to discuss your needs and my qualifications and will call you to schedule an appointment. Thank you for your consideration.

Sincerely,

Ben Jones

Direct mail campaign email with a referral

Dear Ms. Allen,

Several of my former colleagues from ACT Financials, including Jayne Dow and Robert Place, have spoken very highly of Morey Investments and suggested that I let you know of my interest in career opportunities with Morey. I understand that in the recent past you were recruiting for senior programmer/analyst positions and might have current openings.

My background includes extensive knowledge of COBOL, JCL, IBM mainframe utilities, and numerous other systems and applications. At ACT I have gained a reputation for solid technical expertise, reliability, and consistently being an effective communicator and team player.

I have attached my resume to provide further details of my background and have pasted an electronic version below within this email for your convenience.

Regardless of your current staffing needs, I would appreciate the opportunity to meet with you to discuss how my skills and experience could be of value to ACT. I will contact you in a few days to see whether we can arrange a time to talk. Thank you in advance for your consideration.

Sincerely,

Michael Brown

Résumé substitute letter

PHILLIP J. MORALES
5678 Ocean Lane • San Diego, CA 99999
H: (000) 230-6767 • M: (000) 230-9843 • philbrooks5@fauxmail.com

---

November 4, 20XX

Anne Marie Barrett
EVP, Operations
SoCal Industries, Inc.
3000 Padre Blvd.
San Diego, CA 99999

Dear Ms. Barrett:

Are you seeking a seasoned leader with a proven track record of productivity, profitability, and performance improvements? With more than 10 years of experience in operations management, logistics, and manufacturing, I am uniquely qualified to fulfill such a position.

Continuous process improvements, profitability enhancements and performance "above and beyond" at every opportunity are my norm. Given the marketplace challenges SoCal currently faces, you might benefit from a proven performer to turnaround your situation and renew SoCal's position as the industry leader. Evidence that I am that performer includes

- *As a change agent at Bearing Corp where I have served as VP of Operations for the past five years, I spearheaded process improvements and change management programs that improved distribution efficiency by 27% and reduced costs 12% within an 11-month period.*

- *A recognized top performer, I was awarded Bearing's Chairman's Award three out of four years for exceptional dedication and innovation.*

I would be happy to provide a résumé where you will find further examples of my achievements drawing on leadership, initiative, and commitment coupled with seasoned operations management expertise to contribute to an organization's bottom-line profitability and rapid growth.

I will contact you within the next several days to see whether we might arrange a meeting to discuss how I may best meet the needs of SoCal Industries. Thank you for your time and consideration.

Sincerely,

Phillip J. Morales

Enclosure

Putting the finishing touches on your letter

Now that you've seen some examples of cover letters and cover email messages, you have an idea of how effective letters look and sound. Go back through your own letter draft now and put the finishing touches on it, considering the language and flow, layout, font style and size, and the way you'll be sending it.

Language and flow of your cover letter

Imagine that you are a busy employer or recruiter who has just received your cover letter. How does it sound? Is it a chore to read because there's too much text on the page, it's boring, or the sentence structure is convoluted? Is it lively but too lively, to the point of sounding gimmicky or like a pushy sales pitch? Your letter should strike a balance between sounding upbeat but serious and professional.

When writing any job search correspondence, don't forget that you are writing to a fellow human being. Avoid overly formal, stilted language or awkward wording. Follow the tips in the online Bonus Chapter 2, "Honing Your Communication Skills and Tools," on how to write in the plain English style. Make sure the text flows and sounds natural. Read your letter out loud to make sure that it not only makes sense but is easy to read. Your letters should sound as if you are speaking directly to the other person, although with a bit more formality than you would typically have in oral conversation.

Also ensure that all of your word usage is correct and that there are no spelling, grammar, or punctuation errors. Have at least one or two other people who are good writers or editors check over your letter to spot any problems.

Layout

When you are confident that your letter is well-written, you are ready to put the finishing touches on how the letter looks. When sending your letter as hard copy through the mail or via fax, the letter should be laid out on the page in a way that conforms to

 Watch Out!

Never complain, sound whiny, or beg in a cover letter. I've read letters in which job seekers talk about how long they've been looking for work, how tired they are of conducting a search, how badly they need a job, and how they just want someone to take a chance on them. That's a surefire way to turn off the reader.

a standard business letter format. You have three basic choices of formats (displayed on the following pages): indented, block, and modified block. Which one you choose is up to you. Simply pick the style that you like the best or that best presents the content of your letter.

If you are writing your letters on stationery that already has your name, address, and phone number at the top and/or bottom of the page, you don't need to repeat that information. The following examples include the sender's information for people writing on plain paper, not personalized letterhead.

Indented style

Sender's Address
City, State, ZIP
Phone
Email

Date

Recipient's First and Last Name
Job Title
Organization Name
Internal Address (for example, Suite or Floor #)
Outside Address (Street or PO Box)
City, State, ZIP (and country if applicable)

Dear Ms./Mr./Dr. [last name]: (Can use first name if familiar with recipient)

    Indent the first line of each paragraph one tab from the left margin. Continue the rest of the paragraph like this with lines starting at the left margin.

    Skip one space between paragraphs.

Closing,

Sender's Signature
(first name only if the recipient knows you well; otherwise, sign first and last names)

Sender's Name (typed first and last)

Encl. (Can also type "Enclosure;" use this if you send anything with your letter, such as a resume.)

Block style

Sender's Address
City, State, ZIP
Phone
Email

Date
Recipient's Name
Job Title
Organization Name
Internal Address
Outside Address
City, State, ZIP

Dear Ms./Mr./Dr. [last name]:

Justify all lines of the paragraph flush with the left and right margins (also called justified).

Skip one line between paragraphs.

Closing,

Sender's Signature

Sender's Name Typed

Encl.

Modified block style

```
                                              Sender's Address
                                              City, State, ZIP
                                              Phone
                                              Email

                                              Date

Recipient's Name
Job Title
Organization Name
Internal Address
Outside Address
City, State, ZIP

Dear Ms./Mr./Dr. [last name]:

Justify all lines of the paragraph flush with the left and right margins (justified).

Skip one space between paragraphs.

                                              Closing,

                                              Sender's Signature

                                              Sender's Name Typed

Encl.
```

Font style and size

When sending a résumé or bio along with your letter in hard copy by mail or as a fax, select a font style and size that is the same as, or very complementary to, the font of your résumé. The two documents will be viewed side-by-side, so they should match as closely as possible. Follow the guidelines for fonts in the "Résumé Design and Layout" section of Chapter 5 for help in selecting the best font style and size. Note that if you had a difficult time fitting your résumé onto a certain number of pages, you might have used a slightly smaller sized font than you would need to use in your letter. Assuming you followed the advice earlier in this chapter to keep your letter brief, then you might be able to use a larger font size in your letter. You typically would not go larger than a 12-point font, however.

How to send your letter

Whether to send your cover letter—and résumé if appropriate—by mail, fax, or email depends on the circumstances. In many cases, such as when answering a job ad or sending a résumé and letter to someone who has requested you do so, you will already have instructions for how to send it. In those cases, you are likely to be asked to post your letter and résumé onto a Web site or send them by email.

When you are initiating the contact, however, such as in a direct mail campaign to targeted prospective employers, you have a choice for how you send your letter and résumé. Sending by email usually makes most sense when you are writing to people who are likely to prefer email, such as those in the IT field. It is also a time-saving and cost-effective method when you need to get your message and résumé out to a large number of people. You might opt for mailing hard copy, however, if you want to stand out, as many people these days receive more electronic mail than snail mail. You might also be concerned that your email could be blocked by the recipient's spam filter. If you do send hard copy, select a color and weight of paper and envelope that is the same as, or closely matches, your résumé paper.

Just the Facts

- Cover letters really do get read, particularly if they are concise and well-written, and they are an important part of your overall self-marketing strategy.

- Follow the step-by-step guidelines in this chapter to craft cover letters that are not difficult to write and that answer four questions on the reader's mind: Why is this person sending me a résumé? What is this person's background? What could this person do for me or someone I know? What action do I need to take?

- After writing a rough draft of your résumé, read it aloud to yourself to see whether the language flows well and sounds natural.

- How you present your cover letter is almost as important as what it says. Choose a layout and style that makes a clean, professional presentation, and have others proof the letter carefully.

Where Will You Find Your Job?

Now that you've prepared your self-marketing tools, you're probably eager to put them to use. That means it's time to focus on where the actual job openings are, but first make sure that you've carefully identified what you're looking for in your next career move. Review Chapter 3, "Marketing You, the Product," if you need help defining your job objective and determining what sorts of employers are going to be most interested in you. Finding job openings is as much a quality issue as one of quantity. It's not enough just to find job openings, you have to find the ones that are right for you because they match what you're looking for and because they are with employers who need what you have to offer.

This chapter walks you through the two major sectors of the job market—the visible, or advertised, job market that is found online and through print advertisements, headhunters, and job fairs, as well as the hidden market, those positions unearthed through networking and approaching employers directly.

Chapter 7

While the hidden market is usually by far the best direction to head for most job seekers because it lets you tap into opportunities before they're announced to your competition, there are distinct benefits to looking in the visible market as well.

The visible marketplace—your passive approach

The *visible marketplace*—my term for what is often called the formal or advertised job market—is one source of job opportunities. Job openings in the visible marketplace are, well, visible. They're not hiding behind the walls of organizations or in a hiring manager's mind. That's the *hidden market*—positions that haven't been advertised or aren't really even definite openings yet. I discuss these more in the next section of this chapter.

For now, you need to get familiar with what constitutes the visible marketplace. Job openings can be advertised, posted, listed, or announced—whatever you want to call it—in all sorts of places. Essentially, however, you are dealing with four basic categories of opportunity sources within the visible marketplace: the Internet; print advertisements; headhunters; and career or job fairs.

Statistics vary widely on how many positions are made visible versus how many are kept hidden or unadvertised. Experts tend to agree, however, that less than half of all positions are advertised. Some studies have even found that as few as 10 to 20 percent of positions are advertised formally. A word of caution is in order, however: As Internet-based recruiting continues to grow at its current rapid pace, more and more positions will be advertised online, and more job seekers will land positions that way. Networking—learning about positions through word-of-mouth, often before they are announced—will never go out of style. You will also be in the best position to edge out the competition when you hear of a position before it's announced to the world, but the tables may start to turn slightly to have the visible job market play a more prominent role in hiring.

Bright Idea

Don't forget about the job opportunities that might be advertised through colleges and universities on alumni Web sites and on campus in the career or alumni office.

Why employers advertise positions

Formally announcing job openings through print ads or online postings is expensive and accounts for a large portion of organizations' recruiting budgets. Listing positions with external recruiters, a.k.a. headhunters, is also costly in that fees are paid to recruiters when they refer a candidate who ends up being hired, or recruiters might be hired on a retained-fee basis to conduct ongoing searches.

So, why advertise? Employers advertise openings when they need to fill a position quickly or when they need specific skills and experiences that might be in short supply, hard to find, and are not already represented in candidates whose résumés are already on file. (Yes, when employers say, "We'll keep your résumé on file," many really do mean it, especially now that most are easy to keep digitally in résumé databases.)

Employers also advertise positions as a way to have some of the prescreening work done for them. Headhunters, for example, don't just collect résumés to forward on to the employer (their client), many of them do some initial screening or provide other services in the hiring process that offset the cost of the headhunters' fees.

Jobs in cyberspace

For many job seekers, the Internet is the most fruitful source of advertised opportunities. With millions of job listings to browse and the opportunity to post your résumé to be browsed by employers, the Internet is an obvious place to turn in your search.

Moneysaver

To find career centers offering free or very low cost employment advice, tools, training, and job opportunities in your area, go to www.servicelocator.org on the CareerOneStop Web site. CareerOneStop is a federal-state partnership initiative to give access to employment resources across the United States though the site and their "One-Stop Career Centers."

Companies are devoting a large amount of resources to attracting job candidates through online ads. Online recruitment advertising is expected to be a $2 billion business by 2008, according to Forrester Research. Much of this growth can be attributed to the cost-effectiveness of posting jobs online. A recent study out of the Society for Human Resource Management reported that the average cost per hire from an Internet recruiting strategy was $377, as opposed to the average cost per hire of $3,295 from ads placed in major metropolitan area newspapers.

With such a good deal for both job seekers and those seeking to fill jobs, you would think this might be the only place you need to look in your job search—not exactly. Online job searching has its drawbacks, from the merely annoying, such as increased spam mail and the logistical hassles of dealing with online recruiting technology, to much more serious issues, such as the potential for falling victim to scams or identity theft. Chapter 10, "Online Job Hunting," discusses the pros and cons of using the Internet in your search and offers strategies for making the most of cyberspace.

Print advertisements

Throughout the 1990s and even somewhat into the twenty-first century, the move toward Internet-based recruiting and job searching was frequently referred to as a "revolution." It was a growing trend but not necessarily something that had fully taken hold. Employers were still advertising jobs in newspapers and other print publications and only getting their feet wet online. Well, the revolution is over, and clearly Internet recruiting rules the land of employment. As a result, it can feel almost old-fashioned to look for jobs in the paper. Employers and recruiters still list positions in print, however, and candidates still get jobs that way, so don't cast aside print ads just yet.

The obvious place to look is in newspapers of major metropolitan areas, presumably in geographic areas in which you want to work. Some papers of particularly large cities, however, such as *The New York Times*, include ads for jobs well beyond the New York area, so you don't necessarily have to stick with your local publications. In addition to your area's daily paper, check local magazines for job ads as well. Local print publications can be especially good sources if you want to limit your search to your geographic area and if you are targeting smaller organizations that might choose to advertise only locally so as not to be inundated with candidates from all over the country.

A particularly good source of print ads that many job seekers overlook is any publication from a professional or trade association for the field or industry in which they want to work. Newsletters, journals, and magazines for specific fields often advertise employment opportunities. You may have much less competition when applying for positions advertised this way as only those who are in-the-know will see these ads. Check for relevant associations in the online Bonus Appendix 3, "Professional and Trade Associations," to find these publications.

Chapter 8, "Landing a Job through the Formal Marketplace," covers the topic of print ads in more detail and offers tips for evaluating and replying to ads.

Headhunters

Headhunter is the slang term for a consultant who serves as an external recruiter for an organization to identify, screen, and recommend candidates for positions. Organizations list positions with individual recruiters or recruiting firms and pay a commission based on the positions' salary levels if the recruiter recommends a candidate who ends up being hired. One twist on this arrangement is the case of retained searches, in which an organization pays a recruiting firm a retainer fee to conduct a search to fill what are usually high-level positions.

Using a headhunter in your search can be a great way to tap into employment opportunities. In fact, some positions get listed only with a recruiter and are not announced to the public. This is particularly true in cases where employers want to replace a manager or executive but need to keep the search confidential because they've not yet terminated the employee who is to be replaced.

Many job seekers don't fully understand the role of a recruiter and how best to work with them. A detailed discussion of how to find the right recruiters for your search and how to manage the relationship is included in Chapter 8. You'll also find Web sites for locating and learning more about them in the "Executive Recruiters and Staffing Agencies" section of the online Bonus Appendix 1, "Resource Guide." For now, I'll just introduce you to the two basic types of recruiters—contingency and retained.

Contingency

Some recruiting firms or staffing agencies conduct both contingency and retained searches, but the majority of recruiters focus on contingency searches only, which are typically for lower- to mid-level positions paying annual salaries anywhere from the $20,000s to the $80,000s. In contingency recruiting, the firm that places you in a position earns a percentage of your annual salary, often in the 15 to 30 percent range. Unlike retained recruiters, contingency recruiters don't get paid to find you; they get paid only if you are hired by their client.

The arrangement they have with the employer usually includes an agreement that you not only have to be hired but have to remain in the position for a certain period of time— usually a matter of months—before the full commission is paid.

As a result, the smart ones know that it is counterproductive to push you into a job that's not right for you because they won't get paid if you don't stay. There are, however, many disreputable contingency recruiters out there, so beware of any that try to talk you into a position you don't want. They might also push you to give them an exclusive, meaning that they don't want you working with any other recruiters. You do not have to do this. (At times, however, when one particular recruiter is a pleasure to work with and keeps you busy with plenty of good interview opportunities, you might choose to work with them exclusively, and that's fine.)

Contingency recruiters might also broadcast your résumé by blanketing the market with it indiscriminately. You don't want this to happen because it is not only an ineffective way to present yourself to employers, but it can also cause complications if the staffing agency sends your résumé to a company to which you've already applied. Messy situations can result as the agency demands a fee if you are hired, when in fact you're the one who got your own foot in the door before they sent your résumé. Some employers might avoid dealing with you as a candidate when they receive your résumé both ways in order to avoid a sticky situation, so you lose out on potential opportunities. If you don't know whether a particular recruiter will broadcast your résumé without your permission, ask.

Retained

Retained searches, usually conducted by executive recruiters, are typically for higher-level positions, often only for six- or seven-figure salaries. These recruiters are hired on a retainer basis by a corporate client or major nonprofit organization to find and screen candidates. Some larger organizations have executive recruiters on retainer over long periods of time for on-going needs, while others bring in the recruiter only on an as-needed basis.

Employers pay either a flat retainer fee or a percentage of annual salary, often 30 percent or more. Large executive search firms handle a variety of industries or functions, and smaller, "boutique" types specialize in one or two industries or functional roles. Some also provide services such as conducting pre-hire assessments, reference and background checks, and thorough interviews to screen you for the client.

Career and job fairs

Career and job fairs—the terms are used somewhat interchangeably—are events sponsored by professional associations, industry groups, consortiums of employers, nonprofit organizations, government agencies, community groups, and private event-planning firms. At career fairs, employers, and sometimes headhunters as well, set up in a booth, small office, or at a table in a large event room to publicize employment opportunities and meet with candidates. Career fairs range from small events with only a handful of employers in attendance and no formal agenda—job seekers browse the fair and chat casually with employers or have impromptu interviews—to large, highly organized events held in convention centers or other major venues.

Only a small percentage of jobs are landed as a direct result of attending a career or job fair—less than 10 percent is the rate usually cited by most studies—but fairs should be a part of your overall strategy nonetheless. In addition to the chance to learn about actual openings that might be right for you, fairs offer great networking opportunities and a place to practice some of your job search communication techniques, such as your self-marketing sound bite. Plus, it gets you out of the house!

 Moneysaver

Women for Hire puts on career fairs around the country and usually brings in professional résumé writers or career coaches on a *pro bono* basis to offer free résumé critiques to job seekers attending the fair. You can find their schedule of fairs at www.womenforhire.com.

The hidden marketplace—your proactive approach

Most experts estimate that well over half of all job openings are not advertised. Many employers have plenty of résumés already on file from which to choose candidates, or they have qualified internal candidates to promote from within the organization. Other employers do not advertise because even though they anticipate hiring for a particular position in the near future, they are not comfortable formally announcing an opening because of a possible reorganization or budget cut that could make the opening disappear. Some choose not to advertise because the opportunity is confidential—they don't want the person in the position now to know that he or she is about to be replaced, or they don't want to reveal to the competition that a key position is vacant. Still others can't advertise because there is an official hiring freeze in their organization, but some occasional hiring does still go on "off the record."

If you limit your search to the visible, advertised marketplace, you're seeing only the tip of the job iceberg. By using more proactive methods, such as approaching employers directly or networking to get leads to employers, you give yourself a much larger pool of possibilities. You also give yourself much less competition because you learn about positions long before everyone else does.

Direct contact campaigns

For years, job seekers have conducted mass mailings to find jobs. They send out hundreds of résumés by mail or email accompanied by a form cover letter barely tailored to each recipient, if at all. Sometimes, they even pay a career coach or firm big bucks to do the mailing for them. I unequivocally do not advocate mass mailings, nor do most job search experts. As with any direct mail campaign, you're lucky if you get even a one-percent response rate—hardly worth the time, effort, and money. Employers and recruiters view unsolicited résumés with bland, noncustomized cover letters as they would any junk mail. They toss it. This method simply does not work except in very rare cases where the sender lucks into a job this way.

What can work, however, is to target a small number of potential employers carefully and approach them with a cover letter that is tailored to each recipient based on thorough research into how your qualifications might fit the needs of that employer. By approaching organizations directly in this fashion, you benefit from a more wide-open window of opportunity in the hiring process. When a position is advertised, that window of opportunity is just about shut. Employers may already have internal candidates, referrals from their own employees, and word-of-mouth candidates to consider. Then, they advertise and expand the applicant pool even more. Your competition is greater, and employers are already down to picking their short list of most qualified candidates. That window is just inches from being closed. If, however, you approach an employer long before a position is advertised—perhaps even before an opening actually exists—you're there on the ground floor before the competition builds up. You might even end up having a position created for you if you market yourself effectively to show what you could do for the organization.

There are plenty of ways to find organizations to contact and to learn how you can tailor your marketing communications to fit the nature of their business and their particular needs and organizational culture. Keyword searches or databases on the Internet, print directories of organizations, lists of top employers in popular business magazines, and professional and trade associations' publications or Web sites are just some of the ways to do so. The "Researching companies and organizations" section of the online Bonus Appendix 1 directs you to online resources, while the same section of online Bonus Appendix 2, "Recommended Reading List," points you to print directories.

Chapter 8 discusses direct contact campaigns in much more detail, including how to develop your target list of employers to contact, what to say and send, and whether to contact them by mail, email, phone, or fax.

Networking

There's an entire chapter of this book (Chapter 5) devoted to networking. It's that important. Networking is a process of getting to know people, or getting reconnected with people you already know, to build professional relationships for mutual support. Note that I said "mutual." Many job seekers are reluctant to network because they see the process as using people or being a pest. What they don't realize is that networking is a natural part of professional life. People in all industries and professions network on an on-going basis. The reason it's so prevalent is that there is nothing sleazy, mercenary, or bothersome about it—at least not when it's done correctly. Networking works because, when done right, it's a process of give-and-take in which people help each other develop their mutual careers.

Countless studies have shown that the majority of jobs are found through networking—that is, by connecting with people who either know of jobs or who can lead you to the people who have jobs to offer. Networking takes place everywhere from one-on-one meetings, to large group events, to impromptu situations such as chatting with the person next to you on the bus or plane. It can take place in person, by phone, or online. It might take months to cultivate a relationship that eventually bears fruit, or you might get a hot lead from someone the first time you meet. Chapter 9 provides everything you need to know to network effectively, whether you've been doing it for years and just need a tune-up or have never given it a try. Try it; you'll like the results.

 Bright Idea

If you've been working in the private sector and are open to a change, don't overlook opportunities in the nonprofit arena. Visit the Nonprofit Career Network at www.nonprofitcareer.com, a one-stop resource center for paid job opportunities in nonprofit organizations and for volunteer opportunities.

Growth industries

In Chapter 3, you learned that the best way to embark on a job search is to identify what you have to offer and what you want out of your next position and to go after employers that want what you have and offer what you need. You'll be most effective in your search if you follow that advice. It's a better approach than targeting industries just because some expert has declared them as "hot."

With that said, however, there is nothing wrong with factoring industry trend reports and growth projections into your search. This is especially true if in Chapter 3 you identified such factors as stability, job security, or advancement opportunities as being high priorities. It's easy to find information on growing, strong industries. Most major business and news magazines, as well as news Web sites, run feature stories on where the jobs are

Top Five Fastest Employment Growth Areas 2002–2012

The following employment settings are expected to have the fastest growth in job opportunities for the next several years. These are nationwide statistics, so keep in mind that opportunities in your geographic area may vary. The percentages reflect the amount of growth projected from the years 2002 to 2012.

Software publishers: 67.9%

Management, scientific, and technical consulting services: 55.4%

Community care facilities for the elderly and residential care facilities: 55%

Computer systems design and related services: 54.6%

Employment services: 54.3%

Source: U.S. Bureau of Labor Statistics.

(or will be) at least once or twice a year. You can also go straight to the source and review the Bureau of Labor Statistics' projections at www.bls.gov.

Getting interviews

It is a rare situation in which a job seeker can land a position without having at least one interview with the employing organization. It happens once in a blue moon, such as a recent client of mine who was happily employed and happened to call an old colleague to suggest that they get together for lunch simply to catch up. They did go to lunch, and the colleague said to my client, "We have a job opening that you'd be perfect for." He went on to describe the position and concluded with, "So, will you come work for us?" A formal, written offer was sent to my client by fax the next day. Of course, one could argue that the lunch conversation was an interview of sorts, but it really wasn't. This guy received a job offer because his prior reputation and collegial relationship with the hiring authority was all that was needed to get the offer—an offer he wasn't even trying to get!

Most job seekers aren't so lucky, unfortunately. They usually must go through at least one interview, if not an arduous process of screening interviews by phone followed by on-site meetings with all parties involved in the hiring decision. (Types of interviews and how to handle them are discussed in Chapter 12.) So, a key objective in your job search is to land interviews, which is a critical step in landing job offers.

Where to put your eggs—strategy and time allotment

In the online Bonus Chapter 1, "Getting Organized and Planning Your Action," I lay out a typical action plan for getting interviews. I suggested that, although every search is unique, most job seekers need to spend about 60 percent of their time networking, 15 percent researching and making direct contact with targeted employers, 10 percent online, 10 percent in some combination of headhunters, career fairs, and applying to print ads, and the remaining 5 percent on the administrative upkeep of a search.

The exact strategy and time allotment you devise should be tailored to your situation. You may find, for example, that the type of work you are seeking is most likely to be found through executive recruiters, perhaps because you are looking for senior-level positions and have had good luck with headhunters in the past. Maybe you're an IT professional or accountant and are, therefore, more likely to land a position online. You might live in a small community where most positions are advertised in the local paper or listed with the local Department of Labor office, so you'll concentrate your search there. The key is to tailor your strategy to fit the type of work you're seeking and the circumstances of your situation.

No matter what those circumstances are, however, it's important that your search strategy be diversified by taking advantage of all the possible sources of jobs from both the visible and hidden marketplaces.

To HR or not to HR—getting to the person who can grant interviews

If the last time you conducted a job search was 20 or 30 years ago, you might have dealt with a lot of *personnel* departments. These were filled primarily with glorified paper-pushers who prescreened candidates to make sure that they didn't have two heads but beyond that did not have much say in hiring decisions. Fortunately, that situation is a relic of the past. Personnel offices in all but the most nonprogressive organizations have fully evolved into human resources (HR) departments with highly sophisticated recruiting functions and internal recruiters who not only identify and screen potential candidates but have a great deal of say in hiring decisions. So, do not overlook a recruiter in the human resources area of a company as a good person to bring you in to interview.

It is true, however, that oftentimes your best bet is to connect with someone in the department where you would actually want to work (assuming that department is other than HR). If you are approaching a small- to mid-sized organization or start-up that you suspect does not have a formal HR department or one that is actively involved in hiring decisions, then you may be better off trying to get to the hiring manager in the area of the company in which you would want to work. If in doubt, send your email or letter to both HR and the hiring manager and follow up by phone with both.

Getting a name

Don't know who the correct HR person or hiring manager is? If you've replied to an ad—online or in print—then you might see a name within the email address to which you were instructed to send your résumé. If not, or if you're approaching an organization blindly through direct contact rather than in response to an ad, do your homework to try to find some names on the organization's Web site or in online databases of companies. Also ask everyone in your network if they know of anyone in the organizations you're approaching. If all else fails, call the company directly and ask for the name and email address of the head of the relevant department and for the HR rep who handles the sort of position you're seeking. Don't feel that you have to be sneaky. It's okay to say why you want the names.

Getting past the gatekeepers

If the gatekeeper will give you only names and no contact information, don't worry. Get the names and then figure out email addresses by looking at other addresses on the company Web site. You usually can tell if a company's email architecture is something like first name, followed by last name, then "@companyname.com" or first initial followed by last name. You also usually can find phone numbers, or at least be connected to voice mail, by calling a company after hours to hear the employee directory.

Don't Take a Holiday from Your Job Search

During the holiday period of Thanksgiving to New Year's Day, many job seekers let their job searches take a holiday, too, but this is an unfortunate mistake. It's true that hiring activity does slow down in many organizations during that time. Sometimes budgets and decisions about staffing needs don't get set until the new year, and it is often difficult for decision-makers to find time together to interview or evaluate candidates if vacations or busy year-end business activities interfere. It's a myth, however, that there's no point in searching at all during this time. Many organizations want to start the year with new hires fully in place, and recruiters may be motivated to close open cases by the end of the year. Even if you do find lots of employers saying "Contact us again after the first of the year," the holidays are at least a very good time to network. In organizations where business slows down in November and December, people may be more relaxed and approachable, and professional groups often have bigger turnouts at their holiday meetings and parties than at other times of year. Networking during those months lets you get your name in the hat early for positions that may open up in the new year. Plus, those invitations you get to purely social holiday functions are great sources of networking opportunities. Finally, you can also take advantage of any downtime to rework your self-marketing materials and conduct research. However you choose to use the time, be sure to keep your momentum going.

If the gatekeeper won't even give you names and instructs you to apply online or just send in your résumé to some generic address, explain politely that you are happy to apply through the normal channels but have some questions before you do so.

Watch Out!

Don't forget to put yourself in the employer's shoes. You are an expensive commodity to them, so you must show why you're worth interviewing, let alone hiring. It costs employers on average $140 for every $1000 of compensation when hiring someone, according to a 2004 *Benchmark Study* published by Staffing.org and the Human Capital Metrics Consortium.

Be as friendly and down-to-earth as possible with the gatekeeper, and you might be surprised how far you can get.

When you do find a direct phone number for the person you want to reach, avoid the gatekeepers all together by calling early in the morning or in the evening when a manager or executive may be more likely to answer his or her own phone.

Critical preinterview interactions

Many job seekers work hard at preparing to present themselves well in an interview but forget that employers start forming their first impression of a candidate before the interview is even set on the calendar. To establish positive rapport from the get-go, consider the following tips:

- Make scheduling appointments easy. Don't be overly demanding when coming up with a mutually convenient day and time to meet and don't reschedule unless absolutely unavoidable.

- Follow through on all your promises. If you're asked to email or fax another copy of your résumé, send a reference list, make a phone call to schedule an appointment, or engage in any other interaction with the prospective employer prior to the interview, be sure that you do things when you say you will. If you can't do so promptly, then call or email to let them know when you will be following through.

- Be considerate with everyone you speak to or meet. Be courteous and appreciative when working with administrative assistants and receptionists to arrange your interview. You never know who might have input on the hiring decision.

Start showing that you have your act together long before the interview day arrives, and you'll not only be more likely to secure the interview in the first place, you will also predispose the employer to view you favorably.

Just the facts

- The visible—that is, formal or advertised—employment market has distinct advantages in that it is easier to tap into than the hidden market, requires a little less effort, and is more likely to yield definite openings. Beware, however, of taking too passive an approach in your search.

- Over half of all job opportunities are not advertised. The hidden market is an excellent source of jobs and can be uncovered through networking and direct contact.

- Types of jobs and industries that have been identified as growth areas should be considered as one factor in your strategy to discover employment opportunities.

- The best strategy for going after job opportunities is diversified, customized, and focused on quality as much as quantity.

- Use the tips offered in this chapter to respond to the "buy signals" employers may send out and to overcome obstacles and objections as you attempt to get interviews.

Preparing Your Self-Marketing Tools

PART III

GET THE SCOOP ON...
Where the formal job market fits into your overall strategy ▪ Reading between the lines of classified job ads ▪ Heads-up about headhunters ▪
Making the most of career and job fairs ▪ Secrets
of making a direct mail campaign work

Landing a Job through the Formal Marketplace

Chapter 8

As you learned in Chapter 7, the formal, or advertised, marketplace is not necessarily the best place to find jobs. As soon as a position is announced and listed online, in the paper or with a recruiter, your competition increases exponentially. Networking is usually a much better way to go after the jobs, because it enables you to learn about opportunities before the rest of the world gets wind of them. That said, there is nothing wrong with including classified ads, online postings, head-hunters, career fairs, and targeted mailings in your overall strategy. People do land jobs these ways every-day. The key is to be calculated about how you use these methods. They are inherently passive methods, but if you go about them in creative, strategic ways, you can make them work for you.

The issue of job searching on the Internet is a complex enough topic to get its own chapter, so you'll learn about online job hunting, including preparing a version of your résumé for online use, in

Chapter 10. Here, I focus on responding to print job ads, working with headhunters, attending career or job fairs, and conducting direct mail campaigns. As mentioned in Chapter 7, direct mail campaigns aren't technically a part of the advertised marketplace because writing to employers you've identified as a good fit for you is a proactive way to tap into the hidden job market, just as networking is. Targeted mailings tend to be one of the more passive methods of job hunting, however (you send out a bunch of letters and résumés and hope the calls come pouring in), so I've included it in this chapter.

Replying to print job advertisements

Ads for job opportunities can be found in a variety of print publications, including city and community newspapers and magazines, professional association journals or newsletters, and trade publications for your targeted industry. With increasing numbers of recruiters and employers advertising their jobs online, you could just about eliminate print ads from your search strategy entirely because you're likely to find all the job listings you need on the Internet. Print ads can be helpful, however, when looking for jobs in small, local businesses that might choose to advertise only in the local paper and not online. Whether that's what you're targeting or not, there's no harm in browsing the newspaper and other relevant publications just to be thorough in your search methods.

Reading between the lines

One of those rare exciting moments in a job hunt is when you open up the Sunday paper and there, in black and white, staring straight out at you, is the perfect job for you. You know it's just what you want, and you know that you're just what they need. Buyer beware, though! Is it so perfect, and are you so perfect for it? Not to burst your bubble, but you have to read between the lines of job ads because what you see at first is often not what you get. You have to scrutinize the wording of the ad to make sure that it's really what it sounds like and to ensure that you have the qualifications they're seeking.

Make sure the job is what you think it is

Help wanted, or classified, advertisements are usually written to elicit the largest potential pool of qualified applicants in order to justify the cost of placing the ad. Ads make the employing organization sound like the best place on earth to work and make the job sound exciting and rewarding. So, before getting too excited about the position described, read the ad carefully to try to figure out what it really entails. If the sales pitch sounds too good to be true, be very cautious if you choose to apply for the position and get contacted for an interview. Do your due diligence on the organization to make sure they are all they claim to be and ask lots of questions about the position to discern what it really involves.

Make sure you're right for the job

Even though employers and recruiters want to attract as many applicants as possible to justify the cost of an ad, they do not want to be inundated with poorly qualified applicants. As a result, at least 99 percent of the time an ad will specify fairly precise qualifications needed for the position. Those who place the ad are usually quite serious about needing applicants to possess these qualifications. In fact, sometimes employers and recruiters pay to advertise an opportunity only because the requirements for the position are so specialized and mandatory that they cannot find suitable candidates from the pool of applicants who approach the organization on their own. Most

 Watch Out!

Ads for sales positions are notorious for misleading applicants. You might think you're applying for a customer service position to help existing customers, for example, only to find out you would be doing mostly cold-calling for new business.

reputable, well-known employers have plenty of unsolicited résumés coming in and lots of job seekers knocking on their doors, so they don't have to spend money on advertising to fill positions. Therefore, when an employer does pay to advertise, they are usually looking for a clearly defined set of qualifications and don't want to be bothered by candidates who do not fit the bill.

This does not mean that you have to meet 100 percent of the requirements for a position. As long as you're in the 85- to 90-percent range, you should still apply. Just be realistic about the skills and credentials you have and don't waste your time applying for positions that are a major stretch. There will simply be too much competition for your résumé to get noticed.

What to say when you reply

Ads in newspapers of major metropolitan areas can bring in thousands of responses from job seekers. To end up on the short list among that competition, not only do you need to be qualified for the position as discussed earlier, you need to send a letter that provides a powerful introduction to your résumé. Chapter 6, "Job Search Correspondence," includes examples of ad response letters. Be sure to refer to those samples when replying to ads, remembering to be concise and to relate your qualifications directly to those of the job requirements.

The salary issue

Ads for jobs often ask you to state your salary history or salary requirements when applying. Sometimes the ad is worded in a way that makes it sound as though your application will be rejected if you do not address the salary issue. The reality is that this is something of an intimidation tactic and that in most cases your résumé will not be rejected just because you ignored the request for salary information.

Employers would love to know your salary information in advance as a way to get a leg up on negotiations should they end up offering the job to you. It also helps them know that you're

Watch Out!

If the ad to which you are replying was placed by a headhunter, not the employer directly, then you must mention salary history or requirements if the ad asks for that. Recruiters have to know that your desired or previous compensation is in the range of what the client will pay. Do be as broad as possible, though, giving a range rather than exact figures.

in the ball park of what they want to pay, so they won't waste time contacting and interviewing a candidate who isn't the right fit in terms of compensation. But, the reality is that if you are well qualified for the job, they will most likely contact you whether you answered the salary question or not.

Note, however, that I said, "will most likely contact you" and earlier said, "in most cases your résumé will not be rejected." There are no guarantees here; you have to use your own judgment and do what you are comfortable doing. For years, job seekers have gotten call-backs from résumés and letters sent without salary information even though that information was requested in the ad. I've witnessed this with countless job seekers, as have other career coaches. I've also had employers tell me directly that they put in the request for salary information expecting that about half of applicants will provide it, and the other half will not, but that they will consider all candidates on the merits of their qualifications. So, it's your choice to make: to reveal or not to reveal. If you do cave in to the pressure and decide to mention salary, just be sure to be as general as possible. State broad ranges rather than precise dollar amounts.

How and when to reply

If an ad provides only one way for you to respond, use that method, whether it's fax, email, regular mail, or by phone. If given a choice, use whichever method is more convenient for you. You might also want to reply in two ways. For example, you could fax or email your cover letter and résumé (if emailing, remember to send a cover message within the body of the email, not as an attachment) and then follow up with hard copy sent in the mail. This doubles your chances of getting noticed.

After you've determined your response approach, you need to decide on timing of your response. Most job seekers reply as soon as possible after seeing an ad posted. It's understandable to want to reply right away to make sure that you don't miss out on being considered for the position, but there can actually be an advantage to waiting two or three days before responding. Because many ads get huge numbers of responses, your letter and résumé can stand out more if you wait a bit to reply. You don't get caught up in the deluge of applications that hit the recruiter's or employer's mailbox or fax machine in the first couple of days after the ad is placed. The reality is that when a company pays to advertise a job, they are not going to cut off acceptance of applications too early. They want to get their money's worth out of the ad by accepting résumés for at least a couple of weeks, if not more, before beginning the interview process.

Of course, don't wait to reply if the ad is old because you could be near the tail end of the application process. Also, if a cut-off date is given by which all résumés must be submitted, then obviously you would need to meet that deadline. Finally, if it makes you too nervous to hold back your response, go ahead and apply right away. Just be sure to take the time to craft a strong cover letter and tailor your résumé to the position rather than dashing off a response prematurely.

If the name of the employer or recruiting firm placing the ad is provided in the ad, try to follow up by email or phone after sending your résumé so that you won't get lost in the shuffle. If the ad is blind, meaning you can't tell who the employer or recruiter is, then follow-up can be difficult. You might have to sit back and wait for them to contact you. If a phone number or address was provided, however, you might be able to figure out who they are by using one of the online services such as

Moneysaver

Don't post your own position-wanted ad. It smacks of desperation and is usually a waste of money.

www.reversephonedirectory.com or www.anywho.com. Follow-up techniques are discussed in more detail in Chapter 15, "Clinching the Deal."

Hunting for the best in headhunters

Headhunters—the slang terms for various types of recruiters and personnel consultants—can be a valuable part of your job search strategy, but don't rely too heavily on them. You have to be proactive in your search and go after job openings yourself, not just put your name in the hat at recruiting firms and assume that they will find you a job. If you do choose to work with recruiters, be sure you understand the differences between contingency and retained search firms. Review the descriptions of recruiters offered in Chapter 7, "Where Will You Find Your Job?" if you need a refresher.

In the introduction of this book, I mentioned that understanding anthropology helps job seekers work with headhunters. Now you get to find out what I meant by that. Think about what anthropologists do. They study and get familiar with different cultures. They get to know the behaviors and customs of people from different societies and, as a result, are often better equipped to interact with people who are different from them. What this has to do with recruiters is that you must understand how they operate. You need to know how they think, what their customs are, how they communicate, and what motivates them.

Headhunters are a unique breed within the realm of people you will come across in your job search. Career counselors and coaches are in business to help you. Members of your network are at the ready to help you. Headhunters are in business to help themselves (that is, make money) by helping their clients (employers) find the right people to fill positions. Sure, some of the more altruistic among the headhunter species enjoy helping candidates (such as you, the job seeker) and find it highly rewarding to make money by helping people find employment. So, I don't mean to make out all recruiters as mercenaries. The best among them are good people who value helping others. With that said, however, the bottom line is that recruiters are in business to earn a commission or fee for placing the right person in the right job. As long as you understand this, you'll get along just fine with them.

Winning them over

Now that you have a basic understanding of what recruiters are all about, let's look more specifically at how best to work with them. The following tips will help you interact more effectively with recruiters and should minimize the frustrations you could face in dealing with them.

- **Realize that they are busy.** Good recruiters have a lot going on. They spend time developing relationships with new or existing employer-clients and working with candidates they are currently trying to place. Recruiters are hired by employers to identify and screen suitable candidates for positions the employer needs to fill and to shepherd candidates through the interviewing process after the short list of best candidates has been identified and sent to the employer. Some recruiters provide extra services such as reference and background checks, personality or aptitude testing, and other screening services. All of this keeps them quite busy. If a recruiter does not have a suitable job opportunity for you at a given point in time, you are unlikely to get much, if any, of his or her attention. (If a recruiter doesn't seem to be busy, tread carefully because you might be dealing with someone who is very inexperienced or not reputable.)

Watch Out!

If a recruiter offers career counseling services, or if a career counselor in private practice also does recruiting, proceed with caution! Providing both services is usually a serious conflict of interest. You might be coached to make career choices that happen to fit with a job opening for which that person is recruiting, so you could be urged to take a job that might not be in your best interest.

- **Always remember who the client is.** Headhunters get paid, either on a commission or flat fee basis, by the employer. Therefore, the employers are their primary clients. Reputable headhunters know that you need to be treated like a client too in order to make the relationship work, but their primary allegiance is to the employer. Don't expect a recruiter to help you figure out what you want to do with your life, give you lots of job search advice, or write your résumé. Some will touch on these matters, and many recruiters will offer résumé pointers or even tweak your résumé to better match jobs for which they might recommend you. They just won't necessarily be able to spend large amounts of time with you until they have a definite job opportunity for you because that time needs to be spent with clients and with candidates they're currently working on placing.

- **Be realistic about how they can place you.** Recruiters work best with candidates who have a clear job focus and experience directly related to the jobs they're seeking. Rarely can recruiters place people who are trying to make a career change to a new functional role or industry because their clients are paying them to find candidates who are a near-perfect fit for their job openings, not people on whom they should take a chance.

- **Have a laser-sharp focus in all your communications.** Because recruiters are usually busy people who are contacted by more candidates than they can handle, you must be concise and targeted in all your dealings with them. Keep email, voice mail, and letters short and focused. Always clearly communicate why you're contacting them, what you have to offer, and what you're looking for. Pay attention to details such as giving complete contact information and best times to reach you, stating the nature of your correspondence in email subject fields, and including a signature block in every email.

- **Operate with honesty and integrity.** Recruiters put their reputations on the line when they recommend you to their clients, so you must approach the relationship with the utmost integrity. Be up front with them about any skeletons in your professional closet, don't ever lie to them about your qualifications, and don't string them along by having them get you into the thick of the hiring process for a job you have no intention of accepting.

- **Don't circumvent their authority.** If an organization has listed an opening with a recruiter, that organization and the recruiter both expect that the recruiter will serve as the liaison between the employer and candidates. The recruiter also expects and deserves a commission or fee from the employer for introducing the right candidate if that person ends up being hired. As a result, it's critical that you not go around the recruiter and deal directly with the employer, unless you have the recruiter's permission to do so. This means that if a recruiter tells you about a position, you don't try to approach the employer directly, and if you end up being interviewed, you don't communicate with the employer directly during the hiring process without permission from the recruiter.

Following these tips will help you develop a solid working relationship with a headhunter—a relationship that could grow and flourish over your professional career, well beyond your current job hunt.

Buyer Beware: Avoiding Disreputable Recruiters

To help you evaluate the legitimacy and ethics of a recruiting firm or staffing agency, find out whether the firm is a member of any organizations such as the National Association of Personnel Services (www.napsweb.org), American Staffing Association (www.staffingtoday.net), or Association of Executive Search Consultants (www.awsc.org). To have more confidence in an individual recruiter with whom you might work, find out whether he or she holds the CPC (Certified Personnel Consultant) or CIPC (Certified International Personnel Consultant) designation. These are not obligatory credentials, but they serve as a seal of excellence, signifying that the holder has passed a stringent course of study and exams, achieved a considerable level of experience, and promised to uphold high ethical standards.

Beyond that, never work with any firm that wants you to pay them any amount of money for placing you or that makes promises of placement that sound too good to be true. Also be wary of those who cannot guarantee that they won't broadcast your résumé to large numbers of employers—because you want to retain some control over where your résumé goes. Finally, steer clear of those who try to push you into jobs that aren't right for you. Reputable recruiters know that it's not only unethical, it's bad business to talk a candidate into a job that might not work out.

Finding the right headhunters for you

The best way to find a recruiter who is right for you is through personal referral. Not only does this ensure that you'll find someone legitimate and ethical, it also increases the likelihood that the recruiter will respond to you when you first approach. Recruiters like it when their own former candidates refer colleagues to them. You become more of a known quantity and not just some random job seeker approaching them out of the blue.

Short of personal referrals, you can use other, more methodical methods for finding headhunters. Sites listed in the "Executive Recruiters and Staffing Agencies" section of online Bonus Appendix 1 are good places to start. The Web sites I've recommended there include associations to which recruiters and placement consultants belong as well as actual search firms and staffing agencies. You also will find ads recruiters place in print publications and Internet job boards. Get in the habit of browsing those job listings to spot recruiters who consistently advertise positions over time that are relevant to your job objective. These would be good recruiters for you to approach, whether a current opening is exactly right for you or not.

Connecting with headhunters

As you start to collect names of recruiting firms or individual recruiters, determine whether the placements they specialize in match your background and career goals. Sending out mass mailings, blasting your résumé by email, or making cold calls to long lists of randomly chosen recruiters is usually a waste of time. Instead, identify those whose areas of specialization—industry, functional roles, responsibility level, and/or salary level—match yours. You'll have much better luck getting their attention if you are the type of candidate with whom they typically work. After you've narrowed your pool of possibilities to the recruiters who make most sense to contact, approach them with an introductory email and résumé, followed by a phone call a few days later. (Recruiters'

> **❝** As a recruiter, my inventory is time. Job seekers with quick, concise and easily understood email, voice mail, and résumés will have a better chance of getting some of that time. **❞**
>
> —John J. Weiss, CPC, CPRW, Principal, Executive Placement Services

Web sites usually specify how to contact them, so if the instructions differ from my suggestion for how to approach them, go with what the Web site dictates.)

If they don't have any openings that you would be right for, ask whether you may stay in touch with them. Unless they cannot imagine ever having a listing that would be right for you, they will usually say yes. In that case, check in by email or phone periodically, perhaps every two to three weeks, less often if they don't respond very encouragingly to your contact or seem annoyed by it. Each recruiter is unique in terms of preferences for wanting or not wanting candidates to stay in touch. Many understand that it helps job seekers feel more in control of their searches and admire their persistence or appreciate the reminder. Others prefer not to be contacted; if an opportunity comes up that's a good match, they will be in touch but don't want to be bothered in the meantime. So, ask up front what they prefer and respect their wishes.

Interviews with headhunters

You might end up interviewing with a recruiter face-to-face, and certainly by phone if nothing else, as a way for the recruiter to get to know you before working with you or as a screening interview for an actual opportunity. Interviews with recruiters are somewhat tricky because the headhunter is working on your behalf in a quasi-coaching role on the one hand, yet is someone you must impress as you would the actual employer. Although recruiters in agencies and executive search firms are not in the business of acting as career counselors, they do take on a career coaching sort of role in advising you about your résumé, your interviewing style, and your attire in order to best position you for employers to whom they'll be recommending you. They also might need to discuss sticky issues with you, such as why you were fired from a job or how to negotiate for a higher salary. At the same time, their primary allegiance must be to their client— the employer—so they must be highly selective when deciding whom to pass on to their client.

As a result, job seekers often don't know how candid they can be with a headhunter and how much they need to use strategic interviewing techniques with them. In general, a good rule to follow is that your interviewing approach with a head-hunter should be no different from your approach with an employer. You must make a case for why that recruiter should pay attention to you. Use your self-marketing sound bite, your asset statements, and other interviewing approaches that are covered in more detail in Chapter 12, "Types of Interviews and How to Handle Them," and Chapter 13, "Typical and Not-So-Typical Interview Questions." Keep in mind that the recruiter will have to convince the employer that you are a good enough fit for the job to deserve to be interviewed by that employer, so make sure that everything you say about yourself is understood by the recruiter so that he or she can easily and accurately represent you to the employer. In addition, never lie to a head-hunter, because his or her reputation is on the line every time you're sent out; if the employer catches you in a lie, the head-hunter gets blamed. (You don't, however, have to tell your deepest professional secrets. Let your relationship with the recruiter develop fully before you get too candid.)

Finally, remember that the recruiter needs to feel comfortable with you as a person. If you are overly stiff and rehearsed with canned answers to questions, you will not instill confidence in the recruiter. Be real, natural, and genuine.

Career and job fairs

Although only a small percentage of positions are landed directly as a result of attending a career or job fair, fairs should be one element in your job search strategy. They offer the obvious benefit of giving you face time with employers and recruiters, but also career fairs get you out of the house, dressed in nice clothes, and interacting with other human beings. Even if you don't find a job through a fair, you at least can get yourself recharged and avoid becoming isolated during your search by attending one.

Where to find them

Career and job fairs often are sponsored by professional and trade associations. If you aren't already aware of associations relevant to your targeted fields, refer to the listings in the online Bonus Appendix 3, "Professional and Trade Associations." These groups' Web sites usually announce upcoming career fairs. Other career fairs are community-based, sponsored by various non-profit organizations related to employment or by a governmental agency; or they are put on by for-profit, event-planning firms that specialize in job-related events. These are often advertised in city and neighborhood newspapers, as well as on television and radio. Of course, if you're a student, you'll hear about career fairs sponsored by your campus career center or other campus organizations.

Preparing for the fair

Usually, you are able to find out in advance which employers will be attending a career fair, and sometimes you can even find out for which positions they will be interviewing. If the employers and their jobs are a good fit for you, then it's obvious that attending would be worth your time. If they don't fit the bill exactly, consider going anyway. You never know whom you will meet—from both the exhibitors and the fellow job seekers—who could turn out to be valuable contacts for you. As you prepare to attend a career or job fair, keep the following pointers in mind:

- **Research.** Try to find out which employers and recruiters will be there and learn as much as you can about them in advance by reviewing their Web sites and asking around about them. Make notes of your research findings on small cards or in your PDA (handheld electronic device) for easy reference during the fair. This research and note-taking will help you not only zero-in on the employers that most interest you but also sound more knowledgeable when speaking with those organizations' representatives at the fair.

- **Perfect your self-marketing sound bite.** Job fairs are often crowded, hectic environments with all-too-brief and superficial interactions, so you have to make an impact on prospective employers in less than ideal circumstances. A 20-to-30-second version of your self-marketing sound bite (discussed in the online Bonus Chapter 2, "Honing Your Communication Skills and Tools") enables you to convey who you are, what you have to offer, and what you're looking for to a recruiter who has very limited time to spend with you.

- **Plan to dress appropriately.** Most job fairs call for business attire—jacket and tie or suit with tie for men, and a conservative pants suit, skirt suit, or dress for women. If no dress code is specified for the fair, it's best to take this approach. If the code is stated as business casual, then you can take the business attire a notch down, as described in the online Bonus Chapter 2.

- **Prepare your résumé.** Make sure that your résumé content is suitable for the types of employers and positions featured in the fair you'll be attending. Also, make sure that your résumé is laid out well and produced on quality paper so that it's pleasing to the eye and conveys professionalism. Some job fairs have a system for submitting your résumé electronically in advance, but you should still take hard copies to the fair. Try to find out about how many employers and recruiters will be in attendance and take enough copies based on that number.

- **Practice interviewing.** Some job fairs offer opportunities to schedule some one-on-one time with recruiters or employers. These are usually very brief interviews—often about 15 minutes or so, which means you have to have your interviewing technique down pat in order to make the most of that short time.

Ferreting Out the Career Fairs

The following sites list career and job fairs, and some provide advice on how best to work a fair. Also check the Web site of your local city or town newspaper to see whether they list job fairs in your area. For example, *The New York Times* lists career fairs in the New York area at www.nytimes.com/jobfair.

Career Builder: www.careerbuilder.com/JobSeeker/CareerFairs

CareerFair.com: www.careerfair.com

CareerFairs.com: www.careerfairs.com

Career Fairs Global, Inc.: www.cfg-inc.com

Diversity Career Group: www.diversitycareergroup.com/fairs

Equal Opportunity Publications, Inc.: www.eop.com/careerfair

Job Expo: www.jobexpo.com

Job Fair USA: www.jobfairusa.com

National Career Fairs: www.nationalcareerfairs.com

Quintessential Careers: www.quintcareers.com/career_fair_resources.html

Women for Hire: www.womenforhire.com

Making the most of a career or job fair

Most people think of career fairs as only a way to find out about job openings, but they are also a valuable networking avenue and good place to practice your self-marketing sound bite and overall communication techniques. To make the most of a fair, consider the following suggestions:

- **Go early.** Try to arrive at the start of the fair when it's likely to be a little less crowded and when the recruiters are fresh and don't yet have that glazed-over look. If you must attend after the event is well under way, be sure to allow yourself ample time there so that you can meet everyone you want to meet. Be prepared for long lines at some of the employers' booths.

■ **Make yourself memorable.** Recruiters can meet hundreds of candidates at job fairs, so it's important to distinguish yourself from the competition. Besides introducing yourself with your self-marketing sound bite and offering a copy of your résumé, add some bit of information that's likely to stick in the recruiter's mind. You might mention a fact about the organization that attracts you to it (here's where that research comes in handy) or give a brief example of one of your accomplishments.

■ **Follow up.** Follow-up is particularly important after job fairs. When recruiters get back to their offices, the faces that go with the résumés on their desks are mostly one big blur. Send a carefully crafted letter (or email) mentioning something specific that you talked about so that the recipient might be able to put a face with your name.

Contacts Can Turn Up in the Strangest Ways

A client of mine recently attended a career fair sponsored by the career transition firm where I work. While chatting with one of the employers there who didn't have any positions right for her, my client happened to mention the name of a company into which she was trying to break. It turned out the employer's husband works for that company, and she arranged for my client to have an interview there. You never know how a career fair could end up being of benefit to you, even if the employers in attendance are not right for you.

Direct mail campaigns

As mentioned at the start of this chapter, the job search method of applying directly to prospective employers through targeted mailings is something of an oddball category among job hunting methods. In some cases, direct mail campaigns are a passive, ineffectual approach to landing a job. In other cases, they can be highly effective at opening up opportunities because you might write to a company that does have a position open but that hasn't been advertised yet. What makes the difference? The key is in the targeting—in two ways. First, you need to target a relatively small number of organizations to approach—probably no more than about 50. Second, you need to tailor the résumé and/or letter that you send out so that they are targeted to each person you approach.

Developing target lists

If you're going to contact potential employers by mail, the first step is to decide who those employers are. You can develop your "hit list" in several ways. First, you'll know of some organizations off the top of your head, either because you've dealt with them in the past, have read or heard about them, or they are just generally known. Start your list with those organizations and then ask for recommendations from people in your network to expand the list. Remember that a marketing brief (described in the online Bonus Chapter 3, "More Self-Marketing Tools") is a great way to tell your contacts what types of employers you're looking for so that they can think of specific places you might want to contact. Also, keep in mind that about 12 million businesses (97 percent of the private sector) have fewer than 100 employees, so don't limit yourself only to the big guys that might be household names to you and your contacts. Poke around for smaller companies to include on your list, too, unless you are determined to work only for a very large organization.

After getting started on a list primarily of the potential employers already known to you and your network, you'll then

Moneysaver

Avoid purchasing mailing lists from mailing list brokers. You can often get the same names and contact information for free from the databases listed in the "Researching Companies/Organizations" section of the online Bonus Appendix 1.

want to turn to more formal research, using databases that list companies and organizations, as well as doing keyword searches on the Internet to find employers that match various criteria that are important to you. The "Researching Companies/Organizations" section of the online Bonus Appendix 1, "Resource Guide" lists several sites you can use to flesh out your target list.

Researching your targets

After gathering names and contact information on prospective employers as recommended in the previous section, pare down your list to only those organizations that seem to be a good fit for you and for whom you could offer relevant background and skills. Learn enough about each organization to know why you want to write to them.

I live in Atlanta where everybody and their brother wants to work for Coca-Cola or Home Depot, two major corporations headquartered here. Hardly a week goes by that a job seeker doesn't ask me how he or she can get a foot in the door at one of those companies. Before launching into a strategy discussion or handing over contact names, I always ask the clients why they want to work there. Surprisingly, very few can articulate good reasons. They usually just have Coke and Home Depot on their lists because they know those are major employers in our area, and they've heard they are good places to work. Be honest with yourself and see whether your own target list contains names of organizations that are there only because you have some vague notion that you should approach them, not because you have carefully evaluated whether they are a good fit for you. If you can't say that you truly know why you are targeting them, do some research to find out whether the names should remain on your list. Research them by reading the organizations' Web sites, especially the section with press releases, and by asking your network whether they know anything about them. Also, many of the same databases recommended in online Bonus Appendix 1 that you will use to find names for your list in the first place also provide information about the nature of the business, size, financials, and even corporate culture, of those organizations.

Crafting your marketing communications

The same research you conduct to decide which prospective employers ought to be on your list also helps you develop customized letters and résumés to use in your mailing. The more you know about an organization, the better you can tailor your letter and résumé to be relevant to the recipient. Mass mailings in which you use a word processing application's mail-merge function to churn out hundreds of form letters are a waste of time. No one likes getting a form letter, and there is no way you can adequately market yourself with a generic letter. Your time-consuming and expensive letter (if sent via the post office rather than email) becomes nothing more than junk mail that gets tossed.

Cover letter and résumé or just a letter?

Chapter 6, "Job Search Correspondence," included a sample letter that would be sent as part of a direct mail campaign. Be sure to review that sample and the tips offered along with it. Remember that your letter must get to the point quickly, give a brief summary of your qualifications, and mention something about why that organization is of interest to you. Keep in mind also that if you ask directly about jobs, you may close the door on yourself too quickly. Instead, look at a direct mail campaign as just another form of networking and ask for a few moments of the person's time to talk or meet with you to discuss what you have to offer and where they see you fitting in their organization or in their field in general. Also, remember that you do not have to send a résumé. Sometimes, sending a "résumé substitute letter" (also described, with a sample, in Chapter 5) can be more effective than sending a letter and résumé, as the letter alone makes you seem less like any other job applicant and more like a colleague seeking advice and an opportunity for conversation.

Mail, email, or fax?

When you have prepared your letter or letter and résumé, decide whether you want to send it by email, snail mail, or fax. (You could also make cold calls to the places on your list; do this only if you present yourself very well on the phone and have some experience with cold calling.) Many direct mail campaigns are conducted via email these days, but there is something about a letter, or letter with résumé, sent in the mail that makes the approach a bit more formal and polite—and perhaps more likely to be noticed. With email you run the risk of having your email deleted because the recipient doesn't recognize you or having it overlooked if it is one of too many emails backlogged in the recipient's inbox.

The necessity of follow-up

Finally, remember the importance of follow-up. You have initiated the contact with the employer, so it's up to you to carry it through. In your letter, refer to the fact that you will contact the recipient within the near future to see whether you could arrange to meet or speak by phone. Try to have the follow-up method you use be different from the original contact. For example, if you mailed your letter or résumé initially, follow up by email or phone. If you emailed initially, follow up by regular mail, fax, or phone. This increases your chances that you'll hit upon the best method of reaching your target. Don't forget to be persistent in your follow-up, too. It might take several tries to get through, so don't follow-up once and consider it done.

Just the facts

- Networking proactively is usually the best way to land a job, but more passive methods of applying to ads, working with headhunters, and attending career fairs should also be a part of your search strategy.

- When replying to ads in the newspaper or other print publication, read the ad carefully to determine whether you're qualified and whether the organization sounds too good to be true.

- Be selective when using headhunters, targeting those who specialize in your sort of work and watching out for those with unethical business practices. When you do make a good match with the right recruiter, he or she can be a valuable ally in your search.

- Be open to attending career and job fairs, if not because of the actual employers who will be there, then for the networking value and chance to "field test" your job search communications.

- Direct mail campaigns are effective only if you carefully target employers that makes sense for you to contact and if you tailor your letter or letter and résumé to each person on your list. Avoid mass mailings as they are viewed as nothing more than junk mail!

GET THE SCOOP ON...
Common misconceptions about networking ▪
Where and how to network most effectively ▪
What to do if you don't know many people ▪
How introverts can network painlessly ▪
Developing a networking action plan that
ensures you'll do it

Networking

Chapter 9

I n the career transition firm where I work, we have a networking event each month called a landing party. Our clients who have recently landed jobs come back to speak to current clients (that is, current job seekers) about what worked and didn't work in their searches and how they ended up getting their new positions. Invariably, speaker after speaker talks about the significant role that networking played in his or her success. Most report that they ended up landing the new job through someone they had known before or met during their search. But, even those who didn't officially land through a contact speak about how much networking helped them and how they plan to keep their networking relationships active even after starting the new job. Many also describe themselves as "networking converts" who had never done it before or didn't think they would want to or need to do it. These neophyte networkers ended up finding that the contacts they made were highly valuable and rewarding. To make the most of it, however, you have to know what it's all about and how to do it right.

What networking is not

Studies from a variety of sources, including outplacement firms, executive search firms, and the U.S. Department of Labor, have consistently shown that the percentage of jobs found through networking is at least 65 to 85 percent or even higher. At some point, the term "networking" rolls off the tongue of just about everybody who's looking for a job or advising job seekers. That's a good thing because networking is so important. What's not so good is that networking is vastly misunderstood. The following are among the most common misconceptions about networking:

- It's about quantity more than quality—a game of who can collect the most business cards or shake the most hands.
- You have to have a "networking personality" to do it well.
- If you're new in town or new to a career field, you don't have much of a network or much chance of getting to know the right people.
- There's not enough time to network if you're in a hurry to land a job.
- Networking means you have to bother or take advantage of people.

If any of these are concerns you've had, don't give up on networking before you even start. After you understand what networking actually is and how to do it well, you'll be amazed how rewarding it is.

What networking is

At its core, networking is a natural process of connecting with other people in a wide variety of ways. Chances are you already cultivate contacts and seek out information daily for matters ranging from a good restaurant to try or movie to see to help with decisions about buying a car or moving to a new neighborhood. There's really no mystery to networking. It's about building relationships with other people who might help you reach your goals and whom you can help in some way in return. The realities of networking are as follows:

- Networking is about quality more than quantity—the quality of relationships you develop is more important than the sheer numbers of people with whom you come into contact.

- You don't have to be a natural-born networker to do it well. It's a skill that can easily be learned.

- Even when starting from scratch, there are quick and easy ways to develop a network.

- Networking is one of the most effective job search methods, so your search might actually be shorter if you spend most of your time networking.

Experienced networkers know that when they reach out to others to let them know that they're looking for a new job, trying to build a business, or deciding on a new career direction—and when they reach out with courtesy and consideration of others' time—they end up flooded with the generosity of others. People who actively network also find that they actually know more people, or at least have access to more, than they realized and that those people provide all sorts of valuable suggestions, information, and leads.

The remainder of this chapter teaches you the best ways to network so that if you're new to networking, you'll see what I mean about this amazing phenomenon. If you're already a savvy networker, you'll pick up some new tips and refresh your memory about why and how networking works.

Creative ways to make the most of networking

Too many job seekers realize that networking is the name of the game but view networking in overly narrow terms. They often see networking in a job search as simply telling their immediate circle of friends, family, and colleagues to keep an eye out for jobs for them. Although it can be tempting to look at acquaintances and family as "people who can get me a job," the reality is that this narrow approach to networking inevitably leads to a lot of dead ends. Networking in a job search involves more than simply asking people whether they know of any openings or to be on the lookout for openings. Networking for a job requires that you be more resourceful in the way that you use your contacts. It also requires that you expand your efforts beyond your inner circle of family, close friends, and colleagues. Following are some of the specific ways networking can help in your search.

Planning strategy

Instead of just asking your contacts to keep an eye out for jobs for you, sit down with them for advice on your search strategy. In doing so, you're developing a relationship and showing them that there is a way they can help you, whether or not they are aware of actual openings. Most importantly, you're keeping the door open with your contacts because you've given them a more open-ended project—your ever-evolving search strategy—rather than one that has built-in limits, such as asking, "Do you know of any jobs?"

Preparing the tools of your search

When developing your résumé and cover letters or preparing for interviews, it's helpful to have input from others. You might already be getting this help from career and job search coaches, résumé writers, and guidebooks, but it's also a good idea to seek input from people who work in the field in which you want to get a job. Who is better able to tell you what they would want to see in your résumé or to conduct a mock interview with you than people who work in your target field? It's a great way to build relationships while getting some valuable advice in the process.

Uncovering job leads

Here's where networking most often comes into the job search process—asking others for information about jobs that are, or

Bright Idea

Networking is essentially a specialized form of communication, so be sure to read the communication tips offered in the online Bonus Chapter 2, particularly about how to establish rapport and guidelines for communicating by phone and email.

might be, available. This is what's really meant by the proverbial "hidden job market." Instead of just sitting at home answering ads or mailing unsolicited résumés, you talk to people and hear about jobs that haven't yet been advertised.

Enlisting intermediaries in your search

Some people in your network will take the extra step of not only telling you about an opening but actively intervening on your behalf. They might hand-deliver your résumé and recommend you as a candidate to the person who has the power to hire you. Seek out this help wherever you can get it.

Helping you evaluate offers

When you do start to get job offers, it's useful to get advice from the more knowledgeable members of your network to help you decide whether you should accept or decline an offer. They can walk you through the process of evaluating the offer based on the terms of the deal, the nature of the job, the goals you had originally expressed to them, and their knowledge of what is considered to be a good job in their field.

Emotional support during the ups and downs

An often overlooked but equally important function of networking in a job search is to attend to your emotional needs during the often frustrating and demoralizing process of trying to get a job. Any transition in life requires a support system, and the job search is no exception. A strong network can provide this support system for you.

How to network—10 key rules

Whether your networking takes place over the phone, in a one-on-one meeting, or at a large group networking event, keep the following 10 cardinal rules in mind as you prepare to network:

- *Be patient.* "Well, I went to a networking meeting, and nothing came of it," or "I met someone who seemed like they'd be a great contact, but they haven't done a thing for me." These laments are all too common. Allow some time for relationships to build and leads to pan out, and you'll see results. It simply takes patience.

- *Accept that it's a learned skill.* Equally common is to hear "But I'm just not the networking type." There is no such thing as the networking type. Sure, some people are born with an outgoing personality and gift of gab, but even for them, effective, appropriate networking is a learned skill. No matter how natural or unnatural networking may feel for you, it is a skill you can learn.

- *Believe in the process.* Networking works. Period. No matter how long and winding your networking road may seem, no matter how remote a contact may be, you have to keep the faith that it will work for you.

- *Be strategic.* Although networking is a natural, simple process of connecting and building relationships with other people, just as you do in everyday life, it is not to be ventured into casually. Effective networking requires a strategy and a plan. Strategies and action planning are discussed later in this chapter.

- *Have a diversified approach.* Far too often I see motivated, diligent networkers find that their networking isn't paying off because they're relying only on their existing networking, contacting the same people over and over, or are only attending monthly meetings of one professional group, thinking that that's enough. Pull from all the networking venues and sources described later in this chapter in the "Where to Network" section.

■ *Be considerate.* Be kind, courteous, and polite in every one of your networking endeavors, and always be mindful of other people's time constraints and other limitations. It's a surprisingly small world out there, so if you're having a bad day or are just fed up with networking and really don't feel like being nice, think twice before acting in any way you will regret.

■ *Think creatively.* No matter how skimpy your contact database, how remote your hometown, or how shy you are, there is always a way to get to the people you need to reach to network effectively. Use the tips offered in the "Expanding and Identifying Your Network" section of this chapter to see how you might get creative.

■ *Show integrity and reliability.* Show up when you say you'll show up, leave when you've taken up enough of their time, follow through on your promises, don't bad-mouth anybody or anything, and never, ever lie.

■ *Make it easy for people to help you.* Networking is like connecting the dots. You meet with Jim, who refers you to Millie, who refers you to Mary, and so on. You aren't a job seeker with a network, you're the manager of a sales force. Jim, Millie, and Mary are your sales team. Be specific when you tell people what you need and what you have to offer (relying heavily on your self-marketing sound bite as described

---

 Watch Out!

It's easy to lapse into an attitude of entitlement when networking: "If I went to all the trouble to track down this guy, the least he can do is find me a job or give me lots of contacts." Enter every networking encounter with the belief that good things can come of it but with the understanding that no one owes you, and there are no guarantees.

in Chapter 3). This enables them to more easily spread the word about you and what you're trying to accomplish.

- *Give back.* Networking is a two-way street. Make a habit out of asking people how you can help them, and mean it when you say it. And, if some people just never seem to need anything from you or from anyone you might know, then at the very least make sure that they know how much you appreciate them by showing your appreciation through thank-you notes or small gifts.

Now that you have these 10 rules for the right networking mindset and techniques, let's look at where you'll actually find networking opportunities.

Special networking tips for introverts

As a card-carrying introvert, I know how intimidating networking can be. If you are the least bit shy, suffer from social anxieties, or simply prefer to read rather than talk, then networking can seem overwhelming and difficult. It need not be if you follow these suggestions:

- *Don't tackle too much at once.* Ease into networking by setting realistic daily and weekly goals.

- *Don't assume that you're bothering people.* Personality surveys have consistently shown that most people (in the U.S. population) are extroverted, so chances are the people you contact will welcome the overture.

- *Get people to make an entrée for you.* Try to have the members of your network you feel most comfortable with introduce you to others so that you don't have to make so many cold introductions.

- *Take a leadership role.* It's sometimes easier to be a professional association's newsletter editor or treasurer than just to be a member. When you're in an official role, it's easier to meet people than if you had to mix and mingle like a regular member.

Bright Idea

Pardon the plug, but for more detailed advice on networking you might want to take a look at my book *Networking for Job Search and Career Success* (JIST Works, Inc., 2004) available in stores or through www.tullierbooks.com.

- *Don't go it alone.* Rely heavily on your support team to keep you motivated and enlist a buddy to go with you to networking events.

- *Don't underestimate the power of listening.* Introverts are often better listeners than talkers. Listening to others carefully is an important part of building relationships.

- *Go to events with a purpose.* It's easier to talk about the speaker you just heard or the knowledge you just acquired in a class than to make small talk at an event that's purely about networking.

- *Practice, practice, practice.* Get used to saying your sound bite, leaving voice mail messages, conducting networking meetings, or "working a room" by practicing before the real thing.

- *Write before you speak.* Although you have to pick up the phone eventually, there's nothing wrong with relying heavily on email and other written communications to introduce yourself and set up meetings if you're more comfortable writing rather than calling.

- *Make the most of the Internet.* Take advantage of all the online networking opportunities through email, chats, message boards, and groups that might be less intimidating than face-to-face.

Finally, don't forget that networking is a skill that can be learned. With preparation and practice, it gets easier and easier. Believe me, if I can do it, you can too!

Where to network

Networking opportunities range from an impromptu chat with the person seated next to you on a plane, to an official, scheduled networking appointment in someone's office, to attending a large professional event with lots of mixing and mingling. Networking can take place in person or by phone, email, instant message, or through posting on Internet bulletin boards. It doesn't matter where you're networking or whether you're doing it with one person or with hundreds, the key is to network in a variety of places to diversify your approach. This section explores the various avenues for networking along with tips for your networking technique in each setting.

One-to-one networking meetings

One-to-one meetings with network contacts can range from an informal conversation with a friend, family member, or co-worker to an exchange of email with a distant professional colleague to a formal appointment with someone you've never met. One-to-one meetings are often the most productive networking encounters in that they obviously give you quality time with one person to develop rapport and have an in-depth discussion of your needs and goals, as well as of how you can help each other.

Beware of relying too heavily on one-to-one meetings in your networking, though. Although one-at-a-time connections should certainly be a major part of your networking effort, keep in mind that this is the most labor-intensive way to network and could have you putting too many eggs in too small of a basket. You need to add some group events to the mix to make sure that you are covering more ground and expanding your network more exponentially than is possible with the one-by-one approach.

How to set up a networking meeting

The first thing to know about how you ask someone to network with you is not to say "I want to network" with you. If you were inviting a friend out to lunch, would you say, "I want to eat food with you?" You would say something like, "It's been a while since we've gotten together. I'd love to hear what you're up to and get some input from you on things I've got going on. Let's have lunch together." Or, if it's someone you've never met, you would say, "[Name of mutual friend] thinks you and I ought to meet given our similar lines of work. Would you be interested in having lunch one day soon?"

Now, take that same natural process of asking a friend, or friend-to-be, to lunch and translate it to your job search. Let's say you're leaving a voice mail to request a networking meeting with someone you already know. It might go something like this:

"Hi Jim. This is Eleanor Smith. It's been a while since we've spoken. Last time I saw you was at the XYZ conference last summer, wasn't it? I'd love to catch up with you and hear how things are going for you and also get your input on a career transition I'm in the midst of. Don't worry, Jim, I won't be hitting you up for a job. I would just like to get your advice and ideas. Could we do lunch one day soon? I'm free any day the next two weeks except Thursday the 9th and Friday the 17th. I can be reached at 404-111-1111. Look forward to hearing from you."

If sending an email to someone you've never met, the message might sound something like this:

> Dear Ms. Conner (or use first name if the referring party says it would be okay to do so),
>
> Ian Brown suggested I contact you given your in-depth knowledge of the transportation industry. I worked with Ian when we were both with ABC Trucking. As you probably know, ABC recently moved its headquarters to Minneapolis. I chose not to move and am now seeking operations management positions here in the Southeast. I have 10 years of experience in the transportation industry and have gained a reputation as an excellent cost-cutter and team-builder.

I do not expect you to have a job for me or to know of any current openings necessarily, but I would value 20–30 minutes of your time to get your thoughts on my search strategy and to discuss current developments in the industry. Ian spoke highly of you, and I know your input would be valuable.

I will contact you in the next few days to see whether we might meet at your office, or whether I may take you to breakfast or lunch, if convenient for you. Or, feel free to reply to me at this email address. Thanks in advance for your time.

Best Regards,

[your name]

As you develop your own phone scripts or email messages for requesting networking meetings, make sure that you include all of the following:

- How you were referred to the person you're contacting or how you learned about them if not referred by a mutual acquaintance. (If the recipient doesn't already know you.)

- A refresher of how you know the person you're contacting. (If it's been a while since you've been in touch.)

- A very brief version of your self-marketing sound bite to tell a little about who you are.

- Your Reason for Looking statement.

- Why you're writing, that is, specifically what you're requesting, such as a meeting in their office or an invitation to breakfast, lunch, or the like.

- Reassurance that you're not asking for a job. You don't have to hide the fact that you're job searching, but make it clear that there are other ways they can help you (advice, information, thoughts on recent developments in your field) than just telling you about job openings.

- The offer to follow up with them since you are initiating the contact, but also be sure you've included all your contact information so they can reply to you.

- Thanks for their time and consideration.

Including the preceding elements in your requests for networking meetings will greatly increase your chances of actually getting a meeting. Remember, too, that an impression will be formed of you from the first moment of contact, so a voice mail or email that is articulate, polite, and concise will help you get off to a great start.

What to do in a networking one-to-one meeting

After you are in an actual networking meeting, whether it's face-to-face or by phone (or even in a live chat online), be sure to open the meeting by thanking the other person for taking the time to meet with you and restating the purpose of the meeting. Don't forget to offer reassurance once again that you are not there to ask for a job. It's okay to say that if the person knows of any job opportunities you would be happy to hear about them—remember, you don't have to hide the fact that you're a job seeker—but let them know that that's not the main reason you're there.

After spending some time asking the other person about his or her own background, or recent developments if you're catching up with an old friend, move into a discussion of the industry and/or profession you are targeting. Try to have a peer-to-peer dialogue in which you converse about recent news in the field and ask the other person what he or she sees as trends in

 Watch Out!

Be on the lookout for clues that a networking meeting could be turning into a job interview and shift your approach. Step up references to your assets and achievements and minimize the career advice you ask for.

that field. Then move into questions about your own search. Develop a list of questions relevant to you, but some examples you might choose from include the following:

- This is the strategy I'm using to land a job. Do you have any thoughts on how effective this strategy is and ways I might improve it?

- How did you land your job or past jobs in this field?

- Which newsletters, journals, or other print or online publications do you find most helpful for staying on top of this field? Do you know of any that list job opportunities?

- On which job boards do you or your organization post openings? Are there other sites you recommend?

- Are there any professional associations, conferences, or networking groups you recommend I join or attend?

- I've been struggling with how to present a certain aspect of my background (or how to answer a particular interview question). Would you mind if I run it by you?

- How effective is my résumé? Do you suggest any changes?

- If this were an actual job interview would I be dressed appropriately?

- What do you think is the typical going rate of compensation for the type of job I'm seeking?

- Do you have any insights or leads into the organizations on my target list? (Use your Marketing Brief as discussed in the online Bonus Chapter 3.)

- Are there additional organizations you think I should be targeting? Do you know anyone there?

- Do you recommend any executive recruiters (or staffing agencies if you're not senior level) I might contact?

- Is there anyone else you think I should speak with?

    As you wrap up networking meetings, be sure to express your thanks once again and ask whether you may keep in touch to update them on your progress and to discuss any additional questions you might have. Always be sure to send a thank-you note or email within a day or two after the meeting.

Professional groups

Opportunities for networking through professional groups come in a variety of shapes and sizes. Here are some of the most common ones:

Conferences and conventions

Regional or national conferences or conventions in your targeted profession or industry (or ones that encompass a number of industries or career fields) are excellent opportunities to expand your network. Professional and trade associations are most typically the sponsors of these events. For ideas of associations that might be hosting events you could attend, see the online Bonus Appendix 3. Most associations post a calendar of local and national events on their Web sites.

Career or job fairs

As discussed in Chapter 8, career fairs aren't just for job leads. They're a great place to make connections with people who could be key members of your network.

Professional associations

In addition to sponsoring conferences, conventions, and career fairs, professional associations usually have local or regional chapters with a schedule of regular meetings, often monthly. Also, professional associations publish newsletters and journals,

 Moneysaver

If hefty conference registration fees make your wallet groan, be aware that some conferences allow you to register for only a portion of a multiple-day conference, such as just for one day. Pick the day or days that have the most relevant agenda items for you to get the most value for your networking dollars.

which you could write for or be quoted in to gain visibility, and they sometimes have chat rooms and message boards on their Web sites where you can meet and communicate with other members. If you don't already know of the associations for your field, check the online Bonus Appendix 3.

Networking groups

Across the country are many groups for the express purpose of professional networking. Some are informal groups like breakfast clubs or happy hour groups that you'll probably only find out about through word of mouth; others are more formalized networking groups that announce their meetings in newspapers or through an online presence. Some groups consist of people from similar industries or with similar functional roles who get together to share best practices, job leads, and support. Others are formed for women or people of the same ethnic group, and others are exclusively for job seekers. Keep your eyes and ears open for these sorts of groups in your area by asking around as well as conducting a keyword search online and watching for them in local newspapers and magazines.

Internet-based

In a sense, the Internet isn't really a separate category among the places to network because it can be the vehicle for communicating in many of the other networking categories. You can, for example, conduct one-to-one meetings online, participate in group networking events through chat rooms and newsgroups, or attend seminars in Web site auditoriums. But, some online networking avenues don't fit into our other five categories. These are online networking opportunities that aren't sponsored by professional associations or any particular networking organization. Google (http://groups.google.com) and Yahoo (http://groups.yahoo.com) are examples of portals that connect you with online discussion forums and newsgroups for networking. A number of sites focus on connecting people with

Tips for Group Networking Events

Whether attending a national professional conference, major trade show, or small networking club, the following strategies work for most group settings:

- Shake hands with everyone you meet. Introduce yourself as you shake hands, clearly stating your first and last name. Don't wait to be introduced or to be asked for your name.

- Focus on remembering the names of each person you meet. Try to use the name in the first few minutes of conversation to reinforce it in your mind.

- When wearing a name tag, wear it on your right side, a more natural place for people to cast their eyes as they shake your right hand with their right hands.

- Have a few opening lines or questions in mind so that you can discuss something other than the weather. You can never go wrong with asking the person about themselves.

- Use a 20- to 30-second version of your self-marketing soundbite to tell more about yourself after asking about the other person.

- Take plenty of job seeker business cards and keep them within easy reach.

- Soon after each networking encounter, make notes on the back of each card you receive with notes of who each person was and how you plan to follow up.

- Don't monopolize any one person's time. If you want to continue to get to know someone better, say that you would like to stay in touch after the event and then move on to someone else.

Bright Idea

With more than 130,000 schools and 35 million alumni participating, you're likely to find an old friend or make new ones at Classmates.com (http://www.classmates.com).

each other. Monster Networking at http://www.monster.com/networking is one of the best for purely career-related networking. Others that feature professional or business networking include Ryze.com, Linkedin.com, and Spoke.com.

Education and training

Academic and training settings are great places to network. Whether you have all sorts of fancy degrees or your education is mostly work-related training programs, education is an important category in your networking strategy. If you earned a degree from a college or university, check with your alumni office as well as the campus career center to find out about alumni networking events in your area or online. If you are taking, or have taken in the past, classes or seminars through a continuing education program or job skills training institute, your classmates, instructors, and guest speakers can often expand your network significantly.

Social/recreational/community

Valuable contacts are made and relationships are nurtured in such ordinary settings as gyms, cocktail parties, neighborhood meetings, and many other gatherings. Think about any organizations you belong to or would enjoy getting involved with that are civic, community, nonprofit, religious, sports-related, social, hobby-oriented, or recreational. Some of the best networking takes place in settings that are not professionally or business oriented. A word of caution, however—networking in social and community settings has a networking etiquette all its own. The how-to's of tactfully mixing business and pleasure are addressed in this section.

Social events, such as weddings, parties, charity functions, and other nonbusiness gatherings, need to be handled delicately:

▪ *Focus on the socializing.* Don't push anyone into talking business when they would rather be enjoying the party. Be sure not to cross the line between low-pressure networking and being overbearing. Just touch on business or your own career and then turn back to discussing non-business topics.

▪ *Don't try to do business if you've had one too many.* Drinking too much can really foul up professional interactions. Don't get yourself in an embarrassing situation by having too much to drink at a party where potential professional contacts are around.

▪ *Keep your follow-through expectations realistic.* In the relaxed atmosphere of social gatherings, promises might be made that aren't going to be kept after the party's over. Keep your expectations realistic about what might materialize.

The serendipity factor

Sometimes networking just happens. You never know where the next great contact, lead, or tidbit of information is going to come from, so it's important to be open to all possible opportunities, not only to those that are part of your premeditated networking plan. Think of all the places in which you interact with people who might become valuable members of your network. These include the offices of doctors, dentists, accountants, lawyers, and other professionals; your barber shop or

 Bright Idea

Many religious institutions now offer structured networking opportunities for job seekers, and you don't usually have to be a member. Crossroads Career Network (http://www.crossroads-career.net) is one example of an organization that offers networking through churches in several states. Ask religious institutions in your area about similar groups.

beauty salon; realtors' offices; buses, trains, and planes; and the gym or health club. The list is endless—wherever you are, you can network with people. To handle these serendipitous situations with aplomb, keep the following do's and don'ts in mind:

- ▪ DO start a conversation with a simple hello or neutral comment or question.

- ▪ DO stretch past your comfort zone and reach out to meet people.

- ▪ DO maintain a professional tone, vocabulary, and posture so that your overtures won't be misconstrued as inappropriate in any way.

- ▪ DON'T be a pest. If someone doesn't seem to want to get into a conversation with you, don't push it.

- ▪ DON'T put your foot in your mouth by saying something that might be controversial or offensive to a stranger.

- ▪ DON'T go off alone with anyone you've just met and exercise caution even with seemingly friendly people.

Identifying and expanding your network

Is the quantity of names in your Palm™ device puny, and your Rolodex™ a runt? Or, are you the type who has a database or address book stuffed to the gills with names? It doesn't matter which camp you fall into—or if you're somewhere in between. Everyone must begin at the beginning, and that beginning is to take an inventory of your network.

It's time to search your memory banks and go through records and files in your office or home to take stock of the people you already know, including digging deep for ones you've known in the past. You'll also need to learn ways to cultivate new contacts and expand your network well beyond the size you ever imagined possible.

Taking stock of your existing network

As you prepare to take stock of the people you know or have known of in the past, the obvious place to start is with whatever system you currently use, such as an electronic contact management system, a business card file, or a paper address book. Then, gather up every additional possible source of names, such as holiday card lists; company directories from past jobs; alumni directories; neighborhood or community group member listings; files of clients, customers vendors, or others you've worked with; professional group membership rosters; your children's school directories, if applicable; and even your old wedding guest list, if applicable. Also go through email you've saved to jog your memory about people you've communicated with. The point is to get creative about where there might be names of people who could help you.

> **❝** I read somewhere that everybody on this planet is separated by only six other people. Six degrees of separation. Between us and everybody else on this planet. The President of the United States. A gondolier in Venice. Fill in the names. **❞**
>
> —Ouisa in *Six Degrees of Separation* by John Guare

Select one central place to keep all your names and contact information. That might be the system you've already been using or one that you create just for your job search. Concentrate on getting the list up-to-date with all names you can possibly come up with and with accurate contact information on everyone. As you add names to the list, don't censor yourself. It doesn't matter how long it's been since you've spoken with someone or how briefly you knew him or her. Add the name to your list because you never know how pleased that person might be to hear from you and how helpful he or she could be.

Expanding your network

After you've exhausted all current sources of contacts, you'll probably be pleasantly surprised that you know more people than you thought you did. At this point, it's time to look toward expanding your network. To do so, it's helpful to think in terms of categories of contacts. The following sections walk you through several broad categories: personal, work, education, professional groups, career services, personal and professional services, and multimedia. Let these categories remind you of people you already know but had forgotten about and also help you brainstorm about new people you could meet to expand your network.

Personal Contacts

You've probably already thought of all family members and friends to go on your list, but make sure that you haven't over-looked any. Did you attend a family reunion in the past that has a mailing list? Are there friends with whom you've lost touch but with whom you could get reacquainted? Also look for ways to increase your contacts by participating in clubs, community activities, sports and recreation, and religious organizations. Specifically, these might include the following:

- *Clubs & organizations:* social clubs; hobby groups; book clubs; country clubs; parents' groups; sports teams; recreational groups like walking, biking, or hiking clubs; gyms/health clubs; fraternities/sororities, and so on.

- *Community groups:* fundraising or other services for charities; advisory or governing bodies of organizations, such as Boards of Trustees; neighborhood associations and other civic groups; foundations and other philanthropic groups; political organizations; cultural organizations; or parent-teacher groups:

- *Religious organizations:* churches, mosques, temples, synagogues, religious study groups, social groups, or youth groups.

Work contacts

Bosses, co-workers, clients, and customers should all be considered as potential network members. This category is not limited to paid jobs, either. It also includes volunteer work, internships, and other professional assignments. Pull out your current résumé as well as old ones, along with any company directories you've saved from past jobs, and think about who you know from all your jobs, internships, and other work-related projects. Also don't forget about colleagues you might easily overlook such as vendors, suppliers, freelancers, consultants, temps, people at other organizations in your industry, investors, and shareholders.

Education contacts

Whether you are a current student or an alumnus, educational institutions offer ready-made networks. Your classmates from high school, college, or graduate school are often very willing to help you reach your career or business goals. Don't forget about other educational settings as well. If you've taken any continuing education or other part-time, non-degree classes or have been through vocational training or professional development programs on your own or through an employer, you've undoubtedly met people (classmates, instructors, and guest speakers) who could be valuable members of your network.

Professional group contacts

If you don't already belong to professional or trade associations, consider joining any of the organizations for your career field or industry. Attending meetings, conferences, seminars, and

---

 Moneysaver

Professional association membership dues are often steep, but you can sometimes attend association meetings as a guest at no charge or for a nominal fee. Inquire about such arrangements through the association's administrative office or, better yet, track down a member who might let you tag along to the next meeting.

social events sponsored by such groups is an excellent way to expand your network. (See the online Bonus Appendix 3 for a sampling of associations if you need to find ones to join.) You might also want to join organizations whose sole focus is networking, as described in the "Networking Groups" section earlier in this chapter.

Career specialists contacts

If you are working with a career consultant or job search coach or have in the past, be sure to count that individual as part of your network. This group includes career counselors in private practice as well as ones who work in college- or community-based career development or employment centers, such as your local Department of Labor office. Also consider recruiters in employment agencies and executive search firms, as well as outplacement consultants. Some public libraries are also staffed with career resource experts.

Personal and professional services contacts

People who provide personal and professional services are excellent sources of leads, resources, and information. People like your physician, dentist, accountant, hairdresser, or fitness trainer might be just the link you need to the right people or information because they come across a large number of people daily. Don't forget, too, about stockbrokers and financial planners, insurance agents, realtors, pharmacists, mechanics, doormen and landlords, dry cleaners, tailors, housekeepers, and many others. You never know who might turn out to be a wealth of leads and information.

Multimedia contacts

An often-overlooked source of network contacts is all around us every day—media and technology. The Internet has obviously revolutionized the way people can network with email, instant messaging, and online forums, but there are also less obvious networking opportunities through books, newspapers, magazines, television, and radio. Reading or hearing about people

Watch Out!

If you need to keep your job search confidential, be extra careful when venturing into chat rooms or posting on message or bulletin boards. You might not recognize the personal screen name for your boss or nosy co-worker, but they might recognize yours.

whose work interests you or whose career paths you admire is a great source of people who might be willing to help.

Your networking action plan

It's not enough to say things like, "I'm going to network as much as possible" or "My plan is to meet more people." You're more likely to do those things if you define them more precisely and set clear objectives for yourself. Following is a step-by-step guide to taking action when it comes to networking:

- Take stock of your current network, making sure that all contact information is up-to-date.

- Expand your network to include people you might have forgotten about.

- Identify sources of future contacts by listing all the places you might go, people you might contact, and groups you might join, as discussed in the "Where to Network" and "Expanding Your Network" sections of this chapter.

- Set weekly networking goals using a three-pronged approach:

    1. Number of calls to make (or email to send) to develop or reconnect with contacts.

    2. Number of one-to-one networking meetings to have.

    3. Number of group events to attend each week.

As you go through these steps, make sure to keep careful records of all networking activity using the Sample Networking Log and other organizational and time management tools offered in the online Bonus Chapter 1. As for what quantities to set for your weekly networking goals in Step 4, that depends on how much time you have to spend on your search overall and how much networking is a factor in your overall search strategy as opposed to other methods such as using headhunters or online sources. There are no magic numbers, but if putting a full-time effort into your search, you might aim, for example, to contact ten people a day, three days a week, by phone or email and to hold three networking meetings per week and attend two group events each week.

Those are just ballpark figures. Feel free to be much more aggressive with your networking activity or to set your sights a bit lower if you're new to networking or are having to overcome introverted tendencies that make networking intimidating. Finally, remember that networking is as much about quality as it is about quantity. Don't get caught up in a numbers game of making your daily or weekly quotas and forget about taking the time to develop and nurture professional relationships along the way.

Giving back to your network

Networking can seem at times to be a very self-centered activity. You might start to feel like all you're ever really saying is, "How can you help ME?" But the needs of the people who help you should be as much on your mind as your own needs. It's important, therefore, not only to show your appreciation through thank-you notes or small gifts, but also to return a favor when the opportunity arises.

Although each thank-you note should be tailored to the recipient and the situation, the sample that follows could be emailed or mailed. Note that it includes not only an expression of appreciation but an update on action taken since the meeting, a reminder of action the networking contact promised, and a reference to next steps. Include whichever of those elements are relevant in your own letters.

Dear Jose,

I really appreciated the time you spent with me last week to discuss developments in our field and share advice and leads. Your insights were most valuable.

Since we met, I've had a chance to email Ann Bradford and Frank Patel and hope to meet with them soon. I've also reviewed the Web sites of the two recruiting firms you suggested and plan to contact them this week now that I have a better sense of their areas of specialization and guidelines for submitting résumés.

I also appreciated your offer to forward my résumé to your VP of Sales and to the Customer Service Director. I'll check with you in a week or so to see how you advise I handle follow-up with them.

I look forward to staying in touch and hope that you'll not hesitate to let me know if I can help you in any way. Thank you again.

Sincerely,

[your name]

Always remember that networking is based on cultivating and nurturing relationships, not on one-time interactions, so in addition to thank-you notes, consider small (or sometimes large) ways you can do nice things for people in your network—often for no particular reason. Make it a habit to perform "random acts of kindness" such as calling someone when you come across an article that would be of interest or volunteering to help out at the person's favorite charity. Not only are these nice things to do, but they also have indirect benefits to you in that they strengthen relationships and keep you visible.

Finally, look for ways to help out other people after you land a job. Whether you are established in your career or just getting started, it's likely that you have something to offer someone else. Serving as a mentor or just giving occasional advice is an important responsibility that we all have. Chances are you wouldn't be where you are without the help of others, so why not give something back by helping out someone who's a few steps behind you in his or her career or job search?

Just the facts

- Don't get caught up in misconceptions about networking. It's about building quality, give-and-take relationships, not using people or collecting as many names as possible.

- Be creative about how you think of networking. See it as more than just asking people for job leads. It's a great source of strategic advice and ideas.

- Understand that networking is about having the right attitude and strategy, not just randomly making contacts.

- When taking stock of whom you already know, don't assume that you can't reach out to people you haven't had contact with in a long time. It's just about always okay to reconnect no matter how much time has passed.

- Look for ways to expand your network by revisiting old contacts or making new ones in the categories of personal, work, education, professional groups, personal and professional services, and media.

- Ensure that you'll do enough networking by establishing an action plan with clearly defined daily and/or weekly goals for quantities of people to contact, meetings to hold, and events to attend.

- Always show appreciate to the people you network with by sending a thank-you note and looking for ways you can help them.

GET THE SCOOP ON...

The pros and cons of job searching online ▪ Critical tips for protecting your personal security ▪ Finding the hidden jobs on the Internet ▪ Getting an edge on the vast amounts of competition in cyberspace ▪ Clearing up the confusion over electronic résumés and keywords

Online Job Hunting

A chainsaw is great for cutting firewood. Use the tool the wrong way, however, and you could really hurt yourself. The Internet is like that for jobseekers [sic]. It is a power tool. It can aid a job search or prolong joblessness, depending on how it is used.

Those apt words come from an article by Matthew Mariani in the *Occupational Outlook Quarterly* (Summer 2003, Vol. 47, Number 2), a publication of the U.S. Bureau of Labor Statistics. What a vivid way to express the power of the Internet to hurt or help a job search.

During the 1990s, particularly the mid- to late-90s, recruitment and job seeking online secured a firm toehold in the employment landscape, and job hunting has not been the same since. Although connecting with real, live people through a strategic networking process remains, for most people, the best way to land a job, the Internet should play some role in every job seeker's action plan. The key is to make sure that you do it right. You have to take steps to protect your personal safety, gain an edge over the enormous amount of competition, and avoid getting so sucked into cyberspace that you waste precious time. This chapter will help you avoid the pitfalls and rise above the competition.

Not just for jobs

The first thing to get straight about Internet-based job hunting is that it's not all about finding jobs. Sure, that's the obvious reason to spend time online when you need new employment, but there's so much more to online resources than that. Most job seekers go right to the job boards to search for opportunities, but that's only the tip of the iceberg. Some additional ways you need to be using the Internet in your search include the following:

- **Research.** Identify employers to approach, learn about employers you've been contacted by, prepare for interviews, and investigate employers who have extended you an offer. You can also find headhunters and locate salary statistics online. See the online Bonus Appendix 1, "Resource Guide," for suggestions of where to find all this.

- **Networking.** You already know from Chapter 5, "Networking," that the Internet plays a part in your networking efforts, from identifying people to include in your network, to using email to communicate with contacts, to expanding your network through online chat rooms and forums.

- **Career advice.** Don't visit sites like Monster or CareerBuilder only for their job listings. These sites offer a wealth of advice and tips for all aspects of your career planning and job hunting. One of the best sites for advice that's not one of the "household names" is Quintessential Careers at www.quintcareers.com.

- **Education and training.** If you need to update your skills or add a degree to your résumé, the Internet is a great place to locate—and even complete—training and educational opportunities.

- **News and information.** A big part of being a savvy job hunter is being informed about the industry and profession in which you work or want to work, as well as keeping up to speed on economic, political, and social news that affects your world of work. Sites such as www.cbs.marketwatch.com, www.ceoexpress.com, www.cnn.com, http://fullcoverage. yahoo.com, www.bizjournals.com, and more help you tap into the hidden job market and sound more knowledgeable when talking with employers.

So, be sure to let the Web play a much larger role in your search than being only a place to find and apply for jobs.

The advantages of job searching online

Despite the fact that there's much more to online job hunting than just trolling for jobs, there's no denying that identifying and applying for positions online has some huge advantages. These advantages include the following:

- **It's so easy!** From the convenience of your home or wherever you choose to access the Internet, you can find job opportunities from all over the world or your own backyard and apply for them with a couple of mouse clicks.

- **It works for you 24/7.** If you post your résumé online to be browsed by employers, or if you set up a personal search agent to alert you by email when jobs get listed that match your objectives, then you are job searching not only during your waking, working hours but also while you sleep, work out, or vacation.

- **Lots of choices.** Unlike the limitations of newspapers' classified sections or the knowledge of your network, the Internet offers a staggering array of employment opportunities—millions of them.

- **It makes introverts happy.** People who don't particularly relish the thought of getting out "amongst 'em" can apply for jobs in blissful solitude.

Unfortunately, like anything that seems too good to be true, there is a catch. Being aware of the downsides and potential dangers of online job hunting is critical.

The downside and dangers of job hunting online

For each of the advantages of online job hunting, there is a disadvantage, ranging from mere frustrations to serious dangers:

- **It makes you too passive.** Online job hunting lulls job seekers into a false sense of promise and progress. Because it's so easy to blast your résumé all over cyberspace and to have your posted résumé working for you 24 hours a day, it's all too easy to fall into the trap of thinking that you've done enough. You need to be out networking, attending career fairs, contacting headhunters, and approaching employers directly to tap into jobs that haven't yet been advertised. Online job hunting is just too easy, or so it seems....

- **It's not as easy as it looks.** Job hunting on the Internet brings all sorts of technological and logistical challenges. It might seem like you can land a job with the click of a button, but usually it takes much more than that. You have to learn the ropes and devise a strategy, including developing a special résumé for online job hunting, in order for it to work.

- **It makes introverts happy.** As an introvert myself, I have nothing against introverts wanting to be happy. The reason this is a problem, however, is that we need to be getting out there and making direct contact with human beings, not letting ourselves stay isolated in front of a computer.

- **It's a time-eater.** Job seekers waste far too many hours each day or week online. They search site after site trying to find the right job or spend days posting their résumé to yet another site, hoping that it will be the site that gets them hits. Online job hunting should take up only a fraction of your overall job search time allotment. (How to divide your time was discussed in more detail in the online Bonus Chapter 1, "Getting Organized and Planning Your Action.")

- **It's a needle-in-a haystack approach.** With the vast amount of opportunities available to you online also comes the drudgery of slogging through lots of opportunities that aren't right for you or are outdated.

- **It's overwhelming.** If you tend to find the whole idea of job searching to be overwhelming, then all it takes is a couple of hours trying to job search online to make you really want to throw in the towel.

- **Too much competition.** On any given day, more than four million Americans search online for job opportunities, and that number is growing every day. However, if you were to learn about a job through word of mouth before it's advertised, your competition might be only a couple of people, or even no one. Which would you prefer?

- **Your search is harder to manage.** When you search online, you never know in whose hands your résumé will end up. Many job seekers get caught off guard by employers who contact them out of the blue and have to scramble to figure out who the person is, which organization they represent, and which résumé and cover letter they received. When your search involves more direct contact methods, it's easier to keep track of what you've sent to various people, and you usually take charge of the follow-up so you don't have to get caught by surprise.

- **Lack of anonymity.** If you're using the Web for job hunting while employed, be careful when posting your résumé online or replying to postings in which you don't know whom the employer is. Is there a boss, competitor, or client whom you would rather not make aware that you're looking to make a move? They can easily see your résumé online, although some sites, such as Monster.com and others, offer confidentiality services.

■ **An invitation for spam.** Extensive browsing online usually increases junk mail and spam mail in your inbox. Consider setting up a separate email account expressly for your job search, particularly one that offers a bulk mail or junk mail filter.

■ **A sitting duck for scams.** Job postings that sound legitimate but end up having you unwittingly committing fraudulent acts aren't limited to the Web—they've been propagated through classified ads and direct mail for years—but the Web has expanded their reach exponentially. Beware of any position that has you shipping goods, delivering packages, transferring money, or doing anything that makes you the least bit uncomfortable unless you are certain you're dealing with a legitimate organization that you've fully investigated.

■ **Identity theft.** Of all the dangers of online job hunting, perhaps none is more frightening than the possibility of identity theft. Of course, the potential for this exists with any Internet use, but with Internet-based job hunting, you may be more likely to spread your name and contact information around the Web more widely than with other online use. You leave a trail of personal data around the Web as you job hunt, serving as breadcrumbs that can lead to your social security number and the real possibility of identity theft.

As you can see from the prior sections, the cons of online job hunting outnumber the pros considerably. Don't despair, however. You can minimize the risks and hassles and maximize the benefits.

> **Moneysaver**
>
> Steer clear of retail career firms that advertise in newspapers and troll job sites to prey on fed-up job seekers, especially executives, who want someone else to do the hard work for them. They charge thousands of dollars with the promise of contacts and employer databases but don't offer much that you couldn't get for free or do yourself.

Protecting your privacy when job searching online

There is no way to give yourself an absolute guarantee of security whenever you venture online, whether for job searching or any other Internet use. But, the following guidelines can help minimize the risks. Some job seekers don't feel that they need to take any precautions; others follow them all to the letter; and still others find a happy medium somewhere in between. This is a personal decision you have to make after doing some homework on the matter and based on your comfort level.

Don't put your home address on your résumé. List only your email address. If you want to be able to be reached by snail mail, set up a post office box address for your search. If you want employers to know that you live in a particular area (such as when you want to show that you're a local candidate who won't require relocation assistance), you could list city and state of residence, but be aware that this reveals more personal information about you.

Don't put your home phone on the résumé because phone numbers can often be traced with reverse phone directories. If you don't want to list only an email address, consider giving your cell phone or an office number if you have a separate home office line. (Don't use your employer's phone for your search, unless your employer allows it.)

Never give out personal data such as your social security number, driver's license number, or mother's maiden name.

Don't give out personal information such as your marital status, number of children, or appearance (hair and eye color, weight, height) as this can aid in identity theft. No legitimate employer should be asking for this information anyway (with the exception of performing arts or modeling jobs in which appearance is relevant).

Contact any of the three major credit bureaus, Equifax, Experian, and TransUnion, to find out about identity theft prevention and other personal security services they offer. These will cost you a monthly or annual fee but may be well worth it.

Never deal with any employers or headhunters that ask you to wire them money, mail payment, or give access to your bank accounts or credit cards. You should not have to pay for a job or put up any money unless you're investing in a legitimate business.

For insight into the dangers of online job hunting, including articles about the latest scams, along with insiders' tips on how to elude the dangers, visit the World Privacy Forum at www.worldprivacyforum.org.

Gaining the competitive advantage online

If you're competing with more than four million people a day viewing jobs online, how do you stand out from the crowd? It's not that hard, but it does take some effort.

Dig deep

Most job seekers head straight to the big job boards—behemoths whose names fill billboards on the sides of buses and who have their own blimps. Monster.com, for example, has close to 50 million unique visitors per month.

Not only do most job seekers go to the big boards, they tend to stick with the same ones. A recent report out of Jupiter Media Matrix found that job seekers tend to be loyal to one Web site. Sixty-seven percent of Yahoo!HotJobs visitors were found to be exclusive users, for example, and 58 percent of Monster visitors were found to be loyal to that site. What this means for your strategy is that you not only need to vary your visits to the major sites, you also need to dig deeper to find the places the other job seekers aren't flocking to in droves.

Niche sites that specialize in jobs for certain professions or industries, as well as professional association sites, are one place to distinguish yourself from the competition. According to a study by Gerry Crispin and Mark Mehler of CareerXRoads, niche job sites were a larger source of hires from the Internet in 2003 than the leading job boards (Monster, CareerBuilder, and HotJobs) combined. Do use the major sites—70 percent of the Fortune 500 list jobs on at least one of the three major boards, according to iLogos Research—but also make the effort to go off the beaten path to sites that specialize in your targeted type of job. The Riley Guide (www.rileyguide.com), Quintessential Careers (www.quintcareers.com), and CareerXRoads (www.careerxroads. com as well as a printed book entitled *CareerXRoads*), are great sources of niche sites. Don't forget as well that the online Bonus Appendix 1 offers more suggestions for job and career advice sites.

Go straight to the source

In addition to using niche sites, also spend time on employers' sites to find jobs they might list. According to findings by iLogos Research, 94 percent of companies in the Global 500 have employment areas in their corporate Web sites. That number is growing rapidly and likely to be at 100 percent by the time you read this book. The CareerXRoads study cited earlier found employers reported that 68 percent of their hires from the Internet came from the companies' own Web sites.

Even if you're targeting smaller companies typically not represented in such studies, you are likely to find some information on their sites. Developing or expanding career sections on company sites is a hot topic in the world of electronic recruiting.

Bright Idea

A great site for applying directly to companies is www.directemployers.com.

Companies spend huge amounts of money each year to advertise on the big boards, so the more they can attract job candidates to their own sites, the more money they'll save in
recruiting costs.

Work the Net with networking

Job hunting on the Net and networking do not have to be
mutually exclusive job search methods. Set yourself apart from
the competition by combining the two. When you see a job
listed online, contact people you know—even send out an email
to all your contacts—to find out whether they know anyone in
the hiring organization. You'll still need to apply through the
Web, because most employers require that you send your
résumé through the normal channels even if you have a contact.
Your contact, however, might be able to get your résumé directly
into the hands of the right people in addition to the résumé you
submit online. Many companies offer generous bonuses to their
employees who refer candidates who end up being hired, so
even if someone doesn't know you well or at all, he or she may
be more than happy to put in a good word for you.

Understand the technology

You must use a special version of your résumé that transmits
well electronically. Many organizations use electronic methods,

 Bright Idea

Your résumé can become stale after it's been posted on a Web site for a certain period of time, meaning that it might be less likely to be viewed by
employers. To keep it fresh, either delete it and repost it, or just edit it by
making a minor change that causes the site to treat it as a new résumé.

known as Applicant Tracking Systems, to receive, screen, and store résumés. Résumés can be scanned electronically, accepted by email as attachments or within the email, uploaded to Web sites, and accessed from Web-based résumé banks. Consequently, the standard word-processed document saved as a .doc file is no longer enough. You need both a traditional .doc résumé and an electronic résumé, a.k.a. eRésumé. Electronic résumés are discussed in detail later in this chapter.

Use search engines wisely

In addition to visiting popular and niche job sites, you can also set yourself apart from the pack by making thorough use of keyword searches on search engines to dig deep into the Internet for sites that might list jobs in your targeted field or provide insight into industry developments, potential employers, or networking opportunities. Start your search with the large, reliable search engines such as Google.com, Yahoo!Search (http://search.yahoo.com), Altavista.com, and Excite.com. For a slightly different type of search engine, check About.com where human experts, rather than technology, compile links on various topics.

To expand your search reach, use meta-search engines—services that scour multiple search engines at once. These include the following:

- Allsearchengines.com
- Dogpile.com
- EZ2find.com
- Surfwax.com
- Vivisimo.com
- Zapmeta.com

Just be careful not to spend too much time conducting keyword searches through search engines. You can go off on so many tangents that hours can go by before you realize what's happened.

Tips for Yielding More Focused Results from Your Keyword Searches

Besides just typing words into the keyword search field in a search engine, get in the habit of using punctuation recognized by all search engines as a way to narrow your search and to elicit more targeted results. You can do lots of things, but at minimum, you should be using the following techniques:

- Use quotation marks around phrases when you want to find sites that mention those exact words grouped together in the same order. Examples: "marketing jobs" or "sales networking groups."

- Use the plus (+) symbol to find matches with all words you're searching for: +marketing +jobs +atlanta or +sales +networking

- Use the minus (hyphen) symbol to exclude what you don't want. Examples: "security jobs" –terrorism or "IT jobs" –India.

- When you're on a Web page, use Ctrl-F to search for specific terms within the site.

For directories of search engines, links to search engines, and tips on using them, visit www.searchenginewatch.com and www.allsearchengines.com.

To post or not to post

Most job seekers post their résumés on Web sites without giving the action a second thought. More sophisticated job seekers know that it's not always the best thing to do. It's true that the ability to upload your résumé to an online résumé database (a.k.a., résumé bank) is an extremely beneficial feature of online job hunting. Your résumé ends up working for you 24/7. Employers are either given access to the résumé banks to search them for appropriate candidates, or the résumé banks are pro-grammed to search for résumés that match a position's criteria and to alert the employer to suitable candidates. It's also true, however, that there are drawbacks to posting.

Posting your résumé online is a good idea if you are in a hurry to find a job as quickly as possible and if your qualifica-tions are a straightforward match for the types of positions you're seeking. Job seekers with technical, accounting, and cler-ical skills tend to be good candidates for posting their résumés online as their skills are likely to get them lots of hits. Posting also works well for employed job seekers who don't have a lot of free time to browse the Web for jobs.

A downside of posting your résumé is that you lose your anonymity, unless you use a site that has a feature for posting résumés confidentially. Also, you lose control over who contacts you. Not only might you be caught off guard and not sound knowledgeable and prepared when contacted by an employer who has seen your résumé, you might also be contacted by fly-by-night recruiters or disreputable companies. Finally, you aren't able to customize your résumé or tailor a cover message to various employers.

If you choose to post your résumé, be aware of the disad-vantages. Always remember that you do not have to post your résumé online and that instead you might browse job listings and apply only to those employers and recruiters that interest you. Remember, too, that when you initiate the contact, you are able to follow up with a phone call or email to get your résumé noticed.

 Moneysaver

Beware of sites or career professionals that offer to blast your résumé all over the Web for a fee. In most cases, this is a self-defeating strategy. You can't customize your résumé or a cover letter to each recipient, you lose control over who sees your résumé, and many recipients will block your résumé as spam anyway.

Use personal search agents

Many job sites offer a personal search agent service that alerts you to new job opportunities meeting criteria you've specified. This can be a great alternative to posting your résumé in that you still have the benefit of technology working for you around the clock, but you retain control over how you approach each employer or headhunter.

Send a cover letter

If a site gives you the opportunity to post a cover letter when replying for a position, do so. Similarly, if a job posting instructs you to email your résumé as an attachment, be sure to include a cover message within the email as an introduction to your attached résumé. Many job seekers don't make the effort to do this, so you can get an edge on the competition if you do.

Make sure your email gets received and read

More than half of all email is considered *spam*—that junk mail you hate to get, the unsolicited commercial mail of some sort, usually wanting you to buy something you don't need. Companies invest a lot of time and money in technology that lets them block out spam, so your résumé might end up never reaching its destination, or if it does, the human recipient might delete it without reading it.

To increase your chances of getting through to the person you want to reach, follow these guidelines:

▪ If you have already had some contact with the person you're going to be emailing, such as when they've requested you send your résumé or you've cold-called them and want to follow up with your résumé, ask them to add you to their address book or to their company's list of acceptable email addresses.

▪ Avoid Internet Service Providers (ISPs) that are widely considered to be unacceptable sources of email. Most of your major ISPs, such as AOL and Earthlink, to name only a couple, are fine. Others are known as sources of spam and are "black-listed" by many organizations, or they use technology that makes them susceptible to spam blockers. Read more about this issue and check for black-listed servers on www.spamcop.net.

■ Don't do mass emailings. Your mass mailing can look like one of those viruses or worms that sends out infected email to people in your address book without you knowing it. You might not even be able to send out more than about 50 email messages at the same time because your ISP or virus protection software may stop the message from going out. If multiple messages do get sent, the recipient's system may block it as spam. You shouldn't be doing mass emailing anyway, because you need to be customizing your communications to each recipient.

■ Be careful with your subject field. Never leave the subject line of your email blank. What you do put there should clearly state what the email is about. Don't use punctuation, particularly exclamation points or question marks, and don't include the word "free" (as in "free résumé") or all capitalized words as these are hallmarks of spammers. Also avoid putting numbers in the subject line because these can look like tracking codes that spammers use.

■ Use a legitimate-sounding email address that includes some combination of your name and/or initials or your career specialty. Avoid having too many numbers in your address as these can also sound like spammers' tracking codes. The address Jbrown041462@ could be blocked. If you have to include some numbers because all combinations of your name and initials are already taken in your ISP and adding letters would make it too confusing to type, then try to limit it to one or two digits, such as Jbrown99@. Or, add a word that signifies your career field, such as JbrownSrManager@.

- Don't attach your résumé (or any other document) unless replying to a posting that has requested it that way or someone has directly told you an attachment is okay to send. Instead, paste your electronic résumé into the body of the email message. (More on electronic résumés later in this chapter.) If you do send an attachment, never send a compressed file, such as a .zip file as these are not only inconvenient for the recipient but are blocked by many systems as zipped and compressed files are notorious for containing viruses.

- Always follow the instructions that a headhunter, employer, or job posting provides for how to send your résumé. Sneaking in the back door by sending the résumé to someone other than the specified recipient or emailing it to someone in the company rather than sending it through the Web site might seem like a clever, proactive approach, but you could end up getting blocked as spam mail.

Finally, always remember to follow up whenever possible by sending your résumé in more than one fashion. If you have emailed it and are concerned about it being received, call the intended recipient or send a letter and résumé through the postal service.

What you need to know about electronic résumés

You probably already have some idea that you need a special sort of résumé for online job hunting. What you might not be crystal clear on—because most job seekers aren't—is exactly how that résumé needs to be formatted, what it needs to include, and when to use it. Much confusion exists around how to construct an electronic résumé and when to send it rather than the traditional résumé. The remainder of this chapter cuts through the confusion to ensure that your résumé will be effective in all your online job hunting efforts.

Not a pretty sight

To create a proper eRésumé, you have to shift your thinking dramatically. Forget about aesthetically pleasing graphics and eloquent writing all printed out on nice quality paper. Think instead of bits of data arranged in plain fashion on a screen. Electronic résumés don't look nice, and parts of them—namely the keyword section—sound choppy, but they work. You see, in most cases an eRésumé is going to be read by technology before human eyes will ever look upon it. Even when a human does get to it, the résumé is still usually nothing more than one screen of data to give the reader a quick—I'm talking really quick— glimpse of your credentials.

An eRésumé is a résumé created in text-only format, a.k.a. ASCII (American Standard Code for Information Interchange) format, with additional special formatting and content changes made from the Word version (more on those additional changes in the "Converting Your Résumé to an eRésumé" section later in this chapter). When your résumé is saved in ASCII, or text-only, format, it will be readable by just about any software program or operating system the recipient might use. These format changes enable the eRésumé to be scanned, searched, and uploaded electronically.

Scannable, searchable, uploadable, postable—what's in a name

Part of the confusion over electronic résumés is that they are called by so many names. A well-meaning fellow job seeker might caution you to make sure that your résumé is searchable. The person making photocopies of your résumé at your local print shop might say, "Hey, I see you've used italics in this résumé. It's not going to be scannable." Someone else might tell you that your résumé needs to be uploadable or that the line lengths are too long for it to be postable. It's enough to make you call off the whole idea of having an eRésumé and just resort to hand-delivering every résumé. (Even then, however, it would need to be scannable!) Don't panic. Let me explain.

Scannable résumés

A scannable résumé is one that can be accurately scanned from paper and ink into digital data or from electronic form as an email attachment into digital data. When employers and recruiters receive your résumé—traditional or electronic résumé—by hand-delivery, email, fax, or postal service, they often scan it electronically so that the data from your résumé goes into an applicant tracking system (ATS). An ATS is a form of database that stores résumés so that recruiters and employers can search the database by criteria that match the requirements for a particular position.

The technology that transforms your résumé from a piece of paper or file attached to an email into the ATS cannot read certain characters or text styled in a certain way. Scannable résumés must be very plain.

Font style and size

Every character must be clean, with no letters or numbers touching each other. Your safest bet is to use sans serif fonts—plain fonts such as Arial and Helvetica. A point size of 12 is ideal, but 11 or 11.5 is fine, too. Just don't go too small.

Minimal styling

Italic, underlining, borders, vertical and horizontal lines, shading, and columns usually cause problems for scanners. If you must do some styling, use ALL CAPS or **bold**.

No bullets

Scanners recognize only asterisks, plus signs, and hyphens, so replace all your bullet points with any of those symbols.

Margins

Some scanning technology will not read text that is too close to the edges of the page. Keep all margins, top, bottom, left, and right, set at one-inch or larger, to ensure that your text will be picked up.

Bright Idea

To get the inside scoop on what happens to your résumé when it goes to an organization that uses an applicant tracking system, read about one of the most popular systems, Resumix, at http://resumix.yahoo.com.

No headers and footers

Type all text within the regular document, not using the Header or Footer command, as text hidden in a header or footer is often not scannable.

So, is a scannable résumé the same thing as an eRésumé? Yes and no. When you create an eRésumé following the guidelines offered later in this chapter, you will have a scannable résumé. So, yes, your eRésumé is your scannable résumé. You don't need to create a special version for scanning as long as you have an eRésumé. Sometimes, however, your traditional résumé might be scanned. Many organizations receive résumés in the mail, by fax, or by hand and scan them to go into the ATS. You can never be quite sure when this will happen. If in doubt, use your eRésumé.

Searchable résumés

When someone says that your résumé needs to be "searchable," all they mean is that it needs to contain keywords that a hiring manager or recruiter is likely to use as criteria when searching for résumés in an applicant tracking system. The database technology searches for particular words in your résumé that are relevant to the position to be filled. If you create an eRésumé following the guidelines offered later in this chapter, including the discussion of keywords in the "Demystifying Keywords" section, your résumé will be searchable.

Uploadable résumés

As with searchable, the term *uploadable résumé* means nothing more than your regular eRésumé. When you post your résumé into a résumé bank on the Internet, you are uploading it from your own hard drive or from a disk or CD. As long as your résumé is created in ASCII format, it will upload.

Postable résumés

Postable is basically an alternate term for uploadable. The only difference is that many of the fields or boxes in which you post your résumé on Web sites are narrow enough to cause some problems with the length of lines of text in your résumé. Later in this chapter, I include a section on "Electronic Résumés with No Line Breaks." This is a minor modification you'll make to your eRésumé to make it more postable.

When to use an eRésumé versus a traditional résumé

Sometimes it is obvious that you should use your eRésumé; other times you will be certain that the traditional résumé is appropriate. There will, however, also be times when you're just not sure.

Always use the traditional résumé in these situations

Use your traditional résumé (the nice looking one with the .doc extension after the filename) when you want to print the résumé on high-quality paper to mail through the postal system (*snail mail*) or when it is to be hand-delivered to a person. Also use your traditional résumé when you are sending the résumé as an email attachment, unless you've been instructed to attach a text-only or ASCII résumé, in which case you would use your eRésumé.

Always use the eRésumé in these situations

Use your eRésumé when posting in online résumé banks or job banks or when sending within the message field of an email rather than as an attachment. Of course, you would also use the eRésumé any time someone has requested a text-only or ASCII version of your résumé, no matter what the exact circumstances are.

Use the traditional or eRésumé? The gray area

The technology that employers and recruiters use to process résumés is changing rapidly, and it is always difficult to know exactly how your résumé will be handled when it reaches its destination. The gray area comes into play when you are faxing your résumé. You might need to fax your eRésumé because it will be scanned directly into a database. Or, your résumé might be printed on paper from the fax machine and be read by human eyes. In that case, your traditional résumé would work. Generally speaking, the larger the organization, the more likely they are to use sophisticated applicant tracking systems.

If in doubt, fax both versions of your résumé with a brief reference in the cover letter to why you are sending two versions. You may also fax your eRésumé and follow with the traditional résumé by regular mail.

The same quandary applies to sending your résumé via email as an attachment. Typically, you attach the traditional résumé because most, if not all, of the formatting and styling will be retained when the file is opened as an attachment on the other end. There is a chance, however, that your attachment will need to be fed into the database and may have formatting issues that cause the text to become illegible. Plus, your traditional résumé would not have the keyword section that is so important for databases searches. In this case, especially when dealing with large organizations, email your eRésumé pasted into the body of the email message and attach your traditional résumé so that both bases are covered.

 Watch Out!

The issue of when to send your traditional versus electronic résumé is not an exact science! Use common sense and your best judgment to determine which version to use, and send the résumé in more than one way (for example, by both fax and email or both email and snail mail) as a safeguard.

You can also solve some of the problems in this gray area by keeping the layout and design of your traditional résumé simple, following the guidelines listed earlier under "Scannable Résumés."

Converting your résumé to an eRésumé

It's not difficult to create an electronic résumé. You just have to save your traditional (.doc) résumé in a text-only format and make a few adjustments to the layout within the document. You do need to add a keyword section, which often replaces your qualifications summary, but that is discussed in the next section, "Demystifying Keywords." For now, just focus on getting the basic structure of your eRésumé developed, and you'll add the keywords after reading that section. Note that the steps that follow are written for someone creating an eRésumé from a Microsoft Word file. The process is generally the same for users of any word processing program or operating system, but there might be slight variations, such as the names of commands.

Step one: save as ASCII

Locate your traditional résumé on your hard drive, or if not on your hard drive, on the disk or CD-ROM to which you've saved it. Then follow these steps:

1. Open the file with your traditional résumé.

2. From your toolbar, select *File*, then select *Save As*. In the box labeled *Save as type*, select *Text Only with Line Breaks*. Click *Save*. You will be warned that some formatting will be lost. That's what you want to have happen, so click *Yes* to save.

3. After saving as text only, close the file as you normally would close a file.

4. Now open the file you've just created as you would normally open any file in your word processing application. NOTE: The text file you just created might not show up on your list of choices unless you ask for *All files* in the *Files as type*

box. You will know you're opening the correct version if there is a *.txt* extension after the filename and a different sort of icon next to the filename. (In Word, the icon looks like a sheet of paper with lines rather than the "W" symbol.)

Step two: clean up the formatting and layout

You'll see that saving your résumé in the ASCII format has already done much of the work for you. Your document will look very plain with no fancy styling or layout. It will also need some cleaning up. Here's what to do:

■ Bullets usually will show up as asterisks or hyphens after saving as text only, but if some other symbol appears, such as question marks, replace them with asterisks, hyphens, or plus symbols.

■ Most, if not all, styling of text, such as italic, bolding, and underlining will have gone away. Leave the text plain, but if there are places where you want some text to stand out, such as with section headings, you may use ALL CAPS in place of bold or underlining.

■ Make sure that all text is justified at the left margin. Any text that had been centered or right justified in the tradi-tional résumé needs to be moved to the left margin and on its own line.

■ Delete all tabs. To do this, you need to turn on the para-graph marker. This is a command on your toolbar that looks like a paragraph symbol. It resembles a backward capital letter "P" immediately followed by a capital T. Click on it to show all the spacing between words and lines. Tabs will show up as arrows. Remove all tabs by highlighting them and hitting *delete* or backspacing over them.

■ It is best to keep the layout simple and have all text flush with the left margin, but if you feel you must have some text moved toward the right margin, use the space bar to move the text over a few spaces rather than using a tab.

- Make sure that the first line of your eRésumé contains your full name. Follow the name with your email address, and if desired, your phone number, each on its own line, flush with the left margin.

- Where you had multiple items of text on the same line in the traditional résumé, move each separate set of text to its own line. For example, you might have had your job title, employer name, and dates of employment all on the same line. For your eRésumé, spread those out into two or three lines.

Step three: check length and remove page breaks

Depending on the length of your traditional résumé, you may have some additional adjustments to make to the eRésumé.

- If your traditional résumé is two pages long, delete the second reference to your name and any contact information that might have been on the second page in the traditional résumé. Also delete any reference to "Page 2." Obviously, if your résumé was longer than two pages, you'll need to remove the header or footer text from each page. There are no page breaks in your eRésumé—it's just one run-on document—so multiple page headers are unnecessary.

- Check the line count of your résumé to make sure that the most important information appears within the first 75 lines. Many recruiters view only the first screenshot of your résumé, so the information that fits into one screen is critical. Also, some older scanning technology stops reading résumés after a certain number of lines, often about 75. (Note that more sophisticated scanning systems do read beyond 75 lines, so do not be concerned that *every* place you send your résumé will be seeing only a part of it.) Remember that you'll be replacing your qualifications summary section (if you had one) with a keyword summary section, so you'll need to recount lines after doing that. To check the line count, select *Tools, Word Count.*

Step four: saving and testing

- When finished creating the document, select *File* and then select *Save* to save it.

- See Figure 10.1, a sample eRésumé, at the end of this chapter to get an idea of how your eRésumé should look.

- Before putting your eRésumé into action, test it to see how it transmits electronically. Paste the eRésumé into the message field of an email and send it to a friend whose email account is through a different Internet Service Provider (ISP). You can also send it to yourself if you have email accounts through different ISPs, such as sending from AOL to Hotmail or from Yahoo to Comcast. Also try to send it to someone in a corporation to see how it might look when an employer opens it in a corporate system.

Electronic résumés with no line breaks

As mentioned earlier in the explanation of "postable" résumés, there are times when you'll be posting your résumé into narrow fields, or boxes, on a Web site or onto a site that requires you to split your résumé up into text that you paste into a number of fields. Having a résumé saved as text only without line breaks can make it easier to copy and paste your text into those boxes (fields). It's very easy to create a résumé with no line breaks. Follow all of the previous instructions for creating an eRésumé, but in Step one, number 2, save the file as *Text Only* instead of *Text Only with Line Breaks.* Remember also to give your résumé a slightly different filename so that you can easily distinguish between the two versions of the eRésumé.

Demystifying keywords

The term *keywords* strikes fear in the hearts of many a job seeker because they don't know what keywords are exactly, but they hear them mentioned all the time and know that they're important. There is no magic to keywords. If you've ever used a simple database program to search for information by typing criteria, or if you've ever used a search engine on the Internet such as Google to find Web sites that have what you're looking for, then you've seen how keywords work. Not that computer literate, are you? Then, consider this: Imagine you're using a Yellow Pages phone directory to find a particular type of business. You turn to the appropriate page in the alphabet and then scan the page with your eyes to hit on the category that matches what you're looking for. Then your eye might skim the listings and ads in that category to find business names that sound like a place where you would want to do business. If you've done that, then you've experienced what it's like for a recruiter to search a database for résumés by keyword. You just did it in a more low-tech fashion.

Employers and recruiters usually search résumé databases using keywords. Sometimes, employers and recruiters even have technology that automatically does this for them. If you've ever submitted your résumé online and almost immediately gotten a reply that your qualifications do not match the position, this is what was happening. The technology was set up to search résumés as soon as they hit the database.

Your goal is to have the right keywords in your résumé so that you end up on the "hit list." A *hit* is when a keyword search matches keywords in a résumé. Addition of keywords to your résumé increases the likelihood of hits. After keyword matches are identified, many electronic résumé management systems then rank the résumés and score them based on the total number of keywords in each résumé that match the position to be filled. Many automated systems store résumés by keyword only or by extracted summary, not the full text. In those cases, the sentence structure and appearance of your résumé won't matter, but the list of keywords will.

What keywords sound like

Keywords are nouns or noun phrases that reflect areas of expertise, industry experience, functional roles, job titles, education, specific skills, achievements, commonly used trade terms, technical terms, and any other concepts relevant to the positions you are seeking. Examples of keywords are Total Quality Management, Vice President, Direct Marketing, Banking Industry, CPA. Note that the powerful action verbs often found in traditional résumés (for example, Developed, Coordinated, Empowered, and Organized) are not as critical for the keyword section of eRésumés. (Of course, do keep those verbs in the other sections of your eRésumé for when a human being actually reads the résumé.)

The keyword summary is simply a collection of keywords, set off from each other by commas or periods and presented in paragraph form rather than as a list or table. Type keywords in title case (the first letter of each word is capitalized; see the samples that follow).

Sample keyword summary for a business manager

Business Unit Manager. Marketing Manager. Product Manager. Brand Manager. Field Sales. National Sales Team. National Accounts Manager. District Sales Manager. Number One Market Share. Key Account Sales Programs. Joint Venture. Manufacturers Representative Network. Distribution Network. MBA.

Sample keyword summary for a transportation/ logistics specialist

Project Manager, Transportation Systems Planning, Demand Management. Multi-modal Analysis. UGB. 2040 Concept Plan. Transportation Legislation. DOT. TPR. ISTEA. TAC. Citizen Task Force. Public Presentations. Grant Writing. Interagency Coordination. Transportation Planning Processes. BA degree.

Sample keyword summary for an office manager

Personnel Management. Spreadsheet Development. Contract Review. Travel and Meeting Planning. Vendor Coordination. Accounts Receivable. Accounts Payable. Payroll. Written and Oral Communication. Small Business Environment. Sales Support. Quality Assurance. Software Testers and Developers. Computer Literate. Microsoft Office. QuickBooks. Excel. PowerPoint. Multi-task. Problem-solving. Details.

Developing your keyword summary

You would have to be clairvoyant (or a spy) to know precisely which keywords are going to be used by any given organization that you may send your résumé to for any particular position. Professional résumé writers, career coaches, and authors of résumé books continually try to compile lists of keywords for various fields. These can come in very handy, but even they are less than perfect. You simply never can anticipate all possible keywords. Fortunately, there is no real magic to conjuring up at least a handful of accurate keywords. To do so, pull from the following sources:

Keywords already in your résumé

It's likely that your traditional résumé already includes keywords throughout, so begin by identifying important terms that appear anywhere in the text. You don't have to repeat every important term in a keyword summary—you can keep most of them where they are in the regular résumé text—but do select the most important ones and repeat them in the keyword summary that will go near the top of your résumé.

Online and print job postings and ads

Make note of all skills, areas of expertise, titles, and other terms listed in job postings for the types of jobs you are seeking. Include these terms in your keyword summary. (*Hint:* When online, you can copy keywords directly from a job listing and paste them into your eRésumé, *if* they are applicable to your skill set.)

Networking

Informational interviewing is an excellent source of insider information regarding the types of keywords used for résumé database searches.

Expert advice

If working with a professional résumé writer or career coach, ask whether he or she has compiled lists of keywords. Some professional associations for résumé writing and career professionals have keyword lists in the members-only areas of their sites, so even if the person you're working with hasn't put together any lists, he or she might have access to some. Also, check for examples of keywords provided in books on résumé writing. (See the "Online Job Hunting" and "Résumés" sections of the online Bonus Appendix 2 "Recommended Reading List.")

Your knowledge

As a final step, read your keyword summary and judge how well it captures your overall experience and qualifications. Add any words you think are missing. Keep in mind that there is no one, perfect list of keywords for any given job, function, or industry. You are the best judge of terms that reflect what you offer and are relevant to the types of work you seek.

After identifying words that could make up your keyword summary, check to see how many you've come up with. There are no official parameters on number of keywords to include, but about 15 to 20 is usually sufficient. Don't go overboard with much more than that.

When you've pared your list down to a manageable number, it's time to add the keywords to your résumé. Open your text-only version of your résumé and delete the qualifications summary section, if you have one. (First, make sure that any important words you'll be deleting have made it into your keyword summary.) Type the heading "KEYWORDS" in all caps below your name and contact information. Follow on the next line with your keywords typed in title case as in the examples provided earlier.

Jane L. Levin

3333 Brookwood Road

Anytown, GA 30000

Janelevin@email.com

Tel: 770.000.0000

KEYWORDS

Senior Sales Management, Business Manager, Marketing, Food Service, Janitorial & Sanitation, Distributor and End User Sales, Influence Management, Consultative Selling, National Account Management, Multi Territory Management, Field Sales, Exceed Quota, Profit Specialist, BS degree.

PROFESSIONAL EXPERIENCE

COMPANY ONE, Atlanta, GA

2000 - 2005

-BUSINESS UNIT DIRECTOR, 2002-2005

Reported to Director of Sales. Revenue of $16 million. Led a team of five direct reports selling products and services to national accounts and 30+ select distributors in five states.

+ Awarded President's Cup in 2004 and 2005 for ranking in top two teams out of 23 that exceed quota.

+ Achieved five-year Compound Average Growth of 7.5%, compared to 3.4% industry average. Accomplished through team sales efforts and offering products and services as solutions to end users.

+ Delivered 12% growth in FY02. Exceeded plan by 5% despite 9/11 turmoil, recession and loss of largest national distributor. Accomplished through new accounts, new product sales and added distribution.

+ Focused on vendor consolidation with key distributors, resulting in client profit improvement. Worked with end users to develop programs. Decreased costs by 10-25%.

+ Expanded distribution with five new distributors, resulting in $800,000 incremental rev enue.

Figure 10.1. Sample eRésumé

-DIVISION SALES MANAGER, 2000-2002

Managed six direct reports with $12.6 million quota in Southeast Division.

+ Grew business every year through target account management, distributor plan execution and development of team. Respective increases of 8% and 10% in an industry that is virtually flat.

+ Introduced, serviced, maintained and grew multiple location accounts.

COMPANY TWO, Chicago, IL

1992-2000

-MARKETING MANAGER, 1995-2000

Managed marketing and trade deal budgets of $900,000 and reached $90 million sales goal. Led training and new item launches for nine brokers, four field sales managers, and eight territory managers.

+ Successfully supported targeted segment promotions for colleges, manufacturers, and healthcare. Included direct mail and telemarketing campaigns. Exceeded quota by 100%.

+ Awarded two Quarterly Achievement Honors for successful sales and marketing programs.

-REGION MANAGER, 1992-1994

Promoted through four sales positions of increasing responsibility.

EDUCATION

Bachelor of Science degree, 1991
The University of Georgia, Athens, GA

Just the facts

- The Internet is useful for much more than finding and applying for jobs. Be sure to use it for research, networking, and other resources.

- Advantages of online job hunting are the ease and size of it. Disadvantages of online job hunting are the ease and size of it, plus the threats to personal security.

- Distinguish yourself from the competition online by venturing off the beaten path to niche sites and employers' own sites, as well as by fulling understanding the technology involved.

- Having your email and résumé blocked as spam by the intended recipient is a serious potential problem. This chapter offered several suggestions for minimizing the risk of having your mail blocked.

- Proper formatting of an electronic résumé, and the inclusion of keywords, is critical to success in online job hunting. Carefully follow the guidelines offered in this chapter.

Chapter 11

GET THE SCOOP ON...
How to start acing the interview before it even
starts ■ Making your pre-interview research manageable ■ What to take to the interview ■ How
to dress ■ Developing a winning mindset ■
Squashing pre-interview jitters

Preparing for Interviews

E verything I've suggested you do, think about, and work on up to now has been preparing you for your interviews. So, if you've read the chapters leading up to this one, you've actually done most of the hard work already. The foundation you've laid will put you miles ahead of your competition. You're going into interviews understanding the hiring process, knowing your best selling points and what you want out of your next job, as well as knowing how to communicate to employers that you have what they need. Now all you have to do is pull it all together with a pre-interview checklist to make sure you're ready for each opportunity:

Checklist 11.1. What to Do Before an Interview

Research   I've conducted enough research to be knowledgeable about the employer, particularly regarding the company's goals, challenges, and needs.

Marketing Strategy   I've reviewed my assets, selected asset statements that best match the employer's need, and practiced speaking about them.

Props   I've prepared my "interviewing bag of tricks" so that I have all the written materials and other items that I might need to market myself powerfully.

Attire   I've selected appropriate clothing and accessories and have tried them on and checked them carefully in advance to make sure that they fit well, are clean, and are not in need of repair.

Attitude   I've prepared mentally so that I'll go into the interview with a sense of power and confidence.

Researching the employer

Most job seekers don't take the time or have the patience for more than a cursory glance through a prospective employer's Web site, learning only the bare minimum about the organization where they'll be interviewing. Such corner-cutting can have unfortunate consequences. Employers expect you to have done your homework, and you should expect yourself to do your homework, as it's a critical element in developing your self-marketing strategy for each employer. Conducting research before an interview enables you to determine which aspects of your experience and which of your assets are going to be most relevant to the prospective employer.

Conducting this research is about much more than learning obscure financial statistics from an organization's annual report. Unless you're applying for a financial position or very senior management, you don't need to be able to recite every figure in their profit and loss statement. Instead, you need to have a clear idea of what they're in business to do, who their competition is, what their mission statement and goals are, and what the culture is like. By researching strategically, you don't waste your time chasing down useless information, and the information you do obtain will help you answer those three critical questions discussed in Chapter 2, "How Employers Think": Will you add value? Will you fit in? Will you make the commitment? With thorough research, you can set yourself apart from competitors with educated answers to these questions.

Six degrees of information

Almost everyone else interviewing for the job you want will know whether the prospective employer is into widgets or wireless, is expanding or shrinking, and is global or local. To distinguish yourself as the best candidate for the job, you need to be conversant on a broader range of topics that are both directly and tangentially related to the job. A thorough pre-interview research process involves gathering information in the following areas:

> **❝** With the revolution in career and business resource collections, job seekers have access to more information more easily than ever before. Research is vital to speaking intelligently during interviews and to keeping up with the competition. **❞**
>
> —Georgia Donati, Career Consultant and former Director, New York Public Library Job Information Center

- Information about the organization itself

- The nature and responsibilities of the job

- Biographical data about the interviewer(s)

- The nature of the profession or occupation

- Trends in the industry or sector

- Current events and general interest areas

Each of these six areas is explained in more depth on the pages that follow.

What you need to know about the prospective employer

At a minimum, you need to know what the prospective employer's products or services are, where their offices or branches are located, how long they have been in existence, how the organization is structured in terms of divisions and areas, and who the top management is. You can set yourself apart from the pack by digging a bit deeper to find out something about these topics:

- The corporate culture
- Characteristics valued in employees
- The organization's goals and vision for the future
- Projected areas of growth and expansion
- Difficulties facing the organization

When you go into an interview, you are not so much a job candidate as a potential problem-solver and change agent. To show that you could be effective in those areas, you must get at the heart of the employer's needs. What problems do they need solved? What new contributions could they use? In which areas do they need innovation and a new way of thinking? Only when you know the answers to these questions and more can you position yourself strategically.

What does the job itself entail?

To interview strategically, you must know as much as possible about what the job entails and requires. You might not be able to know all the ins and outs of the job until you get to the interview,

 Watch Out!

Research takes time! You'll need anywhere from a couple of hours to a couple of days to conduct sufficient research for each interview. Keep this in mind when scheduling, and whenever possible allow ample time before your appointment to browse the Internet, visit the library, or call your contacts.

but you should, at the very least, know what your target position would typically entail. Make the effort to find out what you can about the specific position at the organization where you'll be interviewing. You may be able to determine some of the following key points:

- Who previously held the job, and why he or she left (or is leaving)
- To whom you would report if you held the position
- Whom you would supervise in that job
- With which other departments or offices you would interact
- Which skills and personal qualities are needed for success on the job
- The biggest challenges of the job

To find answers to these questions, you'll need to turn to your network to track down any current or former employees of that organization, as well their clients, customers, or vendors. If you've been connected with an employer through a head-hunter, then you might be able to learn a good bit about the position if the recruiter has been fully briefed on what it entails.

Who is the interviewer?

Employers don't hire résumés; they hire people. The more you come across as a colleague, a peer, or even a potential friend—not as some anonymous job seeker—the more comfortable the interviewer will feel with you.

It's ideal if you can discover something you have in common with the interviewer to address the issue of how you'll fit in the organization or the department. You need to find out about the interviewer's educational background, past work experience, professional interests, hobbies, family, geographic background, and any pet causes or charities. Even if you find that you don't have much, if anything, in common with the interviewer, you will at least get a sense of his or her interests, values, and personal style so that you can conduct yourself accordingly.

Bright Idea

Whenever possible, obtain the bios of people who will be interviewing you. For the officers of a company, these might be listed on the organization's Web site. You can also try requesting a bio through the interviewers' administrative assistants or the organization's public relations department.

What's happening in the world-at-large?

A common pitfall when preparing for an interview is concentrating all your research efforts on the organization itself and the individual interviewer(s), forgetting about the big-picture context—the profession or industry as a whole, as well as current world and domestic events and news. Awareness of trends and developments in your career field and contact with people from comparable organizations enable you to bring innovation and knowledge to your new employer.

Following the news of the overall industry (finance, real estate, health care, or media, for example) or sector (such as corporate, not-for-profit, or government) also shows that you can add value to the organization. You need to know who has merged with whom, how the economy is affecting a particular product or service, who the major players are, and what the significant trends are.

This research is particularly important for higher-level managers and professionals whose interviews are not so much an interrogation as a conversation between peers. Just as you might discuss general current events at a cocktail party, you need to be up to speed on current events in your industry for the sophisticated conversation that will take place in your interviews.

- Read the current and past three issues of any relevant trade and professional association journals, newsletters, or magazines.

- Read the current and past two issues of magazines such as *U.S. News and World Report, Newsweek,* and *Time,* as well as any specialized periodicals relevant to your field.

- Read your local daily newspaper, as well as a major city newspaper such as the *New York Times* or *Chicago Tribune* if you do not live in a major metropolitan area.

- If possible, attend a trade or professional association meeting or other informative event that would give you insight into economic, political, social, or intellectual issues related to your line of work.

- Have a conversation with at least one of the most savvy members of your network to get the latest inside scoop on what's happening in the industry in which you work (or wish to work).

Being up-to-date on what's happening in the world at large and having a range of personal interests will also make you a more effective candidate. You should never go into an interview without having read that morning's paper, and, if possible, tuned into a 24-hour cable news show or read the latest news online just before your interview. If your research into the interviewer turned up any valuable information about his or her hobbies and interests, then you'll know on which current events to focus. If your interviewer is into tennis, and your appointment is around the time of the U.S. Open or Wimbledon, then don't even think of going to the interview without knowing who's winning, who's losing, and whose serve is faster this year. Even if you don't know what your interviewer is interested in, knowing at least a little bit about current events in sports, film, literature, the arts, finance, and politics will help you hedge your bets.

 Bright Idea

If you are interviewing for jobs in a career field or industry in which you've never worked, pay special attention to the jargon of that field as you do your research. Speaking the "language" of your new occupation will help you sound more like an insider during the interview.

Moneysaver

Get in the habit of reading key publications online on a daily basis. You often have to be a subscriber to read back issues, but the news of the day is usually free, so it pays to sign on daily.

Who has the information you need

For the most part, the information you need to collect in the four areas just described is easily accessible. With minimal effort, you can uncover the basic things you need to know—but with a bit more perseverance and resourcefulness, you can acquire knowledge that will dazzle the interviewer. You can gain that knowledge from a combination of print, electronic, and people resources found through the prospective employer itself, professional associations, the Internet, libraries, bookstores, college and university career offices, and your network of contacts. For a more detailed discussion of the roles these sources play in your job search research, turn to the "Direct Mail Campaigns" section of Chapter 8. Don't forget about the many sources listed in the Research sections of both the online Bonus Appendix 2 and 3.

Researching the hard to research

Not all of your target employers will have thousands of citations on the Web, slick brochures describing the exciting career opportunities they offer, and a staff that fills the pages of *Who's Who*. Small businesses, some nonprofits, individual entrepreneurs, and privately held companies can be difficult to research.

In those cases, you need to be persistent and resourceful in your research efforts. You must have faith that the information you need does exist and that if you keep digging, you will unearth it. Now is the time to turn to reference librarians and other information specialists who are trained in obtaining data that's hard to find. They can point you toward useful resources such as the *Inc Magazine 1000, Directory of Leading Private Companies,* and *Directories in Print.*

Watch Out!

When networking for information on the Internet, you may not be as anonymous as you think. If you need to keep your job search confidential, be careful in chat rooms or when posting on message boards. You might not recognize the personal screen name for your boss or nosy co-worker, but they may recognize yours.

This is also a situation that calls for more networking than book research. Think of whom might do business with or otherwise know about the organization on which you need information. For example, foundation officers and grant writers would know about not-for-profit organizations. Small business administration staff might be familiar with certain small businesses you're researching. And, certainly a keyword search on the Internet is a useful way to cast a wide net for the information you need.

What to do with the information you collect

All the research in the world is useless if your results come in the form of random notes on scratch paper, vague recollections of phone conversations, and file folders too stuffed to wade through before an interview. You'll make your life easier and will be more successful in your meetings if you take the vast amounts of information you collect and put them in a format that is easily accessible and can be read quickly. Before that, however, you need to know when to stop researching so that you don't end up wasting your time chasing down unnecessary information.

Knowing when to stop

When preparing for an interview, you may wonder how much research is enough and how much is too much. Do you need to be able to recite every statistic in the organization's annual report? Do you really have to know where the daughter of the company's CFO attends college? Maybe, but maybe not. Research is important, but you don't need to go overboard. You will find yourself overwhelmed if you try to memorize too many facts and figures or stay on top of too many subjects. Plus, nobody likes a show-off; the interviewer will want to see that you are reasonably well-informed, not a walking encyclopedia.

The suggestions presented in this section are just that— suggestions. The key is to strike a balance between conducting thorough research and also devoting enough time to the other tasks of your job search. If you feel that the knowledge you have gained is reliable, accurate, up-to-date, and unbiased (or at least reflects a variety of opinions), then you have probably done enough.

Organizing the information

To distill the information you collect down to a manageable amount and accessible format, complete a form such as the sample in Worksheet 11.1 for each interview, and review it before every appointment. This form is called "Information Gems" because it should contain only those data bits that will help you dazzle the interviewer with your knowledge.

Worksheet 11.1. Information Gems

Organization name	Year Established

Interviewer(s) name and title: _____

Products/services: _____

Office/branch locations: _____

CEO or director: _____

Other key managers/officers: _____

Organizational culture/style/philosophy: _____

Goals/vision: _____

Growth areas: _____

Problem areas: _____

Skills/expertise/personality needed for the job: _____

Interviewer's biographical data: _____

Profession or industry developments: _____

Current events/news: _____

Best book I've read lately: _____

Best film/theatrical production I've seen lately: _____

Personal interests/hobbies worth mentioning: _____

Also, don't forget about the organizational tools recommended in the online Bonus Chapter 1, "Getting Organized and Planning Your Action." You'll need those to keep track of all the information you collect.

Marketing strategy—tailoring your approach for each interview

If you carefully read and completed the exercises in Chapter 3, "Marketing You, the Product," and Chapter 4, "Your Marketing Plan's Secret Weapon," then you are 99 percent there when it comes to developing a marketing strategy for each interview. All you have to do now is review the Job Search Wish List you developed in Chapter 3 and the asset statements you created in Chapter 4. Those were the building blocks of your self-marketing plan—the answers to the questions What do I want in my next job and employer? and What do I have to offer my next job and employer?

Now, take that information and factor in what you learn from your research on each employer. This enables you to answer the remaining question in the marketing strategy puzzle, which is Who needs what I have to offer and offers what I need? In other words, you review your asset statements and your wish list and pick the items that are most relevant to the organization with which you'll be interviewing. How do you know what is most relevant? You've done your research!

Finally, don't forget to practice. You need to get comfortable talking about your strengths and background, saying your asset statements, answering questions you are likely to be asked, and

Moneysaver

Rather than having to pay a career coach, enlist a friend to conduct and video-tape a mock interview with you, using the questions supplied in this book.

asking pointed questions yourself. (Typical and not-so-typical interview questions are listed in Chapters 13 and 14.)

Props—what to take to the interview

Related to your marketing strategy are the written materials or other self-marketing items you might take to an interview. No matter what the situation, just about everyone needs to take several résumé hard copies to an interview. The person or people you'll be speaking with probably already have a copy of your résumé, but having some extras on hand is a nice convenience in case they do need one. Plus, if they only have your plain-Jane eRésumé, bringing your traditional résumé is a nice way to showcase your experience more attractively. Your job seeker business cards are a must-take, as is a copy of your reference list, a pad of paper, and a pen in good working order.

If you've prepared a job search portfolio, take it. And, if you've put together any sort of presentation, such as a slide presentation showing highlights of your marketing pitch or samples of your work, take that if it seems appropriate for the situation.

If all you're taking to the interview is your résumé, reference list, business cards, and pen and paper, it might all fit into a trim leather folder (the kind that usually comes with a pad of paper and slot for a pen on one side and pocket for loose papers and business cards on the other) or a small portfolio (a pocket folder that holds file folders or loose papers and has a flap that closes). Women can tuck their emergency kit in their purse, and men might be able to fit small items like comb, breath mints or strips, and a packet of stain remover towelettes in their pockets. If you find yourself tight on space, however, or if you're bringing lots

---

Your Interviewing Bag of Tricks

The following items are ones you should just about always take to an interview:

- Several copies of your résumé on nice paper
- Your job seeker business cards
- Reference list
- Pen and paper
- A small personal emergency kit (safety pins, comb or brush, small mirror, breathmints, dental floss, individual packets of stain removal towelettes, extra pair of stockings for women, extra tie for men in case of stains, and anything else you think you might need)

Optional items, depending on what's relevant to the job and employer at hand, include the following:

- Your portfolio
- Work samples
- Slide presentation

---

of the optional items, then there's nothing wrong with carrying a briefcase or laptop case to the interview. Just make sure everything you carry is clean, polished, and in good shape and that the papers and folders you put inside are well organized so you can easily find what you need and can keep the items from becoming crumpled.

What to wear to the interview

In the online Bonus Chapter 2, "Honing Your Communication Skills and Tools," I cover the topic of image and attire in a job search, whether dressing for a networking meeting or an interview. Please review that chapter if you haven't already, as that's where you'll find more detailed advice about how to present yourself. I will repeat, however, some startling statistics that are worth repeating: First impressions are formed within the first few seconds of meeting someone, often before they've uttered a single word, and 93 percent of the overall impression formed comes from nonverbal messages, not what is actually said. How you look when you meet an interviewer sets the tone for how that person is going to receive you. No, it's not a beauty contest, but how you look—your personal hygiene, grooming, and attire—factors heavily into the way the interviewer is going to react to you. If you show up dressed inappropriately or sloppily or with poor grooming, you'll have to put a whole lot of effort into talking your way out of the "first impression hole" and into being considered a viable candidate. If there's lots of competition for the job, no amount of fancy talk is going to dig you out of that hole.

Be sure to dress one notch up from what you would wear on the job. If the organization's dress code is business attire, or if you're going for a senior-level position in any organization no matter what the dress code, wear a suit (and tie for men). If the atmosphere is business casual, with a tendency toward business-like rather than casual, then you probably will still want to go with a suit and tie. If the culture tends more toward the casual end of business-casual, then a suit might not be necessary, but err on the dressier side of business-casual to be one notch up. Finally, if the environment is jeans, ratty t-shirts, and sneakers, don't show up that casual but do dress down more than you might for other environments (e.g., slacks instead of jeans, a shirt with a collar, and shoes that aren't sports shoes). If in doubt about what to wear, there's no harm in asking the human

 Watch Out!

If you're trying to land a position at a higher level than any you've held in the past, be sure your image is congruent with that higher level, even before you have the job.

Bright Idea

If unsure of how people dress at the organization where you'll be interviewing, scope out the situation in advance by dropping by the workplace (as anonymously as possible) to "spy." Try to go in the morning or evening when you'll see people coming and going to work and won't have to enter the building.

resources department about the dress code and for suggestions of what to wear.

Attitude

Preparing yourself mentally prior to an interview is just as important as researching the company, developing your marketing strategy, and deciding what to wear, yet it is often the most overlooked area of preparation. This is the time to remember what I discussed in Chapter 1, "Twenty Secrets of Successful Job Seekers," in the section "Successful Job Seekers Have the Right Attitude."

In particular, you need to remember that you have more power in the process than you might think. Throughout the course of a job search, you are likely to go from feeling confident to cursed, optimistic to hopeless, and capable to ineffectual. Such ups and downs are normal for a process in which you are being judged, in which you face significant consequences for your personal and professional life, and in which you often must face rejection. Attending to your mental state to make sure that you go into each interview with a sense of power and confidence is a critical step toward success.

The psychology of interviews

Whenever two or more human beings interact, the psyche of each participant becomes an ingredient in a sort of group dynamics stew. As with a real stew, the ingredients can mesh well to create something delicious, or they can clash so that you never want to combine them again. Your goal in interviewing is to have all the involved parties want to get together again, either for more interviews or as colleagues on the job. For that to happen, the social interaction must be pleasant and comfortable for all who take part in it. The psychological ingredients must meld well.

As the candidate, you do have considerable control over the success or failure of the interaction with your interviewer(s). First, by paying attention to your own thoughts and feelings prior to the interview, you can develop a winning attitude and not succumb to self-doubt, nervousness, or false confidence. I call this task the *power of balancing*. Second, you can contribute to a favorable social exchange during the interview, employing tactics that give you control over the outcome without steamrolling the interviewer's authority. You can think of this as dealing with the *balance of power*.

The power of balancing

Going into an interview with the right attitude is like walking a tightrope. You have to come across as confident but not cocky, and positive but not starry-eyed. You must convey enthusiasm but not seem desperate. You should let yourself enjoy the experience while maintaining a healthy dose of fear to keep you on your toes. It's a little like the ancient Greeks' admonition of "Everything in moderation, nothing in excess." You can, for example, allow yourself to be apprehensive but not let the fear overcome you. Or, if you tend to err on the side of overconfidence, you need to let that confidence work for you, but not to the point that it distorts your good judgment and makes you blasé. It's all about balance. Trying to banish all negative thoughts and feelings as you anticipate an interview is pointless. Fear, doubt, concern, and false confidence are normal, healthy emotions. Instead of attempting the impossible task of squelching them completely, you simply need to keep them in check so that no one thought or feeling overpowers another. It's a matter of staying balanced.

Table 11.1. How to COPE with interviews

Attitude Element	How to Get It	How to Keep Balance
Confidence	Review your asset statements; recall past successes; realize you've already beaten out some of the competition just to get to the interview stage. If it helps, call upon your religious or spiritual faith for strength.	Avoid getting blindly confident, cocky, or arrogant; be prepared for a tough interview that could shake your confidence.
Optimism	Be aware of what could go wrong. Keep in mind that the interviewer wants to make a match and would prefer to favor you than to screen you out. Your chances for success are good.	Don't dwell on the potential for failure, but be alert to possible pitfalls.
Positivism	Try to minimize feelings of bitterness or frustration you may have as a result of prior job experiences or a difficult job search. Focus on the positives: the fact that you're making an effort to advance your career or that each interview brings you one step closer to a new job.	Don't try to deny or hide your negative feelings completely. If handled carefully, you can sometimes be candid about negative experiences. Remember, putting too much of a positive spin on some inherently negative situations can look dishonest.
Enthusiasm	Treat each interview as an interesting opportunity to learn something about an organization, other people, and even yourself. Look at it as an enjoyable experience, a chance to have a pleasant conversation with a fellow human being. Most importantly, treat it as a chance to start an exciting new chapter in your career and your life.	Don't confuse a pleasant social interaction with a serious meeting of the minds. Remember your agenda and be strategic. Don't get lost in unfocused conversation. And don't overwhelm the interviewer with too much enthusiasm and energy—it can look phony.

Bright Idea

Ask current or former bosses how they perceive your ability to handle the balance of power in a working relationship. Then apply their comments to your role in the interviewing relationship and see where you could use some improvement.

The balance of power

In addition to keeping your emotions and overall approach balanced, you need to strive for a balance of power in the interview. As mentioned before, you do have the right to take some control in the interview. You are there to interview the prospective employer, not just to be interviewed. Only when you have some of the power in the interviewing relationship can you collect the information you need to assess whether you want to work there. You also need control to get your point across, to communicate your asset statements as described in Chapter 4, "Your Marketing Plan's Secret Weapon."

If your attitude is one of "I must be in total control of this interview," you will not only be sorely disappointed when you find out that's not possible, but you will also turn off the interviewer. Coming on too strong upsets the delicate balance of power. You will threaten the interviewer's authority if you're too assertive, but if you hold back too much, you will not be seen as an active participant in the problem-solving and troubleshooting that are cornerstones of an interview.

Anxiety and the interview process

Some degree of apprehension or anxiety is part of the normal range of emotions you may experience throughout your job search. While interviewing is not a game or an act, it can seem at times like playing a part in the school play. You might feel that you're going to be on stage having to deliver a stellar performance. For that reason, it is not at all uncommon to experience some pre-interview performance anxiety or to be struck by stage fright once the meeting is underway. To deal with nervousness, you need to know why it occurs in the first place so you can possibly prevent it from happening.

Viewing the interview as a performance is one common cause of interviewing anxiety. A classic definition of performance anxiety, or "stage fright," is that offered by Mark Leary in *Social Anxiety*: stage fright = the importance of the consequences of the performance ÷ the prediction of a successful performance.

In other words, if you have your heart set on working for a particular company and worry that you're not going to do well in the interview there, then you are likely to experience stage fright. When the stakes are high and you have a lot to lose, you'll probably be nervous. But if you expect to give a peak performance, then you might not be so nervous, even if the stakes are high—much like an Olympic athlete who doesn't choke under pressure.

Related to the issue of performance anxiety is the idea that you are putting yourself on the line to be judged. Being evaluated as a candidate for employment is not the same as having your worth as a person assessed, but many job seekers confuse the two. Certainly, an interview is an assessment in some sense (but not necessarily of your personal worth), and it is one that brings the possibility of rejection or failure. Any doubts about your ability to interview well or the strength of your qualifications can lead to such fears.

Interviewing is a wild card, in many ways. You can prepare and practice all you want, but there will still be variables outside your control. Knowing that the hiring authorities' decision is subject

 Watch Out!

Some anxiety you experience before an interview might have nothing to do with your job search at all. Think about what other aspects of your life are causing you stress and take action against the problems. You need all your mental energy for interviews.

A Special Word About Nerves and Group Interviews

It's especially easy for your nerves to flare up when in a group interview, whether you are a single candidate interviewed by a panel or are part of a group of candidates interviewed by one or more people. Establishing rapport, maintaining eye contact, and reading body language are just a few of the challenges of group interviews.

Group interviews are akin to public speaking. You are expected to answer questions in front of other candidates and/or to address your replies to an audience of more than one. Sometimes you might even be required to conduct an actual presentation if you are interviewing for a training job or a position that would require making sales or management presentations. Countless studies have shown that public speaking consistently surpasses death as Americans' No. 1 fear. So, it's no wonder that the thought of a group interview can get those gastrointestinal butterflies fluttering.

Fortunately, you don't have to let yourself be terrified by group interviews. Try to find a "friend" in the group. Choose the interviewer (or fellow candidate) who has the most inviting demeanor—perhaps a friendly face, open body language, or positive reactions to your comments— and glance at that person whenever you feel the sweaty palms coming on. Say to yourself, "He likes me" or "She seems to agree with what I'm saying." If you can also block out any negative thoughts about how the others are reacting to you, the positive self-talk will be even more effective. Many of the additional tips for dealing with nerves on the following pages will also work well in group situations.

to personal whims, organizational politics, and even large-scale factors such as the economy or fluctuations in your industry can be daunting. There's no denying that interviewing involves an element of luck, and that realization can be nerve-wracking.

Combating pre-interview nervousness

Simply telling yourself not to be nervous or having well-meaning friends or family say "Oh, I know you'll do fine," just isn't sufficient when nervousness strikes before an interview. The thoughts and feelings that accompany anxiety are powerful, and the physical symptoms are all too obvious. To combat these, you must learn, practice, and employ proven strategies. Many surefire approaches to dealing with nerves are provided in the following sections.

Channel your nervous energy into positive action

Instead of wallowing in self-destructive thoughts and feelings, do something. Pour more time and energy into research or taking stock of your assets and less time into unproductive worrying. You can also practice for your interviews, rehearsing what you might say and how you'll say it.

Reflect on your achievements

If you dutifully prepared your asset statements but then put them aside, it's time to pull them back out. Reviewing the strengths, skills, and accomplishments that you have to offer an employer can give your self-confidence the rejuvenating boost it needs to calm your nerves.

Try to have other irons in the fire

That way, not too much rides on any one interview. There will undoubtedly be times when one interview takes on monumental proportions, and you feel as if getting the job (or not) will make or break your career. It is normal for such situations to come up occasionally, but if you approach every interview as though it were the first, last, and only one that mattered, you're

Bright Idea

Approximately 19 million Americans suffer from an anxiety disorder, according to the National Institute of Mental Health. If your nervousness is extreme and debilitating, you might have social anxiety. Turn to www.nimh.nih.gov to learn more.

putting too heavy a burden on your shoulders. You should always have at least a few opportunities in the works. Your job search should be a bit like the ocean tides; when one set of waves hits the beach and disappears, another should follow. If one interview doesn't work out, you can look forward to the next one—or at least you should have lots of feelers out to get more interviews.

Know when to stop preparing for the interview

As you might have experienced during college, it usually doesn't pay to cram right up until the last minute. You need some time to decompress, relax, and let the information you've studied sink in. This downtime also lets you assess how prepared you are for the interview and can calm your nerves if you discover that you are in good shape. Also, try to do something enjoyable and not work-related just before the interview (when time permits). You might get together for coffee with a friend, browse in a bookstore, go for a walk, or do whatever works for your schedule and location.

Don't rush getting to the interview

No matter how you spend your time just before the interview, it is absolutely essential that you avoid a last-minute rush to make the appointment on time. There might be nothing more nerve-wracking than worrying about traffic, a public transportation delay, or getting lost on your way to an interview.

Use classic stress-reduction techniques

Try controlled breathing, muscle relaxation, and visualization. These techniques include:

- Take deep, slow breaths, focusing on and feeling the air entering and leaving your body. For an added benefit, breathe in through your nose and out through your mouth, hearing the air almost whistle its way out through your teeth. Be sure not to take such deep breaths that you start to hyperventilate!

- To relax yourself physically, which usually leads to mental relaxation, close your eyes and concentrate on relaxing every part of your body. Start with your toes and work your way up to the top of your head. It sometimes helps to tighten each muscle first and then loosen it so that you can feel the relaxation in a more pronounced way.

- You can guide yourself in a simple visualization exercise by closing your eyes and picturing yourself in a position that you would define as success. You might see yourself shaking the hand of the interviewer at the end of the meeting, satisfied that you've done your best. You might also see yourself placing the phone call to accept a job offer or entering your office on the first day of the new job.

Keep some perspective

Some job seekers get their hearts and minds set on a particular job and feel that their entire future rides on one interview. What a burden! If you find yourself becoming anxious midstream, try to put the interview in perspective. This is not the last interview you will ever have. You are not interviewing at the last company on earth or with the greatest company on earth. If you fail, you will not lose your friends, your spouse, or your dog.

Just the facts

- Don't just research the organization where you'll be interviewing. Research the position itself, the interviewer(s), the overall career field, and the industry or sector.

- Consult with people—not just books, Web sites, and databases—when seeking information.

- Be prepared to discuss topics not directly related to the job, such as current events or your hobbies and interests.

- Prepare an Information Gems form for each organization and review it before each interview.

- Tailor your marketing strategy (the strengths and asset statements relevant to the employer) for each interview.

- Dress one notch up in formality from the organization's dress code, and when in doubt about what to wear, ask the human resources department or "spy" on workers going in and out of the job location.

- Developing the right mental attitude is just as important as researching the prospective employer and preparing your asset statements.

GET THE SCOOP ON...
Interviewing styles and how to deal with them ▪
Navigating group and panel interviews ▪
Surviving a stress interview ▪ Why preparation is
critical for behavioral interviews ▪
Unconventional interview settings ▪ Psyching-
out the psychological tests ▪ Mastering skills
assessments ▪ What you need to know about
drug testing

Types of Interviews and How to Handle Them

No two interviews are exactly alike, but you can expect that your interview will fit into certain typical patterns. This chapter describes the various formats, settings, and styles of questioning that you might encounter and offers strategies for making the most of each one.

Interviewing styles

Recruiters and hiring managers who know their stuff have a repertoire of interviewing techniques from which to choose. The following pages describe the most popular interviewing styles: behavior-based, traditional, conversational, and stress. You might find that your interviews combine a little of each style, or perhaps start with one approach and then switch gears midstream. For the sake of explanation, this chapter approaches them as four discrete approaches.

309

Bright Idea

To get a sneak peak at what's on that clipboard in the interviewer's lap, take a look at some of the books recruiters read to learn how to interview. (See the "Recruiting & Staffing—Hiring Perspective" section of the online Bonus Appendix 2.)

The behavior-based interview

Behavior-based interviewing (also called "behavioral" or "situational" interviewing) has been all the rage in the world of hiring for a number of years now. Some companies are known for conducting only behavior-based interviews, so from your research and networking you might know for certain that you are going into a behavioral interview. If not, it's a good idea to be prepared for one just in case.

In behavior-based interviews you're asked to discuss your actual behavior in a variety of real-life or hypothetical circumstances. The interviewer is looking for evidence of your achievements and skills more than for details of your job duties. The following questions give you an idea of how this type of interview might sound. After each behavior-based question, a second question shows the alternative nonbehavioral—or traditional—way the same issue might be addressed.

Behavioral: Tell me about a time when you had to manage a team of people who didn't want to work together.

Traditional: What's your management style? or How do you approach team-building?

Behavioral: Tell me about a stressful situation you have faced and how you handled it.

Traditional: How do you handle stress?

Behavioral: A customer is threatening to pull his account from our company because of a billing snafu. What would you do to keep him?

Traditional: Tell me about your customer relations or account
　　management experience.

　As you can see, behavior-based questions require you to give
hard evidence of your skills, experience, and personal qualities—
not just talk in generalities.

Behavior-based interviews—the pros

Looking at the pros and cons of behavior-based interviews, let's
start with what's good about them. If you're well prepared, then
a behavioral interview is the best thing that could happen to
your job search. You can be sure that the interviewer will get a
complete picture of not just what you claim to offer, but what
you really can do and how you can add value. This type of interview can also be more stimulating and interesting, unlike the
rather dull format of the traditional interview or the less challenging conversational one (traditional and conversational
interviews are described in the sections that follow). Also, this
type of interview provides clues to the employer's needs and
goals because the situations you're asked to talk about are likely
to reflect ones that are commonly found in that organization.

Behavior-based interviews—the cons

With behavioral interviews, lack of preparation spells disaster.
Thinking of examples off the top of your head is often difficult,
so you need to develop a versatile set of examples before you're
put on the spot to come up with them. You also need to conduct
sufficient research on the prospective employer and individual
interviewer to reply effectively to the hypothetical situations
posed. Knowing what the interviewer is looking for helps you

 Bright Idea

If you can't think of an example in a behavior-based interview, turn the question around to be a hypothetical situation and describe what you would do if
faced with such a situation.

know which of your asset statements to use when discussing what you would do in a particular situation.

Strategies for a behavior-based interview

Luckily for you (if you did the exercises in Chapter 4), solid asset statements are just about all you need to ace a behavior-based interview. But, don't get so caught up in describing your past accomplishments that you forget to talk about what you could do for the employer in the near future. Link your past achievements to the needs of the employer, as best you can discern them from your pre-interview research or questions you ask during the interview.

Don't go off on a tangent when talking about your past achievements. Only hit the highlights, focusing on the qualities you demonstrated in that situation and the actions you took to bring about particular results.

The traditional interview

Traditional interviews are sort of the "do-it-by-the-book" type of interview. They are likely to be highly structured, with the interviewer following a clearly defined protocol for what to ask and when to ask it. In a traditional interview, the interviewer directs the course of the conversation. He or she fires off questions that aren't particularly thought provoking but are simply straightforward inquiries into your experience and skills. Most commonly found at the early screening stage; they are usually first interviews conducted by a human resources representative or by someone in the department in which you would be working but who is not real high up on the food chain. That's because the traditional interview will only get the employer so far. From that

Bright Idea

Interviewers often make a point of keeping a poker face, so don't assume that a neutral expression signals displeasure with your responses. Try to remain confident even if you're not getting any positive feedback through body language.

interview, they'll know that you have the basic qualifications to do the job and that you are reasonably articulate, but the questions posed don't let them dig very deep to find out how you'll add value or to get to know you as a person.

The typical flow of a traditional interview might go something like this:

- The interviewer begins with small talk to put you at ease and to establish rapport.

- Some interviewers next move right into describing the position and/or discussing the organization itself. Others save that until the end.

- Next you might find yourself confronted with that wide-open, often dreaded opening line, "So, tell me about yourself. . ." (How to answer that question is covered in Chapter 13.)

- What follows is usually a review of your résumé and questioning you about its contents, including work experience, education, and credentials. This is where you might hear such comments as "Tell me more about your role as a call center manager at XYZ Company. . ." or "What sort of courses did you take as a communications major?"

- The interviewer then might move into a discussion of your capabilities, asking you to describe your skills and personal qualities. You might be asked some of the classic old questions such as "What three adjectives best describe you?" or "How would your last boss describe you?" or "How do you function under pressure?" (These and many other questions are discussed in Chapter 13.)

- The interview closes with a chance for you to ask questions about the position, the organization, or the hiring process.

- Before parting company, the interviewer might provide some information about the next steps in the process, such as if and when you could be called back for another interview, how many more candidates are to be interviewed, and so on. (The "Starting Your Follow-up Before the Interview Ends" section of Chapter 15 covers ways in which you can elicit this information if it is not volunteered.)

Traditional interviews—the pros

Traditional interviews are relatively easy to prepare for and to deal with because the line of questioning is straightforward and follows a logical progression. Rarely are these interviews stressful (other than causing the normal amount of interview jitters), nor will you be thrown many curve balls. This type of interview also works in your favor in that it is likely to be thorough, so the interviewer probably will gather most of the necessary information about your qualifications without you having to worry about working it into the conversation.

Traditional interviews—the cons

Traditional interviews can be too structured, making it more of a challenge to work your own agenda into the interviewer's agenda. This type of interview puts you in the role of a somewhat passive, powerless job seeker with the interviewer calling all the shots about what is discussed and when. Having the opportunity to ask questions only at the end is also problematic because it keeps you from being able to assess the employer's needs as you go along and get the interviewer into more of a peer-to-peer dialogue. Also, because it is not likely to be very conversational, an interview based on this somewhat mechanical approach might not let the interviewer get a feel for you as a person.

Strategies for a traditional interview

To make a traditional interview a more effective process for both you and the interviewer, keep the following strategies in mind.

- Take the initiative to be an equal player in the discussion. Try to get a dialogue going by asking questions throughout the interview rather than waiting until the end. And, subtly steer the conversation toward topics that you want to be sure to touch on to best showcase your selling points.

- Because you will not be specifically asked for examples that demonstrate your assets, you have to volunteer examples. For example, don't just say three adjectives that describe you. State the adjectives then tell a short story that shows how you demonstrated those qualities or skills. Use your asset statements!

- Find some common interest on which you can build rapport so that you make a human connection with the interviewer.

The conversational interview

In a conversational interview, you might feel like you're chatting with a friend or professional colleague instead of a prospective employer. Rather than following a question-and-answer format, the interview flows informally from one topic to the next, as in a typical conversation. The interviewer might talk at length about the position or the organization as a whole and might want to discuss current events in the industry or world at large.

Conversational interviews often take a circuitous route with no apparent agenda. They are sometimes conducted by an unskilled interviewer or a disorganized person, or perhaps by someone who was asked at the last minute to interview you and isn't prepared or is preoccupied with other obligations. Conversational interviews are, however, conducted by some experienced, trained interviewers who simply prefer to gather information in the context of a conversation rather than a question-and-answer format.

 Watch Out!

Don't assume that conversational interviewers don't know what they're doing. They might be judging you with a more critical eye than you suspect or lulling you into a false sense of security with the relaxed conversation.

Conversational interviews—the pros

Conversational interviews are often more relaxed in tone and thus more comfortable for the interviewee than any other type. Rarely are they stressful (unless you find making conversation to be taxing). They don't pose much of a challenge because you aren't being grilled with tough questions. And, the interviewer is likely to get a good feel for you as a person because you're communicating in a more casual way and discussing thoughts and opinions.

Conversational interviews—the cons

Conversational interviews can lull you into complacency, leading you to forget what you came to talk about—that is, how you can add value—and leaving the interview with nothing more accomplished than a pleasant round of chit-chat. Furthermore, interviewers who use the conversational approach might not collect the hard data they need to make an informed decision. You might find that they end up selecting a candidate who won the congeniality contest rather than emerged as the most qualified.

Strategies for a conversational interview

To avoid having a conversational interview turn into nothing more than a chitchat session, employ the strategies recommended below.

- Make a concerted effort to work your agenda—your asset statements and how you can meet the employer's needs—into the dialogue.

- Use conversation topics as springboards for discussing your assets rather than getting caught up in a conversation that goes nowhere.

- Pay special attention to questions you ask, such as, "What qualities do you need in the person who will do this job?" By asking the right questions, you force the interviewer to address the issue of what's needed and how you might meet that need.

- Watch your tongue. The rapport and comfortable atmosphere in a conversational interview might lead you to open up too much or say something foolish.

The stress interview

A stress interview is easy to spot. It's the kind that has you squirming in your seat, tugging at your collar, and developing sweaty palms. It is designed to intimidate and to find out how you operate under pressure.

In a stress interview, the interviewer might seem angry, gruff, disinterested, or distracted. You might find that almost everything you say is met with disagreement and that your opinions and claims are challenged at every turn. A stress interviewer might probe for information until you feel like the victim of the week on "60 Minutes."

Stress might also be created through skillful use of silence. You reply to a question or make a statement, and the interviewer stares at you with a blank expression for longer than the normal pause in a conversation. (See the strategy tips that follow for ways to deal with unnatural silences.)

Another way to know you are in a stress interview is if the room seems unusually uncomfortable. You might have a harsh, artificial light or sunlight shining in your eyes, be seated in an uncomfortable chair or one that is very low, or find the room extremely hot or cold.

An additional way stress is introduced into an interview is through tough questions that seem like tricks. The interviewer might ask you to perform an impossible task, such as open a window that isn't designed to open. Or, you might be asked a

 Bright Idea

When an interviewer seems disinterested or argumentative, don't take it personally. Remember that you might simply be in a stress interview, so his or her reaction is only a test, not a personal vendetta against you.

mind-teaser question such as how many manhole covers would be found on the streets between your home and interview location or how many trees are in your town's largest park.

> 66 A high station in life is earned by the gallantry with which appalling experiences are survived with grace. 99
>
> —Tennessee Williams

Such tactics are fairly common when interviewing for stressful jobs or for high-level ones in which you are likely to face pressured situations often. They are not unheard of, however, as a way of weeding out applicants for jobs that are not at the high end of the stress scale but simply require that you be assertive, confident, and good at thinking on your feet.

Stress interviews—the pros

If you handle it well, you can really shine in a stress interview. This format lets the interviewer see you in action, not just spouting pat answers to routine questions. A stress interview keeps you on your toes, so for those who like a challenge, this type of interview can actually be fun.

Stress interviews—the cons

For those who don't thrive on the adrenaline rush that stress interviews bring, or those who are the least bit doubtful about their abilities, stress interviews can obviously be quite unpleasant. Also, it can be difficult to determine whether you really are in a stress interview, as opposed to dealing with an interviewer who simply dislikes you or is in a bad mood.

Strategies for stress interviews

To keep your cool during a stress interview and show the employer that you can pull through under pressure, use these techniques.

- Don't panic. No matter which curve balls come your way, whether it's a room that's overly warm, an off-the-wall question, or an adversarial interviewer, retain your composure at all times. The interviewer's primary objective is usually to see how easily you get rattled.

- Deal with silences by keeping a confident, pleasant look on your face and maintaining eye contact until the interviewer speaks again. Don't shift around in your chair, rub your hands together, clench your fists from nervous tension, bounce your foot up and down on the floor, or let any other fidgety body language give you away. If the silence goes on to the point of absurdity, ask whether the interviewer would like you to elaborate on the last point you made.

- If asked a mind-teaser question, don't worry so much about the answer as about the thought process you would use to get to an answer. You're usually not expected to know the answer but are expected to show how you would find it, demonstrating logical thinking and resourcefulness.

Interviewing venues and formats

The classic format and venue for an interview is the one in which you interview with just one person at a time on-site at an organization where you've not worked before. But, what happens when that interview takes place by phone or with a group of people? Those and other twists on the traditional format are discussed here.

Group interviews

In a group interview, you and a few other candidates are interviewed simultaneously by one or more interviewers. This approach is often used for positions in which teamwork is

 Watch Out!

When you've had a panel interview, don't try to get away with writing a thank-you note only to the head decision-maker. You must write to each person individually.

particularly important, or where leadership style is critical. Group interviews not only let the employer observe how you operate in a group, they also save the employer time and money.

Group interviews—the pros

You get to demonstrate your capabilities in a setting that simulates the workplace. You might also find that you don't experience some of the pressure found in a one-on-one interview because the interviewers' focus does not rest solely on you.

Group interviews—the cons

You have to work extra hard to distinguish yourself within the group, making sure that your assets clearly stand out. You might also have to deal with some overt competition.

Strategies for group interviews

To outshine the competition but still come across as a team player, try these strategies.

- Realize that you are more likely being observed to see what role you adopt in the group and how you behave on a team than having your specific comments and answers judged too closely.

- Figure out which qualities the interviewers are seeking— such as leadership, teamwork, or organization—and play that part.

- Be courteous and helpful to your fellow candidates.

- Balance a cooperative, collaborative approach to the task or discussion with the more self-serving comments necessary to promote your candidacy. For example, say things such as, "I think John makes a good point. When I've faced similar situations, I handled it by. . ."

Panel interviews

In panel interviews, you are the sole candidate meeting with more than one interviewer. These interviews are typically formal in tone and usually are conducted by an official search committee, as opposed to a collection of colleagues who just happen to be free to speak with you at the same time. You are most likely to come across panel interviews in academia, government, and for senior-level positions in the corporate world. This approach is also used in situations in which a job would require you to make presentations to groups of people, such as in consulting, sales, and training.

Panel interviews—the pros

Panel interviews have a logistical advantage over one-on-one interviews. Although it may be intimidating to meet with several people at once, chances are you would have to meet each one individually at some point, so at least you benefit from the convenience of meeting them all together. Additionally, panel interviews are often part of a more formal—and, therefore, more organized and efficient—recruiting process. As such, you might get an answer sooner than when you have to meet with each decision-maker individually, which often drags out the process. Also, you don't have to keep repeating your story and your asset statements because everyone hears them at the same time.

Panel interviews—the cons

Obviously, panel interviews can be intimidating. I'm reminded of a client who told me about an interview he had for a high school guidance counselor position. He found himself seated in a straight chair looking up at a panel of faculty and administrators perched high on a dais, even though he had been told he would just be meeting with the school principal and "might chat with a few teachers." Although he quickly composed himself and did fine, he said he felt as if he were testifying to a grand jury.

Panel interviews are also a challenge in that you must mesh with multiple personality types and communication styles, not to mention various personal styles with regard to formality, seriousness, and dress.

Strategies for panel interviews

The tips below will help you treat every member of a panel interview like a VIP.

- Vary your eye contact and body position to alternate your focus on the different members of the panel so that each panel member feels he or she is being paid attention by you.

- Determine who is the head of the panel, if there is one, and defer slightly to that person while paying sufficient attention to the rest of the group.

- When answering one interviewer's question, focus on that person for most of your reply and then vary eye contact.

Internal interviews

An interesting twist on the interviewing process occurs when you're applying for a position in an organization where you are already employed. An internal interview might result from the initiative you take to find a more satisfying position at your company, or from the efforts of a superior who sees your advancement potential and recommends you for a better job. Internal interviews are also common in companies that are undergoing restructuring or downsizing. If your position is eliminated, you might be offered the opportunity to apply for other positions within the organization.

Internal interviews—the pros

Whether you're meeting with someone you know well or someone with whom you've not had contact, you are at least interviewing in familiar territory. This makes the whole process easier for you in terms of research, mental preparation, building your case, and the logistics of scheduling and getting to interviews. Because you already know—or should know—the organization's needs, culture, and goals, you have an advantage over candidates coming from the outside. Also, the interviewer might see you as a natural choice because you are a known quantity.

Internal interviews—the cons

Some of the advantages just described might also work against you. The fact that you are a known quantity can be detrimental if your employer is looking for some "fresh blood." No matter how innovative your ideas or how high your energy level, you're not a new face—and that can be a major stumbling block. Organizational politics also might be at work. If you've ever rubbed anyone the wrong way, whether intentionally or unknowingly, the slight can come back to

> 66 When interviewing internally, don't assume the job is 'in the bag' just because you come highly recommended from within the organization. You have to interview as impressively as you would for an external interview. 99
>
> —Kevin Waxman, Vice President, Career Services, JPMorgan Chase

haunt you when you try to make a move internally. No matter how stellar your track record with your current employer, a co-worker with a grudge can do some significant damage to your reputation and candidacy.

Strategies for internal interviews

To make the most of internal interviews consider the tips below.

- Don't take an internal interview any less seriously than an external one. Build your case with powerful asset statements, as you would in a less familiar environment.

- Don't skip the research phase just because you think you know your company inside and out. Speak to key players in the organization to find out what's really going on in the area where you would be working, or to learn about the concerns and objectives of upper management, if you are not already privy to such information. (If your desire to make a move is confidential, you can still have these conversations carefully without letting anyone know why you want the information.)

Bright Idea

If you interview with several people at a particular company on the same day, don't assume that everyone will compare notes in detail at the end of the day. Start fresh for each new meeting and be willing to tell your story all over again. Never say, "I told that to the last person...."

- If you are trying to advance to a higher level within your organization or transfer to a different functional role, pay special attention to your image. Make sure that your attire and demeanor fit the culture of the area or level to which you aspire and be prepared to build a strong case—with concrete evidence—for why you can handle the new responsibilities.

Follow-up interviews

After you have had an initial interview, you might make the cut and be called back for one or more follow-up meetings. Although an offer is sometimes extended after just one interview, more often it is necessary that you come back to meet more people who have a say in the hiring decision.

At the follow-up interview stage, rarely are you asked for basic information about your background. The interview is more likely to focus on the issue of fit and commitment. People you meet at that follow-up stage want to get to know you as a person. They already know you meet the basic requirements of the job. Now they want to see whether you would fit in and if you really want the job. They also want to make sure that their good first impression of you wasn't a fluke.

If you are called back for a third or fourth follow-up interview, it's usually safe to assume that the pool of applicants has narrowed to as few as two or three, or that you are the sole candidate but are just having to go through the formality of meeting more key people. Don't be complacent, though! Keep fighting for the job as if you were still trying to get your foot in the door.

Follow-up interviews—the pros

Follow-up interviews are an obvious good thing. You've been asked back, so you're moving in the right direction. Beyond that, consider these reasons why follow-up interviews are a welcome opportunity.

- You've gotten through the first hoop and no longer have the challenge of having to prove that you can do the job and will add value. You now just have to be yourself and see whether the fit is right.

- You get to ask even more pointed questions about the organization and the position. This helps you better evaluate whether you even want the job, and if you decide that you do, the answers to your questions give you further insight into the needs of the employer—insight that's valuable as you try to clinch the deal.

Follow-up interviews—the cons

While it may seem hard to imagine, there is a downside to follow-up interviews. Consider these pitfalls:

- You can too easily develop a false sense of confidence, assuming that you have secured a job offer and that the call-back is just a formality.

- Or, you might put undue pressure on yourself because you know you're close to an offer.

Strategies for follow-up interviews

To get yourself one step closer to closing the deal, approach follow-up interviews with the strategies below.

- Stay on your toes; don't take the interview too casually just because you've gotten this far.

- Pay particular attention to establishing rapport and showing that you can fit in as that's one of the main factors being judged at this point.

Moneysaver

If you're expected to foot the bill for traveling to an out-of-town interview, ask whether anyone from the company will be traveling on business in your area around that time, and see whether you could arrange for that person to meet with you locally instead.

- Be assertive in your requests for information about where things stand, such as how many other people are being considered and when they expect to make a decision.

- Be sure to ask about any doubts the interviewer might have with your candidacy. At this point, you can be knocked out of the running over one seemingly minor deficit that you could easily have corrected if you only had known about it.

- Ask for the job! Don't hold back on your enthusiasm for the position. Of course, you don't want to sound desperate or so enamored with the organization or position that you would work for nothing. This can do obvious damage to your bargaining power when it comes time to negotiate compensation. But, there's no need to play coy at this stage. Let them know you want the job.

Interview settings

Where an interview takes place raises important questions about which communication strategies, attire, and etiquette are appropriate for the setting. How you conduct yourself during an interview in a quiet corporate conference room may not be appropriate for an interview that takes place at a bustling job fair or by telephone. The following are typical—and not so typical—sites for interviews along with tactics for navigating them.

On-site interviewing

The most common place for an interview is at the prospective employer's location. Although the employer in this case has the "home court advantage," this setting presents few special challenges. Just be sure that you know where you're going and how long it will take to get there.

On-campus interviews

If in college or graduate school, you might have the chance to participate in an on-campus recruiting program in which you meet with employers who come to your institution to spend the day interviewing graduating students. In this case, you have the home court advantage and might find that meeting in a familiar spot is not only convenient but comforting. On-campus interviews tend to be fairly brief because several interviews are usually tightly scheduled into the day. They also tend to be standardized so that uniform information can be collected throughout the day. You're more likely to find that the interviewer's approach is traditional or behavioral rather than stress or conversational.

An important element in your strategy for this setting is to distinguish yourself from the pack. On-campus recruiting becomes something of an interviewing mill for the prospective employer, so all candidates blur together by the end of the day. And, because the format of each of the interview is roughly the same, there is even less for the interviewer's memory to latch onto.

Be sure to make good use of your asset statements and also try to steer the conversation away from academic topics such as grades and what classes you've taken. Although your academic background is important to address, many on-campus recruiters do so at the expense of discussing your work history and your extracurricular experiences.

Conferences and conventions

At some professional conferences or trade shows, you might have the opportunity to interview with employers from all around the country or the world. Some conferences provide a designated time and place for interviews as a formal part of the agenda. If not, you might have to arrange interviews yourself.

Although you might have to deal with more than the usual distractions—unless the interview is held in a private room—conferences can be a nice place to interview. The simple fact that you're attending the event shows your initiative and commitment to expanding your knowledge, so the interviewer is likely to view you favorably before the meeting even begins. In addition, the shared experience of being participants in the same conference provides common ground with your interviewer and plenty of conversation topics for your encounter.

Job fairs

Job fairs are not just window-shopping events where you browse exhibitors' booths to pick up literature about various employers and find out for which sorts of positions they're hiring. They also provide the opportunity to have mini-interviews with representatives of numerous organizations under one roof. As with conferences and conventions, job fairs offer a slightly more relaxed environment in which to talk with prospective employers. You know that the employers are looking to hire—otherwise, they wouldn't be attending the fair—and they appreciate the initiative you've taken to attend the event. Instead of just sitting home sending out cover letters and résumés, you're getting out and making direct contact, which is an effort that many employers appreciate.

If you do get to sit down with a recruiter for 10 or 15 minutes at a fair, keep a few pointers in mind.

- Try to block out the distractions of noise and people around you and focus on the person to whom you're talking.

- Realize that the recruiter's time is limited, so you have to make a big impact in a short period of time. Be sure to cut to the chase, and if possible, prepare in advance what you want to say to various recruiters so that you have one or two achievable objectives for each meeting. Using your self-marketing sound bite is key here.

Bright Idea

When following up with someone you've met at a job fair, be sure to send some documentation, such as your résumé, portfolio, or other work samples— not just a thank-you note—so that the recruiter has something tangible to remember you by.

- Keep in mind that employers might be meeting with many candidates during the job fair, so you need to make yourself memorable. Add *flavor* to your story with lively anecdotes and power words and phrases. And, of course, be sure to work in at least one asset statement.

- Find out who else at the organization, if anyone, is involved in hiring for the types of positions for which you're looking. Get the names of any key decision-makers with whom you could follow up so that you're not relying just on the representative at the fair to advocate on your behalf.

Interviewing over meals

You might find yourself having breakfast, lunch, or dinner with a busy recruiter or employer who has only those times to interview you, or who uses this as a supplementary activity to a traditional interview in the office. Interviews over meals take place on neutral territory (unless you are taken to the interviewer's private club or regularly frequented restaurant), so the experience can be less intimidating than in an office. Getting out of the office also creates a more natural atmosphere for getting to know you as a person and for you to learn more about the interviewer.

But, for those who panic when they have to choose between three different sizes of spoons and face cherry tomatoes that just won't get on a fork, interviewing over meals can be terrifying. The solution is simple: Learn the basics of table manners and watch what you order. Some of the books listed in the "Image/ Etiquette/Attire" section of the online Bonus Appendix 2 can help you do just that. And for those of you who already know your fish fork from your salad fork but still find mealtime interviewing intimidating, consider these quick tips:

- Keep an eye on your drink glasses (and those of your companions) at all times and limit your hand and arm gestures so that you minimize the risk of knocking over a glass and sending iced tea splashing onto your interviewer's favorite tie.

- Order wisely, avoiding foods that are difficult to eat, including long noodle pastas, some salads, oversized sandwiches, and anything you have to peel or eat with your hands. Stick with simple things you can eat with a knife and fork in small, manageable bites such as vegetables, fish, chicken breast, steak, and so on.

- Don't drink alcohol—at least 99 percent of the time you shouldn't. At times, however, your interviewer(s) might order a drink at an evening meal, and you would seem like a nonconformist if you didn't take one. If you usually are a nondrinker, then you don't have to have one. But if you do enjoy a drink and your hosts are having one, then there's no harm in doing so as long as you limit your intake so that you can keep your wits about you.

By the way, you might come across interviewing advice that suggests that if the circumstances are appropriate for consuming alcohol, then at least order something light, such as a white wine spritzer. Well, picture yourself out for dinner at a steak-and-potatoes kind of restaurant being interviewed by a table of robust people downing scotches and bourbons. What do you think they would think if you order a dainty wine spritzer? Remember how important that old issue of fit is. I'm not advocating imbibing hard liquor if it's not your habit to do so—never feel pressured to drink alcohol at all or something stronger than you really want—but don't order what would be viewed as a "wimpy" drink just to be drinking something. You're probably better off having a soda!

In addition to being careful about what you order and how you conduct yourself at the table, be sure to follow the strategies suggested throughout this book for interviews in office settings. Just because a mealtime interview takes on a more casual, relaxed feel doesn't mean you shouldn't use your asset statements, powerful language, and all the other ammunition at your disposal.

Telephone interviews

The telephone is frequently used as a way to screen applicants before devoting precious time to meeting with them in person, and it's also useful for interviewing candidates who are in another city or town. Hiring decisions rarely are based solely on a phone interview, however, so a phone interview is usually followed up by a face-to-face one.

Interviews over the phone not only are convenient for the interviewer, but they can work to your advantage as well. You don't have to agonize over what to wear or worry about your body language, and you can't be discriminated against based on your appearance or how old you look. You might also feel more relaxed in a phone interview because you are likely to be doing it from the familiar surroundings of your own home (or your office, if there is adequate privacy).

For every advantage, however, there is a downside. Obviously, all the nonverbal cues that are so important for reading the interviewer or for communicating part of your message are unavailable. Also, rapport is more difficult to establish when you're not looking each other in the eye. And, if you aren't thrilled with the sound of your voice, you might worry—and rightly so—that the interviewer will misjudge you based solely on how you sound.

By employing a few simple strategies, however, you can make the most of this interviewing format. (For more tips on telephone communication, consult some of the books listed in the "Communication—Oral" section of the online Bonus Appendix 2 and check out the tips in the online Bonus Chapter 1.)

Watch Out!

Just because your clothes won't be seen when you have a telephone interview doesn't mean you should dress like a slob. You may find that if you wear business attire—or at least something fairly pulled together—you will feel more confident and professional, which will come across in your voice.

- Stand up while talking to keep your energy level high but avoid pacing the floor—you might sound out-of-breath without realizing it.

- Keep notes handy to remind you of your asset statements and other points you want to make to build your case.

- Minimize all distractions by making sure that your background is quiet, and avoid technical interference by disabling call waiting and speaking from a well-functioning phone—preferably a land line rather than mobile phone.

- Be extra concise and avoid speech fillers such as "uh" and "um." Using these or being long-winded is more pronounced when you're on the phone because the listener has nothing to focus on but what you're saying.

- Be conscious of keeping your voice sounding positive and energetic and be sure to vary your pitch and tone.

Just the facts

- The most popular style of interviewing is the behavior-based approach, in which you give evidence of your behavior and achievements in actual past situations or describe what you would do in a hypothetical situation.

- If your interview has a structured question-and-answer format, as in a traditional interview, be sure to maintain an equal balance of power with the interviewer and work your asset statements into the conversation.

- Don't be lulled into complacency by a conversational interview. You're still being judged.

- When faced with a stress interview, the most important thing to do is stay composed and mentally sharp.

- Vary your strategy to fit the setting of each interview.

- Don't be intimidated by psychological tests. Remember that understanding how the test is constructed helps you affect the outcome.

- Due to the risk of false-positive results, you should be knowledgeable about how, why, where, and when drug tests are done.

Landing the Job and Moving Forward

GET THE SCOOP ON...
Strategies for acing any interview question ▪
A step-by-step guide to avoid sounding like a
robot giving canned answers ▪ What interviewers
really mean when they ask certain questions ▪
Tips for answering more than 90 of the most
commonly asked and less common questions

Typical and Not-so-typical Interview Questions

This is a dangerous chapter. Any time you see typical job interview questions and suggested responses written down on paper, there's a danger that you'll feel the need to memorize answers to every type of question you could face in an interview. That's just not possible because there is an infinite number of questions you could be asked. Plus, memorizing answers means you run the risk of sounding overly rehearsed and insincere. So, before you feel caught in a Catch-22 situation of never being able to prepare for everything you might face in an interview, yet knowing you need to do some preparation, but trying not to do too much lest you end up sounding robotic, let me put your mind at ease.

Sure, there is no way to anticipate every question you might face in a job interview—the possibilities are endless—but you can relax in knowing that there are basically only three questions being asked in any interview. No matter how an interview question is worded, almost every question is basically getting at one of the three bigger questions on the minds of employers: Can you do the job and add value? Will you fit in? Will you commit to the job and to this organization? As long as you know enough about your most marketable assets and each employer's culture and needs, you can answer these three questions. You'll see how this plays out as you read the sample questions explained throughout this chapter. First, however, let's examine some guiding principles to help you through any interview.

Guiding principles to get you through any interview

You're likely to have a lot on your mind as you go into an interview, but two simple sets of tips are just about all you need to be focusing on—six keys to effective strategy and six steps to fielding any question. I recommend that you jot these down on a small cheat sheet that you review right before going into an interview.

Six keys to acing the interview

The first set of tips consists of the six keys to an effective interviewing strategy. These are the main things to keep in mind as you conduct yourself throughout an interview:

1. *Remember you're talking to a fellow human being.* The person interviewing you is a human being. Simple as that. Be real, sincere, thoughtful, and relaxed.

2. *Put on your consultant's hat.* Go into every interview prepared to assess the employer's needs and show how you can meet those needs. In other words, do what consultants do. Consultants identify problems to be solved or challenges to be met and develop solutions to overcome problems and reach goals. That's what you're doing as a job seeker. The employer has needs; you're there to help.

3. *Maintain the balance of power.* Related to the concept of the consulting approach is to remember that you hold a great

deal of power during an interview. You are not a lowly job seeker desperate for a job but a talented professional with skills and expertise that can help the employer reach goals. Don't go so far as to be cocky, but do keep this in mind during the interviewing process.

4. *Make it a dialogue, not an interrogation.* No matter how structured an interview format might be, there is always room for a two-way dialogue. Try at all costs to keep interviews from turning into interrogations where you feel like you are having questions fired at you, and all you can do is fire back answers. Ask questions throughout the interview, showing that you are curious and interested about what's going on at that organization.

5. *Use your asset statements.* Remember that asset statements are key for distinguishing yourself from the competition. Anyone can give a decent answer to a question, but you set yourself apart from the pack by giving hard evidence of your assets through stories that are unique to you and your experience.

6. *Know when to stop talking.* It's so easy to talk yourself right into the ground. Rambling and being long-winded not only taxes the interviewer's attention span beyond its limits but also increases your chances of saying something you'll later regret having said. Concentrate on answering each question fully but stopping when you've said enough, which is usually after about 30 to 60 seconds, though, of course, that depends on the exact nature of what you're talking about and the overall time allotted for the whole interview.

 Bright Idea

Always read the latest issues of journals and online publications related to your field just before interviews to be able to sound knowledgeable and savvy about developments in your industry or profession.

Six steps to fielding any question

The next set of guiding principles to review as you go into each interview is a list of six steps to walk yourself through each time you're asked a question.

1. *Listen up!* First, be sure to listen to the interviewer(s). If you're at all nervous or preoccupied with making sure that your body language is appropriate or by any other distractors, you might forget to listen to the questions being asked. Before going into each interview, remind yourself that you need to concentrate on using your best listening skills.

2. *Determine what's being measured.* As soon as a question is asked, quickly analyze it in your mind to determine what the question really means. Figure out whether this is a can-you-add-value, will-you-fit-in, or will-you-commit kind of question. Think about what the employer is trying to get at so that your reply will be on point.

3. *Ask for clarification if needed.* If the question wasn't clear, don't be afraid to ask for some clarification. Try not to do this too often during an interview, but asking occasionally is fine.

4. *Pick an asset statement.* Call up an asset statement from your repertoire (as developed in Chapter 4) that you think best demonstrates the qualities, knowledge, or experience being measured by the question at hand. Remember that even if the interviewer does not explicitly ask you to give an example from your past, you should offer one anyway because examples—that is, your asset statements—provide evidence of the claims you make about yourself and your abilities.

5. *Answer the question.* Of course, you answer the question after determining what it's measuring and thinking about which aspects of your assets and background are most relevant.

6. *Pause after 30–60 seconds.* After you've given what you think is a sufficiently detailed reply, pause and ask the interviewer whether he or she would like you to elaborate.

Having the six strategic keys and the six steps in mind will help you ace any interview that comes your way no matter what sorts of questions are asked. Of course, you do need to do some additional preparation to make sure that you won't be caught off guard by some of the questions you might be asked. The remainder of this chapter covers sample questions and ways to respond.

Sample questions: can you do the job and add value?

Just about every interview will focus heavily on questions to determine whether you have the skills and experience necessary to do the job at hand and to look for clues to how you might go above and beyond the basic job requirements to make a real difference. The samples given here show some of the ways that recruiters and employers might try to get at that information. You'll see that these samples—plus all samples in subsequent sections of this chapter mix behavioral, situational (that is, hypothetical), and traditional/general questions. The reality is that almost all questions can be asked in any of those formats. The traditional-style question, "How do you solve problems?" is essentially the same as the behavioral-style, "Tell me about a problem you faced and how you resolved it," and as the hypothetical question, "How would you handle a problem such as. . .?"

So, for each of the samples you see in this chapter, realize that you might be asked that same question in a different format or with different wording, but that your approach for answering will be basically the same.

The résumé-based questions

The following questions are ones that have you elaborate on, explain, or summarize information on your résumé.

- **Tell me about yourself.**

"Tell me about yourself" occupies a place of honor in the Hall of Fame of difficult interview openers. Because it provides no parameters to guide a response, job seekers usually find this interview opener bewildering. Sometimes that reaction is unwarranted, as this is often an innocuous icebreaker, a simple conversation starter not meant to challenge you but intended to let you say a few words of your choosing. More often, however, "Tell me about yourself" is a calculated way of finding out how you organize your thoughts, how you articulate them, and on which information you choose to focus. The good news is that if you've prepared a self-marketing sound bite (see Chapter 3), then you have the makings of a powerful, concise reply. Just make a few adjustments to fit the situation, and you're all set. Here's how one job seeker's reply to "Tell me about yourself" sounds:

"First I'd like you to know that I'm really pleased to be here talking with you today because I'm confident I have what you're looking for and I've long admired the work you do here at XYZ Company. My family and I just moved here last month from Raleigh, North Carolina, where I had worked for 12 years in quality control and as a production manager for two furniture manufacturers. In my last position, I increased production 26 percent and cut costs 17 percent. I'm an effective team-builder, a good trouble-shooter and expediter, and a hard worker. And, I'd be happy to elaborate on any of those points if you'd like."

- **Summarize your career for me.**

The best way to respond to this is to treat it like the "Tell me about yourself" request but provide more details of your work history. Most candidates walk the interviewer through their résumés, basically narrating the written chronology of their career. This can get extremely boring and does nothing to market you. Instead, if you quickly give the chronology but weave in references to your key strengths, personal qualities, and accomplishments, the summary will be much more interesting and effective.

Watch Out!

Interviewers are often on the lookout for inconsistencies in your story, such as employment dates that don't add up or an incomplete account of what you did on a job, so be prepared to deal with any negative aspects of your background that they might get out of you.

▪ **Tell me more about your last job.**

This request is tailor-made for your asset statements, so it should be easy to answer. Start by providing a brief overview of your responsibilities and then describe in more detail two or three aspects of the job that are most relevant to the prospective employer. And, of course, talk about the skills you acquired or demonstrated while doing the job and how they might relate to the needs of the prospective employer. In other words, use your asset statements rather than simply reciting the job description off your résumé.

▪ **How did your last job change over time?**

This question is clearly getting at how adaptable and flexible you are. It's likely to signal that the organization you're interviewing with is undergoing change, or is about to, and they need to know whether you'll be able to handle it. They might also be looking for evidence that you have grown and developed, taking on new responsibilities and showing an ability to be innovative in the way you do your work. Reply to this one somewhat in the way that you would reply to "Tell me more about your last job" but be sure to comment on what you learned and the versatility you demonstrated as the job changed. If your last job didn't change much over time in terms of actual responsibilities, think long and hard about subtle ways it might have changed (new boss, new customers, anything at all that was new). Or speak about a job you held before that one that did change or require innovative approaches.

Looking for what you bring to the table in skills and knowledge

These questions ask you to speak about your subject matter expertise, skills, and talents to make sure that you really know what you're talking about when it comes to doing the sort of work for which you're applying.

- **What is your greatest strength? What are your greatest strengths?**
- **What are three adjectives that describe you?**
- **What are your three best qualities?**

No matter how they're worded, these questions are all asking you to hand the interviewer your top assets on a silver platter. The interviewer is saying, "Make my job easy. Show me that your top strengths match what I'm looking for." Select the most relevant assets you bring to the table and state them. Most importantly—and here's where most of your competition will fall short—give examples! Use your asset statements to provide evidence of these strengths.

Example: "Team-building is one of my top strengths. For example, at XYZ company I was selected to supervise a team that was not working together effectively. Productivity was way down in that group, and there'd been a lot of turnover. I met with the team members individually and as a group, getting input from each on what was going on. Bottom line was that no one had been listening to them. By hearing their concerns, I was able to resolve some conflicts and implement process changes that got them all on the same page working as a more motivated, cohesive team. Productivity increased 26 percent over the next 12 months."

- **What have you done to improve yourself?**
- **What have you learned in your career?**

These questions are basically getting at the same information. Pick two or three assets (remember that's the catch-all term for content knowledge, skills, and personal qualities) that are most relevant to the position at hand. Give examples of how you've grown and enhanced those assets in the recent past through formal or informal training, seeking a mentor, or just self-improvement efforts.

Questions about how you do your job

These questions take the previous category to the next level by probing into not just what you know but how you go about using your skills and knowledge. They let the employer glimpse how you operate and help them judge whether you know what you're doing.

- **Describe a method/approach/process you would use to do X.**
- **How do you plan out a project?**
- **How do you manage multiple priorities?**
- **What's your approach to problem-solving?**
- **Tell us about a time you anticipated and prevented a problem.**
- **How do you meet goals?**
- **How do you deal with upset customers/clients?**
- **How do you get teams motivated and working well together?**
- **Give me an example of a time when you had to be detail-oriented.**
- **Give me an example of a time you successfully dealt with a challenging situation.**
- **How would you handle this problem. . .?**

There are lots of ways to ask, but all of the questions are asking you to describe your methodology. Whether it's multi-tasking, problem-solving, process improvement, client relations, people management, or project management that's most relevant to the job for which you're applying, you're being asked to walk the interviewer through how you operate. There are two things to do to prepare for this. One is to make sure that you have a method to your madness—that you can articulate the methodology you use to do these things. It doesn't have to have a fancy name out of a textbook, although if it does, that's fine. You just have to be able to describe how you do these things. The next preparation step is to have an example. Remember that your asset statements are the key differentiator between you and the competition, so be sure that you not only describe your approach but also give examples of times when that approach has produced successful results.

- **How do you make decisions?**
- **Tell me about a difficult decision you've had to make.**

If asked the first question, turn it into a behavior-based question like the second statement by giving an example of a challenging decision you've made and describing the process you used. On the surface, your reply to this statement tells the interviewer what kinds of decisions you've dealt with in the past—and, thus, whether you are used to handling the kinds of issues that the job in question would entail. And, it lets the interviewer know how skilled you are at making decisions.

On a deeper level, it says something about your values and work style. You might describe a decision-making process that is autocratic or one that involves others. You might talk about the pressure and stress that accompanied a decision or a tug-of-war between head and heart.

 Bright Idea

To arrive at interviews at the right time, aim for being 30 minutes early to allow for unforeseen delays. If you do actually arrive that early, take a stroll around the block, wait in your car, sit in the building's lobby, or pass the time in some other way until about 10 or 15 minutes before your interview time.

To answer this question effectively, choose a decision that is similar to ones you would have to make on the target job. And, be conscious of the values and work style that you are exemplifying when describing your decision-making process.

▪ **On average, how many hours does it take per week to get your work done?**

Interviewers usually have multiple objectives in asking this question. First, they want to see how effective you are. If you begin to rant and rave about how many hours you work—thinking that you are making yourself sound very industrious—you might actually sound like you don't use your time efficiently during your regular business hours. If you do say that you work considerable overtime, make it clear that you do so because the workload calls for it—not because you're using the time to catch up.

Second, interviewers want to know whether you will fit into the collective work ethic at their organization. Do you seem willing and able to work long hours if required, or do you sound like you would do so only grudgingly?

Looking for evidence of how you can add value

These are the challenging questions that force you to show how you could make a difference. Although these can be more difficult to answer than some others, consider yourself lucky if you get asked them. It's these questions that let you shine by giving examples of how you've added value in the past and could do it again.

▪ **Why should we hire you?**

This question can easily throw you off track, but it need not be nearly as intimidating as it sounds. It begs for you to use your asset statements, so it is really quite simple to address. What the interviewer is saying with this question is, "Please do my work for me. Tell me how you are different from the last five people

I interviewed and the next five candidates I will meet." What you have to do to ace this question is to be aware of the employer's needs, to assess what you have to offer related to those needs, and to give an example of how you have met similar needs in the past.

The worst answer you can give to this question is one that is completely undistinguished, such as "You should hire me because I'm a hard worker with excellent skills and experience." So what? Anyone can say that. You have to zero in on the two or three qualifications the employer cares most about, and the one or two problems that need to be solved, and then deliver a powerful punch of a reply, such as this:

"From what we've discussed this afternoon, it sounds like your department needs someone who can hit the ground running to get your operations streamlined, reduce your production costs, and boost the staff's morale. I've done that before, and I can do it for you." (At this point, the candidate would continue with one or two asset statements as examples to back up that last claim, or would cue into the listener's signals to pause before continuing.)

- **What can you do for us?**
- **How long would it take you to make an impact here?**
- **How long would it take you to learn this job?**
- **How are you different from other candidates?**

If you get any of these questions, pretend you've been asked the why-should-we-hire-you question and reply accordingly. Be realistic about how long it would take you to make an impact, acknowledging that you would need a short time to get the lay of the land but that you would get up to speed quickly and make a difference. Give evidence of how you've gotten up to speed quickly in the past and use your asset statements to show how you've added value in the past, linking those past successes to the prospective employer's needs, of course.

- **Tell me about your greatest professional success.**

This is simply a different way of asking "What can you do for us?" The interviewer wants to see how you've added value in the past as a way of determining how you might do it again. This question also gets at how you measure or define success as a way of assessing fit, which is discussed in the next section of this chapter. When selecting a success to speak about, be sure to pick one that is relevant to the needs of the prospective employer.

- **Tell me about a time when you had to take initiative.**
- **Tell me about a new idea you presented to your boss in the last six months (or other time period).**
- **Tell me about a time you had to go above and beyond the call of duty.**

Again, you're being asked to show that you can make a significant contribution. By showing that you have ideas or have taken initiative to make things better, you're proving your value. Don't be thrown by the "last six months" constraint that is often included in these sorts of questions. That's simply the idea of "what have you done for us lately." Employers want to know about recent achievements. Try as hard as you can to think of something recent, but if you must go back a bit further in time, that is usually acceptable as long as the example is a strong one.

- **How have you increased revenue or profits?**
- **Can you give me examples of ways you've cut costs/expenses?**
- **Have you improved productivity/quality/processes/systems?**

These are only a few examples of questions you might be asked that get at some specific aspect of your work. If the type of work you do doesn't fall within these examples, don't worry. Just be aware that you need to be prepared to give examples of improvements you've made or contributed to the making of. In general, you would answer these questions just as you would any of the "what can you do for us" type of questions described earlier in this section.

Sample questions: will you fit in?

As you already know, hiring decisions are not based only on who can best do the job and make a difference. They're also based on who will best fit with the organizational culture and the team. The questions that follow are designed to provide the employer with clues to your work style, temperament, and ethics.

Who are you?

These questions try to get at what makes you tick. In fact, you'll see "What makes you tick?" is an actual question some interviewers ask.

- **Do you have a personal mission statement?**
- **Describe your leadership philosophy.**

All executive-level job seekers need to be able to answer these questions, and anyone seeking a management role needs to have a reply to the second question at least. The mission statement doesn't have to be the sole domain of the top ranks, however. Everyone can benefit from developing a personal mission statement that expresses the values you uphold and promote in the workplace, motivators that drive you, and broad goals you strive to reach. If you're at management level, your leadership philosophy would be part of your mission statement as well. For example, I am not currently functioning in a management role, but my mission statement is as follows:

"I will seek out and seize opportunities for intellectual challenge or knowledge contribution and will tackle them with gusto using creativity, strategic thinking, and attention to detail, in order to produce results that better the lives of others."

Your mission statement can be longer than one sentence but do keep it brief. It should not be an essay but a concise statement that captures the essence of who you are.

- **What makes you tick?**
- **What motivates you?**
- **How do you like to be rewarded?**
- **How do you define success?**
- **Why do you work?**

The what-makes-you-tick question might throw you for a loop when you first hear it, but it's really the same as the more specific questions that follow it. What makes you tick is essentially the same as what motivates you. The rationale behind these questions—and the strategy for answering them—however, are fairly straightforward, so you need not be stumped.

Most interviewers use these questions to determine whether your values are in line with those of the job in question or the organization as a whole. When determining how you will answer a question about your definition of success, start by simply thinking about it. What motivates you to work hard? When have you felt successful, what were the circumstances? Then compare your findings with what you think would be valued in the organizations where you are interviewing. If there is a match, then you have nothing to worry about. But if you suspect a conflict, then you must decide how much you are willing to modify your true feelings to tell the interviewers what they want to hear, or how much you would prefer to look elsewhere for an employer whose values would match yours.

- **What did you like most (or least) about your last job?**
- **What were the most repetitive or tedious tasks on your last job?**

Here's another way the interviewer can try to determine whether the job is a good fit for you. The obvious rationale is to find out whether the elements of your work that you find most interesting and motivating are in line with the position for which you are interviewing. If you've been able to find out in advance what the position would entail, or to ask questions early in the interview if you weren't able to learn much beforehand, then you'll have no problem choosing one or two aspects of a past job that are relevant to the target job. Be sure you choose aspects that reflect a strong work ethic and other admirable qualities, as opposed to saying that what you liked most was the short workday or ample vacation time.

Every job involves some degree of tedium, so it is best to be candid and name something you didn't like rather than pretending that you loved every moment of the work. To soften the blow, however, couch your candor within a positive statement and an example of how you got the tedious task done despite the boredom. For example, you might say something like, "Fortunately, I genuinely enjoyed just about every aspect of my work, but if I had to single out one thing I wouldn't mind doing less of, I suppose it be the monthly sales reports. But, I developed a system for doing them that made the process go more smoothly and painlessly.

- **How would your last boss/peers describe you?**
- **What will your references say about you?**

You will obviously answer this question by saying all the positive things that your colleagues would say about you. To make that reply less subjective, try to interject direct quotes wherever possible: "I'll never forget the time my manager told me I was the most effective customer service rep he'd ever supervised" or "When I left my last position, one of my direct reports called me a 'master of motivation.'" You might also refer to language used in a performance review.

Some interviewers might also ask this question because there is a chance it will trip you up. If you become visibly agitated when the subject of references is raised, and if you hesitate when replying, a red flag is raised about how well you have performed on your jobs, or a particular job, and how well you have gotten along with co-workers and bosses in the past.

- **What do you do in your spare time?**
- **How do you relieve stress?**

These questions help the interviewer get to know you better. Although sometimes this topic is merely an innocuous conversation tool to put you at ease by letting you talk about something you enjoy, it is usually brought up as a way to find out about your values, personality style, and skills. It is important that you not launch into a lecture on the wonders of bee-keeping or recite the 200 ingredients in your favorite paella recipe. Just say a little something about one of your more interesting pursuits, then pause and ask whether the interviewer knows anything about that topic or activity. Getting a read on his or her interest level keeps you from being boring or from preaching to the converted.

If asked about your personal interests during an interview, it's to your advantage to take the bait and discuss them as this helps you appear more interesting and well-rounded and helps establish rapport with the interviewer. Be aware, however, of the legalities involved when the interviewer inquires about your personal activities. You are not obligated to discuss any interests or activities that are not related to the job for which you are being interviewed. If you would prefer not to discuss any aspects of your personal life, you can reply to the question with a tactful brush-off, such as, "I manage to rest and relax during my spare time so that I have a balanced life and am fresh for the next day of work." If you do choose to speak about anything more specific, be aware that the prospective employer has no legal right to know about your personal beliefs, such as religion, sexual orientation, or political leanings. This issue is discussed in more detail in Chapter 14, "Interview Curve Balls."

Bright Idea

If being interviewed in someone's office, look for clues to that person's hobbies and interests and comment on them. It's a good way to establish rapport.

■ **What else should we know about you?**

Consider yourself lucky if asked this, and if not asked it, volunteer the answer anyway. In Chapter 11, you learned that preparing your marketing strategy and assembling your "props" are two critical things to do before an interview. They ensure that you go into an interview knowing which key selling points you need to cover and with any supporting documentation for them. When asked whether there's anything else the employer should know about you, this is your chance to make sure that everything on your self-marketing agenda has been covered and that any documents you've brought have been seen. If not, now's the time to talk about them.

■ **How do you interact?**

Short of having the opportunity to observe you on the job, employers use these questions to gather clues about how you do interact with your colleagues, whether peers, bosses, or subordinates.

■ **What kinds of people do you get along best with?**

The best way to answer this question is to cover all bases and say that you get along with all types of people. Try to get away with a short answer and move onto another topic so that you don't have to get into a discussion of the personalities of people with whom you've worked. Such a discussion invariably requires that you voice judgments about various temperaments and work styles, thus, opening the door to offending the interviewer. If the interviewer does press you for more specific definitions of types of people you have worked with or would like to work with, never mention race, ethnicity, gender, or sexual orientation when describing with whom you do or don't get along well. Cite characteristics that you know reflect the organizational culture, such as being hard-working, creative, motivated, intelligent, and the like.

- **How do you feel about teamwork?**
- **What role do you typically take on a team?**

Teamwork is such an important part of most every job that you obviously need to sound enthusiastic about teamwork. Beyond that, answering these questions involves two steps: The first is to determine with which role(s) the employer is most concerned. If the job you are going for requires leadership qualities, then you need to talk about how you usually emerge as the natural leader of a team (but a democratic one, of course). If you aren't sure which roles would be most valued, your safest course of action is to describe how you can play two or three different roles, depending on what the situation calls for. The second step in preparing is to identify an example of a team effort in which you have taken part and describe your role(s) in that function, as well as its successful outcome.

- **How competitive are you?**
- **Define cooperation (or collaboration).**
- **Describe a time you had to collaborate with someone who didn't see eye-to-eye with you.**
- **How do you communicate with people who have different work styles?**
- **How many different levels of staff and management did you interact with on past jobs?**

These questions are only several examples of the many ways that interviewers can get a feel for how you interact with colleagues on the job. Whether the question is couched in terms of competition or communication, or a related aspect of interpersonal interaction, the interviewer wants to know that you are easy to get along with, collaborative and helpful rather than ter-ritorial, and competitive only as the job requires that you be. To answer this question, it's critical that you provide an example of a time when you've demonstrated effective interpersonal skills. You might be asked specifically about interacting with different levels or types of people or customers on the job, as in the last example, but if not, offer this information anyway. You want to show that your interpersonal skills are versatile and that you work well with all types of people.

- **How do you take direction?**
- **What type of manager/supervisor do you work best with?**
- **What kind of support do you need from your boss?**
- **How did you get along with your last boss?**

Tread very carefully with this topic, especially if you are speaking directly to the person who would be your boss! If you have done sufficient research and networking prior to the inter-view and have uncovered inside information about the nature of your prospective boss, then you will have no problem with this question. If you're going in cold, however, and don't know what makes the prospective boss tick, you need to play it safe. Your best bet is to say something innocuous, such as, "I like working for someone who is fair and who shows me respect as long as I'm deserving of that respect" or "My last boss and I got along very well." If the interviewer does not accept an off-the-shelf answer and presses for more detail, just be sure that you don't sound demanding or picky when describing what you look for in a good boss or negative when speaking about a past boss. As always, leave the battle scars out of the interview and talk about anything positive you can possibly come up with to describe the relationship if it was less than rosy. Discussing what you learned from your boss is usually a good option, since we often learn valuable lessons from even the most unpleasant bosses.

Bright Idea

If you've taken any career-related tests (assessment), refer to the results for ideas of how you might speak about your style or typical role in teams or as a manager.

- **What's your management style?**
- **What kind of boss are you?**

Obviously, this question will be asked only if you are applying for a supervisory or managerial position. If you're aiming for such a job, you must have a management philosophy in mind—even if you are more inclined to wing it in reality. Your management style does not have to be a formal doctrine off the pages of an M.B.A. course textbook (unless you're interviewing in the type of organization or with a type of person who would appreciate your citing formal theories). Just be able to describe the thought process underlying your behavior and also make sure that the approach you describe fits with the organizational culture.

Try to sound balanced: fair but firm, democratic and egalitarian but able to take charge, empathetic but objective, or collaborative but self-directed. Your pre-interview research comes into play here, as well as your active listening during the interview. Both skills enable you to pick up on clues the interviewer might give as to what is needed for the position at hand. Listen for words and phrases used to describe what is needed in the new hire and adapt your own style to fit those needs.

- **What does diversity mean to you?**
- **How do you deal with diversity in the workplace?**

The term "diversity" has been so overused and misused that it has just about become a cliché. If you're asked this question, you are probably being clued into the fact that the environment you'd be entering has a diverse workforce or is possibly having problems with diverse groups getting along well. Avoid giving clichéd answers and try to give one that you've put some thought into.

Example: "To me, diversity means success. A wide variety of opinions, backgrounds, points of view, and skill sets enriches any enterprise and means that the organization is more likely to achieve great results. Of course, a diverse workforce needs to act as a cohesive unit, and that means not just tolerating differences but truly respecting them. For example, when I was with XYZ Company, we. . ."

Make sure that your own answer involves speaking thoughtfully about what diversity means and giving an example of how you've dealt with it positively.

What's your work style?

These questions help the employer get a sense of how well you'll fit into the environment and corporate culture. Are you used to a fast-paced, ever-changing environment, or a steady, routine one? These and issues related to ethical standards are discerned by this set of questions.

- **Describe your energy level.**

Most employers want to hire people with high energy levels who will work hard, put in extra hours as needed, and keep up with a fast pace. Be careful, however, that you don't go to extremes in describing your energy level. Present a balanced picture, saying that you are a high-energy person but that you don't overwhelm people when a situation calls for a more low-key, composed approach.

- **Tell me about a time you had to work under extreme pressure.**

This request gets at your character and work style. It is a behavior-based one that doesn't merely ask how you deal with pressure in a hypothetical sense; it also asks how you have handled it in an actual situation. Be sure to choose an example that mirrors situations you might face on the job for which you are interviewing. In describing it, be sure to sound balanced and fair, not placing the blame on any one person or set of circumstances for causing the pressured situation. Also, don't sound overly negative as you describe the situation. Make the description brief, giving just enough facts to set the stage. Then move on to an account of how you handled it, citing assets you used to remain calm and clear-headed. Conclude by describing the outcome of your efforts. Did you prevent something catastrophic from happening? Did you protect your boss's reputation? Did you keep morale up in the people working around you? Did you set a good example by remaining on an even keel in the face of adversity?

- **Do you prefer to work with others or alone?**

While being a willing and able team player is an almost universally desired trait in job candidates, there are positions that require you to be considerably self-sufficient and comfortable with autonomy. If you know something about the job and organization as a whole, then you should have no difficulty answering this question. Give a balanced answer that makes you sound versatile and able to work well alone or in groups but put the emphasis on the one aspect that best describes the job in question. Also, be sure to give an example of how you have done both, along with one showing how you have performed well either alone or in groups, depending on which aspect you need to emphasize.

- **What is your preferred work environment?**

This question gets at your work style and directly relates to the issue of fit. Interviewers not only want to know whether the kind of environment you seek is the one they have to offer, they also want to identify any character flaws you might inadvertently reveal in answering the question. Be careful that you don't sound like you require any extremes, such as too much structure or too much autonomy. And don't slip up and contrast your desired work environment with that of your past or current job. There's no need to volunteer negative information about other workplaces.

Sample questions: will you make the commitment?

Remember that employers want to know that you want them. They need to ensure that their investment in you will pay off by having you stick around long enough to get the job done. They also want to make sure that your career goals fit with what they can offer and that you're not looking to move up more quickly than they could accommodate or that, on the flip side, you are as ambitious as they want you to be.

Do you want the job?

Remember that employers want to feel courted as much as a job seeker wants to feel wanted. You've got to let them know that you're interested in not just any old job, but a job with that organization.

- **Why do you want this job?**
- **What do you look for in a job?**
- **Describe your ideal job.**

The answer to this question is straightforward: State responsibilities and opportunities that you know the job offers. In doing so, focus not on what your employer can do for you, but on what you can do for your employer. Come across as looking for the chance to use what you have to offer—whether that's creativity, the ability to cut costs, or strong management skills. Don't sound like someone looking for perks and prestige.

- **Why are you interested in this organization/company?**
- **Why us?**

Here's an example of why conducting research prior to an interview is so critical. When interviewers ask outright "Why do you like us?" you must have credible, thoughtful reasons for doing so. If you have done sufficient research, this should be a welcome question—one that really lets you shine. You get to show how well prepared you are and can state your case for why that organization is the right place for you. Just be sure you don't overwhelm the interviewer with a dull recitation of facts and figures gleaned from your research.

Could this be the start of a beautiful friendship?

These questions get at whether your long-range plans mesh with the opportunities that could become available in the organization down the road.

- **Where do you see yourself in x# of years?**
- **What are your career goals?**
- **What are your short-term career goals?**
- **What are your long-term career goals?**
- **How quickly would you expect to advance here?**

No matter how the question is worded, most employers are looking for three types of information here:

- Is your projected career path in line with what the job and organization in question can offer?
- Are you willing to take the initiative in determining your own course rather than expecting the employer to coddle you?
- Are you too eager to move up? Are you going to get impatient if you don't advance quickly?

In responding to this question, be sure that your expectations for advancement are realistic and fit with the structure of the prospective employer. Also express your willingness to be responsible for your own success and patience to move when the opportunity is right for the organization as a whole, not just for yourself.

The best way to answer is to balance specific information with broad brush strokes. Employers' eyes will roll if you are too broad, giving a canned response such as "I hope to grow and advance with a company that can offer challenges and opportunity." That means nothing. Talk instead in terms of function, level, and areas of contribution.

When to Keep Your Career Plans to Yourself

If you're planning to make a career change but need a job in your current field for now just to pay the bills while you gradually make the career change, be careful what you say about your future plans. One employer I know was interviewing a man for a sales management position in the office supply industry. The candidate was coming across as well-qualified and interested in the work until he was asked about his career goals. Without skipping a beat, the applicant replied that he hoped to become a chef and was currently taking courses in a culinary institute. In a friendly and interested manner, the interviewer subtly pressed for more information, asking what the courses were like and how the culinary program was structured. Unwittingly, the candidate talked about how he was nearing the end of his course requirements and that the school required a three-month apprenticeship for the degree. As he spoke, the applicant realized that he had let the proverbial cat out of the bag and that there was no way he would get the job. The interviewer spoke about her need to hire someone who would stay at least a couple of years and politely brought the meeting to a close.

You might not be concerned that you will be so candid about career goals that don't mesh with the employer's needs, but be aware nonetheless of how a seemingly friendly conversation can close doors for you. If you do plan to go in an entirely different direction, you have two choices: (1) lie about it and face the moral consequences when your true goals are revealed later on; or (2) seek only jobs that do fit into your career plan so you don't have to lie.

You might say, "Well, of course, I can't say exactly where I want to be five years from now because career paths are unpredictable these days, but I know that I will still be involved in IT and will be continually learning and applying cutting edge technologies. I also know that I would like to move into more of a supervisory role. And, I'd like to be able to say that I have made significant contributions to my employer's bottom line."

Do you know what you're getting into?

These questions test your knowledge of the employer or industry to make sure that you know what you're getting into. These would be most common if you are attempting to make a career change into a new functional role, product or service, industry, or labor market sector (such as private sector to nonprofit).

- **What are you looking for in your next job/employer?**
- **What do you know about us?**
- **What interests you most and least about this job?**
- **How did you choose this career?**
- **Why do you want to move into this industry (or new functional role)?**
- **What do you know about this industry (or new functional role)?**

No matter which wording is used, these questions test your knowledge of the specific job, organization, industry, or profession you are attempting to enter (or re-enter). In describing what you know about the employer or the field or in discussing why you have chosen them, let the interviewer in on your thought process. Demonstrate that you are making choices based on a thorough, logical thought process and based on accurate data. If, however, you describe "falling into" a career field, your credibility will be called into question unless you can show convincingly that the career has turned out to be right for you, even though you did not consciously choose it.

Watch Out!

While expressing your interest in working for a particular organization, don't go overboard with your enthusiasm. Employers these days can't make a promise of lifelong employment, so they'll be turned off if you sound like you're already too attached.

■ **What do you think about [current event/recent development in the industry or profession]?**

This question demonstrates the importance of keeping up with developments in your industry or profession—and not just limiting your research to information about the organization itself. The specific content of your answer is not as critical as the fact that you demonstrate some awareness, knowledge, and opinions in discussing that content so that the interviewer sees you as well informed and interested in keeping up with developments in your field.

Will you meet our needs?

Here's where the employer tests the waters of your flexibility and commitment. Will you go where they send you and work in the way they want you to work?

■ **Will you be willing to travel anywhere we need to send you?**

■ **How much travel are you open to?**

Before an interview, you will probably be able to find out how much travel, if any, the job will require, so you won't be caught off guard by these questions. Decide in advance where you stand on the issue of travel, and if your preferences match those of the job's travel demands, then your answer to this query is a no-brainer. If, however, you are hoping for less travel than the job requires but decided to interview anyway, or if you didn't think it involved any travel and don't have a ready opinion, then you need to proceed carefully. Try to evade the question slightly by putting it back to them: "Do you know how much travel the position would require?" or "Where might the travel take me?"

If at some point you have to give more of a straight answer, say that you are open to consider any terms of the position after you have a better sense of the position as a whole and can evaluate the travel factor in light of other job requirements. The idea is to keep the dialogue going and the door open as long as possible before closing the door by refusing travel from the start.

▪ **Are you willing to relocate?**

Answering this question is fairly simple if you are indeed willing to relocate. You simply say "yes." You can make your case stronger by giving an example of how you have been flexible with past employers, relocating as needed. If you don't want to relocate, or if you're not sure how you feel about it, but you don't want to miss out on a job offer, answering this question becomes a little more complicated. If you say "yes" but don't mean it, then you will face problems down the road when your employer expects you to pull up stakes and move. If you say "no," then you might not get the offer. Because this question is sometimes asked despite the fact there is little or no chance relocation would be required, it is unfortunate to miss out on an offer because you said "no."

To take a safe middle ground, handle it in much the same way as the business travel issue. Say that you are open to the possibility but would prefer to discuss that matter in more detail if and when an offer is extended. Of course, if your pre-interview research shows that relocation is a standard part of a particular job, then you have no choice but to say "yes" if you want an offer.

▪ **Are you willing to work the night shift (or any other particular shift)?**

▪ **Would you be available to work on weekends?**

▪ **Are you willing to work overtime?**

As with relocation and business travel, try to know as much about the position as possible before going into an interview so you'll be prepared to address the issue of weekend work,

overtime, or handling a particular shift. If you are caught unpre-
pared for this question or hope not to have to meet this require-
ment, then handle it as advised with the relocation and travel
examples. Say that you never say no to any requirements until
you have the full picture of the overall job and an offer in hand.
In other words, keep your options open.

Just the facts

- You can ace any interview with these six guiding principles: remember you're just talking to a fellow human
  being; act like a consultant there to assess needs and solve
  problems; realize that you have power in the process;
  make it a dialogue, not an interrrogation; back up your
  claims with evidence—your asset statements; and know
  when you've said enough.

- The six steps to fielding any interview question are listen
  carefully; figure out what's really behind the question; ask
  for clarification if you don't understand; pick a relevant
  asset statement to use; answer the question directly; and
  stop talking after about 30–60 seconds, offering to elaborate if desired.

- There's no way to prepare answers to every possible interview question, and you'd sound too canned if you did;
  instead understand that all interview questions are getting
  at the three basic things on an employer's mind: Can you
  do the job and add value? Will you fit in? Will you make
  the commitment?

- Even though you can't anticipate every interview question
  because the possibilities are infinite, you can prepare a
  strategy for answering some of the more common and not
  so common questions. More than 90 sample questions
  were discussed in this chapter to help you prepare those
  strategies.

The meaning behind questions that seem designed to trip you up ▪ Best strategies for the toughest interview questions ▪ Diplomatically dodging illegal questions ▪ Building a strong case to overcome obstacles and objections ▪ Knowing what to ask when it's your turn to ask questions

Interview Curve Balls

Chapter 14

What's an interview "curve ball?" It's all in the "squirm-factor"—a question that stumps you or makes you feel uncomfortable, questions that dance on the edge of being illegal, or obstacles to employment that you can't see any way around. This chapter helps you hit those curve balls with confidence by preparing for the tough questions, learning how to deflect illegal questions tactfully, arming yourself with tactics to get around objections, and finally, with a surefire list of questions to ask when it's your turn to do the asking.

Tough questions you might be asked

In some cases, the way a question is worded can throw you. Most people find it easier to respond to "Tell me what kind of person you are" than to answer "If you were a tree, which kind would you be?" Yet, the tree question is seeking the same information— who are you?

Similarly, the scope of a question can be intimidating. Remarks like "Tell me a story" give you few parameters with which to structure a reply. You wonder where to begin, what to put in the middle, and when to end. But the rationale behind a request like this is not much different from that of more specific requests, such as "Name three skills you possess" or "Tell me how you would solve this problem we have." The broader questions call for the same information as the more specific ones; they just require that you choose which information to provide.

Finally, some of the questions discussed in this section are particularly difficult because they ask you to discuss negative personal qualities, failures, or controversial topics: matters most job seekers would prefer not to bring into the conversation.

In this section, you'll find examples of more than 40 questions that might give you pause due to their wording, scope, or "squirm factor." For each one, I provide strategies to guide your responses; in some cases, I offer actual sample answers. Keep in mind that the issue of how to reply to these questions is highly debatable. If you surveyed 10 people who know anything about interviewing, you would get 10 different takes on how these questions should be handled. What you will find on these pages are the approaches that have been found to be most effective by the many successful job seekers with whom I've worked, recruiters to whom I've spoken, and research I have conducted to bring you the inside scoop. Where relevant, I've also given you more than one option from which to choose when structuring your replies. How to deal with tricky questions is a matter of personal choice. Use your own judgment to decide what works best for your circumstances, personal style, and desired level of risk taking.

Sample questions: negatives

Questions that require you to discuss negative aspects of your character or experiences go against the grain of every job seeker who wants to make a positive impression in interviews. The examples that follow typify this perplexing line of questioning and offer strategies for navigating them.

■ **What is your biggest weakness?**

■ **What are your weaknesses?**

■ **In past performance reviews, what were your suggested areas for improvement?**

Next to "Tell me about yourself," the question about weaknesses has got to be one of the most dreaded in the history of employment interviewing. You go into an interview wanting to discuss your assets, so the last thing you want to do is talk about your deficits. The key to being comfortable with this question is to remember that you'll be more successful in an interview that lets the prospective employer get to know you fully than in one in which you come across as too good to be true. After that realization sinks in, you then need to craft a reply that is at once candid and positive.

The most important thing to keep in mind when answering this question is to avoid a canned response. There's a long-standing myth in the world of job hunting that says you should answer this question by choosing a positive quality and making it sound negative. Don't even think about it! Saying that your weakness is that you're a perfectionist to a fault, or too detail-oriented, or a workaholic is a thinly veiled attempt to dodge the question. Everyone has weak areas, and employers want to know about them. They wouldn't ask the question if they didn't. Your best bet is to give an honest answer involving a genuine deficit— but to do so strategically. Here's how:

■ Choose a weakness that is not critical to success on the job in question. Obviously, you shouldn't talk about your poor math skills if you're going for a job as a bookkeeper. Select an area that would be a minimal part of the job.

■ Discuss a weakness that relates to content knowledge as opposed to an innate personal quality or a transferable skill. Saying that your weakness is lack of knowledge of a particular computer application is preferable to saying that your problem is in managing people or following through on a task (even if those are minimal parts of the job). Content knowledge can be learned and is less connected to your basic character and aptitudes.

■ Select a weakness that the interviewer is already aware of— or is likely to discover—so that you're not raising a negative that wouldn't have been noticed in the first place. With this strategy, the question "What is your greatest weakness?" can actually work in your favor because it gives you a chance to address a concern before it festers in the interviewer's mind.

■ Always talk about how you are working on the problem. Give tangible evidence of your efforts to improve in that area, such as courses you've taken, books you're reading to teach yourself something, or mentoring you've sought to help with your professional development. If you've already shown improvement, give an example of it.

Ask a question as soon as you give your answer. Say, "How important is X for success on this job?" If your deficit is a major concern, then you have the chance to address that concern right then and there.

■ **Tell me about a time you failed.**

■ **What is your biggest professional blunder?**

■ **What mistakes have you made?**

■ **What regrets do you have?**

These questions are similar to "What are your weaknesses?" in that they force you to make yourself look less than positive. You have similar choices here in that you can be evasive and say you've never made a mistake and have no regrets, or you can admit to a mistake—remember that everyone on this planet has made at least one—but do so in a way that doesn't damage your credibility. Choose one that does not reflect a serious error of judgment or a character flaw and that is not central to the work you would be doing for the prospective employer.

Watch Out!

When choosing a weakness to talk about, don't choose one that has absolutely nothing to do with the job for which you're interviewing. Your answer will sound phony and like an obvious attempt to dodge the question.

As before, use your own judgment to decide how direct you want to be. Keep in mind, however, that as long as your answer is carefully crafted, you usually will come across as more sincere if you do admit to a mistake or two in your past. If you opt for the direct approach, choose a mistake that is somewhat related to your professional life but not a critical error and emphasize what you've learned from it. For example, the sample answer that follows uses relocation as a mistake:

"Fortunately, I've had a pretty good track record, but, of course, everyone makes mistakes on occasion. I guess the one that has been on my mind lately is the decision I made to leave Boston two years ago. I uprooted my family and left all the family and friends we had here to go to the West Coast, where the economy was stronger at the time. Although we adjusted pretty well considering the culture shock we faced, and while I thrived in my work with California Capital, I knew soon after the move that we all belonged back in New England. I had made the decision on purely objective data, overlooking the more subjective aspect of a decision like that—would we feel like fish out of water? So, I'm eager to get back here in my old stomping ground. I even miss shoveling snow! And, as with all mistakes we make in life, I learned a great deal. This incident reminded me not to make a decision based solely on how something looks on paper, so I think in an ironic way, this mistake has made me a better manager."

▪ **Have you ever hired or fired the wrong person?**

This is commonly asked of managers or human resource professionals involved in staffing. If the true answer, is no, then don't try to concoct a situation that never existed, but answer this question as a hypothetical, speaking about how you would handle the situation if you did hire or fire someone mistakenly. If you have experienced this, own up to the fact that it was your mistake rather than blaming it on others and speak about what you learned from the experience.

- **Have you ever been fired or asked to resign (for reasons other than a lay-off/downsizing)?**

Whew! This is a biggie. If the answer is yes, and you know that either: (a) a past employer will reveal this when a reference is checked; or (b) you operate in a small professional world where word could easily get around that this happened, then you have to own up to it. Explain the circumstances in a matter-of-fact, succinct manner. But, if you have verified that your past employers will say that you resigned, rather than being terminated or asked to resign, then you can fudge it a bit and talk only about decisions you've made to leave positions.

- **Why haven't you landed a job yet?**

Job searches come in all shapes and sizes. Some people work diligently at their search 40 hours a week but take months or even more than a year to land a job. Others work in starts and stops, not putting a full-time effort in the search, so it takes them a long time to land as well. Others luck into a job early on regardless of the level of effort they put in. So, the first thing to remember when asked this question is that your value should not be judged by the length of your search. In a troubled economy, or when the industry in which you're searching is experiencing a downturn, you can cite those factors as the reason for not having a job yet. If you've taken some time off since leaving your last job or have taken on some temporary assignments, talk about that so that it's clear you've not been searching steadily all this time. If you're still employed, explain that your search has to be very part-time and, thus, you haven't landed yet. If you're attempting to change industries or professions, remind the interviewer that such a shift usually lengthens a job search.

If you can't blame it on any of those external reasons, try to sound positive and play up any activity you've generated, mentioning that you've spoken with a number of employers, but nothing has been the right fit. (You can conveniently omit that it was the employers who felt it wasn't the right fit, not you!) Of course, if you've received offers that you turned down, mention that to show that you've been in demand and that you've chosen to extend your search. Online Bonus Chapter 4 discusses how to deal with a search that's dragging on, so if you are particularly concerned about this issue, you will find some tips and solutions there.

Sample questions: conflicts

Interpersonal conflicts are an inevitable part of work life. The questions below are examples of how employers might try to determine your style of handling conflicts.

- **Give me an example of a time you disagreed with your boss (or co-worker).**

- **Give me an example of a time you had to resolve a conflict between yourself and a colleague (or between two colleagues).**

- **Have you ever had a personality clash with a colleague/ boss?**

- **If someone or something is standing in your way of reaching a goal, how do you handle it?**

Regardless of exactly how it's worded, this type of request is particularly difficult because the issue of personality clashes and interpersonal conflicts is one you want to avoid like the plague in interviews. Personality conflicts between bosses and subordinates, between co-workers, and between employees and clients or customers are rampant in the world of work, but they are a taboo topic for interviews almost 100 percent of the time. The reason for this is that it is nearly impossible to discuss a personality clash without having yourself end up looking like a bad person. If you own up to your role in the conflict, you come across

as someone who is difficult to work with. If you place blame for
the clash on the other person, you look like you are not only difficult but, at minimum, are not a team player; at worst, you look
like a back-stabber.

In asking this question, the interviewers are getting at that
issue of fit. They want to know whether you have problems getting along with other people. They are also trying to find out
how tactful you are—do you say negative things about others, or
are you diplomatic in how you describe a situation? This question also serves as an indirect way of asking what you look for in
a boss or co-workers, to see whether your work style and preferred way of managing or being managed is congruent with the
prospective employer's workplace.

Your best bet here is to say as little as possible. You basically
have three options for answering these types of questions, options
that are presented here in order from safest (but most evasive)
to riskiest (but most direct):

1. Say that you have been very fortunate in that you've gotten
    along well with everyone you've ever worked with and that
    no personality clashes or conflicts come to mind. In other
    words, evade the question.

2. Answer the question in a seemingly direct way, but inter-
    pret the wording of the question to your advantage.
    Define "personality clash" (or "conflict") as a clash of val-
    ues or work ethic rather than one of personality or work
    style. Talk about how a boss wanted you to do something
    illegal or unethical, or how a co-worker disagreed with
    how to approach a problem.

3. Be more candid, and talk openly (but tactfully) about the
    lunatic boss or psychotic co-worker with whom you've
    had to deal. You would usually choose this option only if
    you know the interviewer is familiar with your situation
    enough to know about this person. This actually happens
    more often than you might think, particularly in tightly

knit industries where everyone knows everyone else and knows who the notorious bosses are.

A word of caution is in order if you choose the second or third option, however. Whenever you even venture near candor when discussing a personality conflict, do so very diplomatically. Be brief and matter-of-fact. Don't sound emotional, angry, bitter, or whiny. Don't sensationalize the issue or sound gossipy. Always bear some of the blame for the problem and talk about what you did to resolve it, what you learned, and how it has never happened since then. Also, mention that you were not the only person to have a problem with this boss or co-worker. If you can cite turnover rates or formal complaints other employees filed, you objectify the situation and make it sound less like your problem and more like fact.

- **Tell us about an ethical/moral dilemma you've faced and how you handled it.**

- **What would you do if you knew someone in this organization was committing an ethical violation?**

The first request listed here is typical of behavioral interviews in which your integrity and work ethic are assessed through real-life examples you provide. The interviewer wants to know what sorts of moral issues you've had to deal with, how you handled them, and what you learned from them. The other is obviously a hypothetical. If you can't think of an actual example to answer the first one, reply in a hypothetical sense, saying what you would do if an ethical situation were to arise. In describing an ethical dilemma you actually have faced, consider the following:

- Choose one in which you were involved only as an observer or secondary participant. You might describe witnessing someone violating a company policy, cheating, or stealing. This is preferable to choosing one that involved your own behavior. (An interviewer might press, however, for you to discuss one in which you were directly involved. In that case, you have to respond to that request.)

- Be tactful and diplomatic in the way you describe the situation. Speak of it in neutral terms instead of sounding self-righteous or like a snitch.

- Don't reveal confidential information that violates the rights of past co-workers or the proprietary rights of your employer. Obviously, you should not identify anyone by name and should provide only as many details of the incident as needed to tell the story.

When speaking about how you would handle the hypothetical situation (or did handle an actual one), use the following guidelines:

- Say that you first would define the problem to make sure that there was indeed a breach of ethics taking place before jumping to conclusions.

- Explain that you would deal directly with the parties involved to let them know of your concern and to give them a chance to explain their position before reporting them to any relevant authorities.

- Conclude your account with a discussion of what you learned (or would expect to learn, if foreseeable) from the incident.

Sample questions: nosy ones

Some lines of inquiry make you want to snap back at the interviewer with "That's none of your business!" Before making that assumption, however, think about what the rationale might be behind the question. You'll see that each of the questions has an

 Watch Out!

Be sure you don't confuse seemingly nosy questions with illegal ones. Illegal questions ask for personal information that can be used to discriminate against you. The "nosy" questions are ones that try to shatter the illusion of the rehearsed job seeker to uncover the real you.

intent that goes deeper than the superficial information sought. The interviewer is not trying to be nosy but is looking for clues to such matters as your integrity, work-related skills, level of interest and commitment, and professionalism in general.

■ **How are you finding the time to interview while employed?**

This question (asked of job-seekers who are currently employed, obviously) might be used to determine whether you are the type of person who takes unfair advantage of your employer. Are you the sort who lies and abuses company time for your own gain? Do you say you're going on a client call when you're really heading for an interview?

It is also asked to find out how you manage your time. Never let down your guard when answering this question, saying something to the effect of, "Oh, what a time I've had trying to fit appointments into my work week—it's been a nightmare!" The best approach is to say that you're using vacation time and personal days, also called "floating holidays," to go on interviews and to conduct other job-search activities. You can also say that you are interviewing at breakfast, lunch, and after work whenever possible. Of course, if you haven't been managing your time that way and have been sneaking around, calling in sick, or using your employer's time for your search, then you'll have to limit your reply to something short-and-sweet like, "It hasn't been too difficult to interview and still do my current job effectively. I tend to manage my time well."

■ **How does this job/organization compare with others you're looking at?**

This question is not all that difficult to reply to. It's essentially asking you to tell why you are interested in this organization and to indicate your level of interest. See the "Do You Want the Job?" section of Chapter 13 where I discuss such questions as "Why are you interested in this organization/company?" and "Why us?"

Watch Out!

Don't be concerned if an interviewer gives you no indication of your chances of getting the job. Interviewers are often trained to keep a poker face and not to make promises they can't keep, so you might get only neutral verbal and nonverbal signals.

▪ Where else are you interviewing/have you interviewed?

This question often throws job-seekers for a loop because they assume that they have to keep other prospective employers a secret. It's no coincidence that the term "courting" is sometimes used to describe the mating ritual in which employers and prospective employees engage. You might feel that if you mention other organizations, you will sound less interested in the one where you are interviewing. On the contrary, interviewers know that a smart job seeker is going to investigate every possibility and will rarely approach only one place at a time.

A direct approach to this question is usually the best approach. It will also have the added benefit of getting the employer's competitive juices flowing when you sound like you are in demand, being "courted" by others. A decision you have to make when replying is whether to mention specific company names or just to speak of them in generic terms. If you do mention the actual name of another organization, do so only if you have a definite interview scheduled or have already been there. The person you're speaking to might know someone at the other organization and can catch you in a lie—or at least a stretching of the truth—if you say you're being considered somewhere you're not.

If you have no other interviews scheduled—or likely to be scheduled—but don't want to sound like you're not in demand, you can speak euphemistically. "I'm in the early stages of discussing opportunities at other firms" is a handy euphemism for saying that you have placed preliminary calls to a human resources representative who told you that some opening might exist and that you should send in your résumé and they'll call you—maybe. Of course, if you are not interviewing anywhere else because you are not in an active search, you can simply say so.

▪ **How long would you envision staying with this organization?**

This question might catch you off guard, but there's really nothing tricky about it. This is simply an attempt to see whether your career goals fit with the employer's needs. It's a way of assessing your level of commitment. Be sure to review the suggested strategies in Chapter 13 for such questions as "Where do you see yourself in x# of years?" and "What are your career goals?" for ideas of how to approach this.

▪ **What have you left off of your résumé?**

An employer does have a right to know about your complete employment record. In fact, you might have to complete an employment application that asks for a detailed work history. Employers know that your résumé—when done correctly—is really a marketing tool that presents your background in the most favorable light. They also know that space limitations might prevent you from listing all your jobs and activities.

If you choose not to include certain jobs on your résumé simply because they are from more than several years back or from a previous career field not relevant to your current target, then you have nothing to worry about. You can give the employer a brief run-down of that part of your work history and then shift the focus back to your more recent employment or educational experiences.

 Watch Out!

Headhunters will almost always expect you to discuss salary in a first interview with them, so be prepared to disclose your current and previous earnings and your salary requirements. Otherwise, they won't be able to work with you effectively.

If, however, you omitted jobs because you were in them only for a short time—usually a few months or less—or because you left on bad terms and don't want to have a reference checked, this question is trickier to answer. If you are interviewing in companies that do comprehensive background checks, you must reveal all prior employment because it will probably be discovered anyway. Also, if interviewing for jobs in tight-knit industries in which everyone seems to know everyone else, it is usually wise to disclose everything. For other situations, you have the option of committing a sin of omission by simply forgetting to mention the firm that fired you after only 30 days. The choice is yours to make, but do keep in mind that any lies you tell or information you conveniently forget can come back to haunt you.

Sample questions: putting you on the spot

- **Why are you leaving your current job? Why did you leave your last job?**

The online Bonus Chapter 1 offers tips for preparing a "reason for looking" statement. If you follow these suggestions, then this question will be a breeze.

- **How would you rate me as an interviewer?**

This is no time to be overly critical. Give the interviewer a good rating and try to leave it at that. If the interviewer presses for you to give some constructive criticism about something that could have been better, mention a question they could have asked you that didn't get asked, rather than saying something negative about what they did ask or how the interview was conducted in general. Pick a question that you would like to answer–one that will bring up positive information about you.

- **Are you going to go after my job?**
- **When would you expect a promotion?**
- **When would you expect a raise?**

Strike a balance here. You need to sound ambitious but not chomping at the bit to snag the boss's job. Say that you would expect to advance and have salary increases as you prove yourself and earn the right to do so after achieving successes at the level where you begin. Also try bouncing this question back by asking about the typical career path for the position so that you know what you're dealing with.

- **What sort of salary/compensation are you looking for?**
- **What were you making on your last jobs?**
- **What's your salary history?**

The issue of how to answer questions about salary history or salary expectations is complicated. I've dealt with this in detail in the "Getting the Money and Benefits You Deserve" section of Chapter 15. Please refer to that chapter for guidance on how to deal with the compensation questions.

- **Have you heard anything bad about our organization?**

If you have, try to keep it to yourself, unless the negatives are so widely known that you would sound ignorant if you didn't mention them. Instead, deflect this question by bringing up all the positive things you've learned about them and showing you've done your homework.

- **How long do you think you would stay with us?**

This can be a tricky question because you have to know how long the employer would want you to stay. As discussed throughout this book, most employers these days do not expect you to stay with them until you retire and get the proverbial gold watch. It is something of a myth, however, that they don't care at all about how long you stay. Hiring and training of a new employee can be an expensive endeavor. Add to that cost the effort that goes into analyzing staffing needs and carefully plotting where personnel are needed, and you find that employers invest a great deal in a new hire. So, when answering a question about how long you'll stick around, take these factors into account and don't sound like you'll be out the door when the next great opportunity comes around.

Also rely on your research about the company—particularly the networking you will have done to get the inside scoop on what's happening at a given organization. Your research findings should give you some indication of what the norm is for tenure in various positions, as well as how much job-hopping is the norm for a given industry. If your research does not turn up any clear signals, or if you simply want to hedge your bets, a safe answer is something along the lines of: "I'd want to be with [company name] as long as I'm making a valuable contribution."

- **Do you think you have done the best work you're capable of?**

This is an interesting question because it presents a damned-if-you-do, damned-if-you-don't dilemma. If you say that you have done your best work, you'll certainly be saying something positive about your past performance but will be implying that you have nothing left to offer. If you say you haven't, then you are indicating that you have a lot to contribute but that your past work has been less than stellar. This is one of the few interview questions that has only one satisfactory answer: "I have always tried to perform to the best of my ability and have done some excellent work, but I also strive for continual improvement, so I know I can do even better." It's a bit corny, but it works. (And, remember, you need to put this in your own words, so you can make it sound natural for you.)

- **What would you want your obituary to say?**

Your response to this rather morbid question tells the interviewer what you value, how you define success, and which accomplishments you are most proud of. It is also an indirect way of getting at your career goals. If you say that your obituary will mention a particular career that is not part of your current target career path, your reply might call into question your commitment to that current career direction.

This question can also be a sneaky way of finding out about your personal life. For example, a nosy interviewer who suspects you're gay might be looking to see whether you include "devoted family man" or "loving wife" in your obituary. Similarly, if someone wants to know whether you have children, your obituary might mention that fact.

To answer this question effectively, be sure to give it some thought in advance, as it is not an easy one to deal with off the top of your head. As always, balance being yourself and reflecting your true values with emphasizing the qualities and accomplishments that would fit with the prospective employer's values and needs. And, reveal only as much personal information as you are comfortable doing.

Note: A related question you might be asked is, "What would you want the epitaph on your tombstone to say?" This, too, can be a tough one to answer because you must come up with a pithy statement that captures the essence of you. That can be particularly difficult to do on the spot, so it's a good idea to prepare for it in advance.

▪ **When is it okay to lie?**

Whew! This one's a doozy. Everyone knows that most every mere mortal has been known to tell an occasional white lie when the situation calls for it. Don't admit to it, though. It's best to evade this question by answering with humor: "It's okay to lie when my girlfriend asks whether her hair looks nice" or "It's okay to lie if my husband asks whether he's lost more hair on the back of his head." Always add to the humor with a serious comment about how honesty should be the only policy in professional environments.

▪ **Tell me a story.**

This one can really catch you off guard. "Tell me a story" often simply means "Tell me *your* story." In that case, you would reply in the same way as you would for "Tell me about yourself." Other times, "Tell me a story," means literally tell a story— perhaps an amusing anecdote from an activity outside of work or an account of one particular incident from your professional life. (The latter could be one of your examples from your asset statements, as described in Chapter 4.) If you choose to tell a story from your personal life, make it one that demonstrates your skills, personality, or values in some way and doesn't reveal too much personal information.

For example, I know of one man who wanted to make a career change from advertising account management to management in a social service agency. When I asked him what had been the catalyst for this transition, he said that it was the day his six-year-old daughter asked him whether his work "made his heart feel good." He realized that he would be lying to her if he said "yes." This incident, coupled with the fact that he had been contemplating a career change for more than a year, led him to make some changes. When he went on interviews in the not-for-profit sector, he found that this story was a powerful statement that proved his commitment to their work.

"Tell me a story" might also be a way to find out how creative or entertaining you are. If you'll be interviewing for creative positions or ones requiring the gift of gab, such as sales, be sure you have a good story or two at the tip of your tongue.

If in doubt about how to approach this question, don't hesitate to ask for clarification, requesting that the interviewer tell you a little more about what he or she has in mind in the way of a story. However, if you're interviewing for creative or sales positions, as mentioned, go ahead and tell a story without asking for clarification. This question could be a test of your creativity or charisma.

 Bright Idea

Always have in mind names of books you've read recently or movies you've seen because some interviewers ask about them as a way of getting to know you better. Pick one or two that are career-related and some that are not.

Deflecting illegal questions tactfully

Deflecting or confronting a question that asks for personal information completely unrelated to the job or for information that could be used to discriminate against you is tricky business. You might not know whether you should stand your legal ground and refuse to answer an illegal question such as, "What kind of child care arrangements do you have?" or to simply answer the question because you don't find it particularly offensive and have nothing to hide—even though you know it's not related to your qualifications for the job.

Fielding illegal questions is also tricky because you are trying to build rapport with the interviewer and gain some power in the process without being overly aggressive. In an interview that has been going smoothly and cordially, refusing to answer a question on the grounds that it is illegal can be as jarring as standing up and throwing your chair out the window.

Illegal questions also cause discomfort because they lead you to question your own judgment and doubt your knowledge. You might not know whether you're merely being an alarmist—turning an innocuous line of inquiry into a federal case—or whether you are objectively and accurately reading the situation as discriminatory. The only way to trust your judgment is to become as knowledgeable of hiring law as can reasonably be expected— "reasonably," because it is a complex topic that you should not expect to master unless that happens to be your field of expertise.

Knowing your rights

Simply put, everything asked of you during the interviewing or assessment process must be relevant to the job for which you are applying. You cannot be discriminated against based on any factor that does not relate to your ability to do the job, such as your race, gender, national origin or ancestry, religious beliefs, citizenship status, age, marital or family status (as in asking the number and ages of your children, if any), appearance, or physical or mental disability.

Bright Idea

To learn more about illegal questions and laws governing employment discrimination visit the U.S. Equal Employment Opportunity Commission at http://www.eeoc.gov.

Handling illegal questions

When faced with an illegal question—or an illegally worded question you have three choices:

1. *Answer the question.* You might come across some questions that are technically illegal but that do not offend you in any way. You might not mind if an employer knows that you are married or what your native language is. If so, there is nothing wrong with answering such questions, as long as you see no reason why the information you provide could work against you. Actually, in some cases, it can work in your favor. Because interviewers want to get to know you as a person, they will feel more comfortable knowing a little something about you personally and usually have no evil intentions.

The reality is that seemingly illegal questions are asked all the time by employers who have no intention of discriminating against you but who are simply curious to know more about you than what's on your résumé. If you feel completely comfortable with such questions, you can answer them. It is important, however, that you be attuned to the potential for bias and not get too chatty. If you start talking about what a hassle it is to get your child to daycare on time and still be at work by 8 A.M., you might raise a concern that the interviewer hadn't even thought of.

Use your judgment to determine the spirit in which a question is being asked, and answer it only if you believe it is being asked out of genuine and harmless curiosity.

Watch Out!

Employment laws vary from state to state, so you can't fully understand a federal employment law until you know how it is affected by state statutes.

2. *Evade the question.* If you would prefer not to answer a question because you find it offensive or because you know that the information it elicits could be used against you, you do not have to answer it. You can choose to dodge it. Using humor is often one way of doing that. For example, if asked, "Do you have any children?" you can say, "Well, if you include my husband, my tank of fish, and our two cats, I suppose I have 17 children." (Of course, this reply presumes that you don't mind having the interviewer know you're married, and I wouldn't include the husband part if speaking with a male interviewer!) The interviewer is left not knowing whether you have two children and 12 fish, or no children and 14 fish—and will probably be so taken aback and perplexed that she will move onto another question.

3. *Openly refuse to answer the question.* If a question is blatantly discriminatory, offensive, or just plain stupid, you might want to respond in a more direct manner. You can say, for example, "Does my religious affiliation have any bearing on this job?" However you reply, don't be defensive, and try not to make a major ordeal out of the situation. Keep in mind that some interviewers will ask illegal questions simply because they don't know any better, not because they are biased. There's no need to alienate them unnecessarily.

 Moneysaver

For a one-stop source of legal information, visit FindLaw at www.findlaw.com for a treasure trove of legal resources on the Internet.

Sexual harassment

Of all the legal issues in the workplace, the matter of sexual harassment may be the one with which the general public is most familiar. Major legal battles in the public eye over the past several years have made all of us armchair employment attorneys. Yet, it often seems that the more we know, the less we know. If the legal scholars on major networks and cable TV programs can't agree on how to interpret sexual harassment laws, then how can the average person be expected to do so? The answer is: Don't try.

If you're in an interview and think that the interviewer's behavior might constitute sexual harassment, but you aren't sure (assuming it's a subtle verbal cue or action rather than an overt sexual advance), keep your cool until you get out of there. Then consult with an employment law expert. Don't try to make the call yourself. Of course, if the harassment is more overt—attempted physical contact or a statement or clear insinuation that you will not be hired unless you perform a certain act—then you don't have to sit tight. Make a beeline straight for the door.

Overcoming objections

You're overqualified. You're underqualified. You'll be bored. We think you'll leave us within the year. We can't afford you. These declarations on the part of interviewers leave job seekers frustrated and often unsure of whether they should fight back with a counter argument. And if so, how hard and for how long should they fight?

Some objections are legitimate. If you've held 10 jobs in the last 9 years—assuming you're not a freelancer, professional temp, or consultant—a prospective employer might have just cause for concern that you won't stick around for too long. Other objections are not so justified. Some are based simply on ignorance, bias, or paranoia. The employer creates a problem where there really doesn't need to be one and assumes you shouldn't be hired when, in fact, you would make a top-notch employee.

Let's look at some general strategies that can help you get around any barrier thrown in your path to a job. Then we'll explore some of the specific objections job seekers often face.

Strategies for dealing with interviewers' objections

Whether the interviewer is concerned about gaps in your employment history, why you were fired from your last job, or anything else, the following tactics can help you talk your way out of a sticky situation:

Anticipate objections in advance

If you know that something about your background or qualifications is likely to be problematic, don't wait until you're in the interview to think of how you're going to explain it. Discussing negatives about yourself—and building a case for why those negatives shouldn't knock you out of the running—is hard to do off the top of your head. So, even though it might never come up if you're lucky, take an objective look at what might concern interviewers—or ask someone else to help you identify the potential objections—and be prepared to address them.

Understand the root of an objection

To build an effective counter argument, you must know why something is a problem in the first place. For example, let's say someone left the corporate world to open and run a restaurant, but he couldn't make a go of it and is now back in the job hunt. You might assume that when an employer says, with raised eyebrow, "I see you had a restaurant for 18 months. . ." that she is concerned that the business failed. In fact, that interviewer probably doesn't care that it didn't succeed—everyone knows how tough it is to make a restaurant successful and that lots of businesses fail. What might be of concern to her, however, is that the candidate's entrepreneurial leanings could make him antsy and unable to settle back into a 9-to-5 job. So, don't make assumptions about what the objection is or where it's coming from until you find out what is really at the heart of the objection.

Ask questions

Before launching into a major counter argument, ask what specific concerns the interviewer has. If that former restaurant owner started making a case for why he's still a good businessman despite the fact that his restaurant didn't succeed, he'd be missing the boat. He should instead be talking about his desire to make a commitment to a particular employer and how he has done so in the past.

Don't be defensive

The worst thing you can do for your case is to act agitated, aggressive, or overly apologetic. Half the battle in overcoming employers' objections is to keep a positive attitude. If you are not overly concerned about or ashamed of any flaws in your employment history, you will convey confidence in yourself, which means the employer will have confidence in you.

State your case succinctly

This is one time when it's not such a bad idea to script out what you are going to say. Explaining something that has the potential to do major damage to your candidacy (such as having been fired from a job) must be done with finesse. You need to know exactly which words and phrases you will use, and you need to have your story straight. Hemming and hawing will only make matters worse.

Keep it in perspective

Many objections you expect an employer to have might never surface at all—or, if they do, they're not the big deal you assumed they would be. I've worked with countless job seekers who think that they are virtually unemployable because they were fired from a job, left their last job after only a few months, or got a bad reference. As you'll see in the sections that follow, there's almost always a way to break down seemingly impenetrable barriers to employment.

You've been fired

This is one of the toughest situations to deal with in a job search. No one trying to make a good impression in an interview wants to get bogged down in a discussion of having been fired. Inevitably the issue will come up, however, so you need to have a well-crafted plan of how you will address it. Consider the following strategies and options:

> **66** The ultimate measure of a man is not where he stands in moments of comfort and convenience, but where he stands at times of challenge and controversy. **99**
>
> —Martin Luther King, Jr.

Don't blow the issue out of proportion

People get fired every day. You might feel like the only person on Earth who has suffered this degradation, and the emotions you are experiencing might be painfully raw, but try to remember that it is quite common and that it does not spell the end of your career.

If you left your bosses on terms even the least bit cordial, speak to them about how you might discuss the termination with future prospective employers

You would be surprised how many are willing to let their former employees say they resigned.

Don't overlook honesty as possibly the best policy

Rather than weaving a tangled web of lies and deceit, consider stating the facts of your termination concisely and matter-of-factly. Many employers will appreciate the candor and will understand that these things happen. As long as you describe the firing in a tactful way, citing a difference of opinion and a willingness to acknowledge your role in the problem, you might be pleasantly surprised to find that the matter is not such a big deal.

Consider not mentioning the job at all if you were employed there for a short period of time, such as only a few months

As long as you are not applying for a job with the type of organization that does an "FBI-style" background check, and as long as you are not interviewing in a tight-knit industry where everyone knows everybody else's business, you have the option of not listing the job on your résumé or on an employment application. Remember, however, that lying in a job search is usually not a good idea for many reasons. So, I'm not advocating this strategy but just letting you know it's one that many people resort to when more honest alternatives just don't seem to exist.

You have gaps in your work history

If you have been out of work for a period of more than several months at some point since your career began, employers will most likely want to know why. You have nothing to worry about if the gap in your work history is due to valid reasons such as being a full-time student, being a full-time parent, recovering from an accident or illness, caring for a critically ill family member, or taking time off to travel.

If, however, you were not working because you couldn't find a job, you need to prepare a defense for objections the employer might have. If your unemployment was due to a recession or wide-scale job shortage in your field, most employers will understand that the problem is no reflection on your character or qualifications. Also, if you have made a major career change, prospective employers understand that it can take time to define your new focus, get the necessary training, establish new contacts, and make the transition.

But if the reality is that you left a job, spent a few months lying on the couch before getting motivated to look for a new job, then spent several months or more trying to find one, the gap might be more difficult to explain. If you have been employed since the gap occurred, then the problem is not as pronounced, but if you are currently job hunting after having been unemployed for the past several months, you have some explaining to do.

People don't like to hire people who have been rejected by lots of other potential employers. So, if you say that you have been actively searching for several months, or even a year or more, the prospective employer might assume that something is wrong with you. You'll need to account for your time. Exactly how you do that is a bit controversial.

The reality is—you didn't hear it from me—that people lie. They might talk someone at their former job into stretching the end date of their employment out by a month or a few months to buy them some time. Then they say that they traveled for a month or so to take a break before starting a job search. Then, they took time off to re-evaluate where they wanted to move next in their career. (Actually, that last excuse might very likely be true and is certainly acceptable and plausible.) By the time all those activities are factored in, the active job-searching process gets reduced to just a few months, which is a reasonable period of time to be looking. In addition to—or besides—those excuses, some people go so far as to concoct stories about caring for sick relatives or other seemingly noble deeds to account for their time.

Others who did have some sort of professional activity going on while job hunting get creative about how they describe it. Someone might spend a couple of weeks helping out a friend start a business by doing a little public relations, but in an interview this person calls it a six-month consulting job. Someone who volunteers for a few charities might list the title "fund-raising consultant" on a résumé. Whether you tell a bold-faced lie or merely stretch the truth to your advantage is your call.

Note: If you have been out of work for a significant period of time in the past due to psychiatric problems or incarceration, you are protected by laws that prohibit employers from rejecting you on those grounds (with some exceptions, such as for jobs in financial institutions or those that involve public safety).

That doesn't mean, of course, that they won't find some objection to your candidacy that is a legally justifiable reason for rejecting you.

You look like a job-hopper

As changing jobs and career fields have become more the norm over the past several years, job-hopping is less common a concern among prospective employers than it used to be. The massive downsizings and reorganizations of the 1990s forced many well-qualified professionals to move from job to job more frequently than was customary in previous generations. This movement created a climate of tolerance in which short tenures at jobs are now more acceptable, even if they are due to the employee's own desire to make a move. Added to this phenomenon is the fact that some industries—such as the media, advertising, public relations, and high-tech, among others—are characterized by revolving-door employment patterns.

Nevertheless, if your résumé lists so many jobs that it sends up a red flag, be prepared to explain the movement. The key to doing so is to be brief and to the point when explaining why you left each job. It's best if the reasons for leaving have little to do with you and as much as possible to do with problems on the employer's side: a company that went out of business, a not-for-profit group that lost funding, an organization that downsized, or an organizational structure that offered little room for advancement. In describing your work history, don't sound bitter, negative, or passive. Show how you took charge of situations, such as leaving before a business failed or cutting your losses if a job just wasn't the right fit.

To put an additional positive spin on the situation, think of something you have stuck with for a considerable period of time. If your résumé says you've had five jobs in five years but you've served meals at a soup kitchen every Saturday morning for those five years, tell the employer about it. Any example you can give of your ability to make a commitment and stick with it will help your case.

Bright Idea

Keep in mind that we are living in the Age of the Comeback and a culture of forgiveness. We excuse major transgressions on the part of prominent figures such as celebrities and politicians, so that little skeleton in your professional closet is unlikely to keep you from getting hired.

You started a business that failed

As mentioned with the restaurant example earlier, this problem is more likely to be a concern in your own mind than an objection the employer will voice. As long as you don't give evidence of poor judgment or management skills when describing the failure, you don't have much to worry about. Focus on how you showed initiative, ambition, and a tolerance for risk-taking by striking out on your own. Also, talk about what you learned from the experience and any successes that you did have. Make it clear that you have now sewn your entrepreneurial oats and are more than ready to commit to working for someone else.

You're overqualified

When employers say that you are overqualified for a position, 99 percent of the time they're really saying that they assume you want more money than they can pay. The way to know whether that's the case is, of course, to ask.

If salary is the issue—and if you don't mind earning whatever they can pay, even if it's less than what you've been making—then deal with it by building a strong case for why you don't mind taking a salary cut. Discuss how you are making a career transition and that you are well aware that you have to make some sacrifices to get where you want to be. Don't just sound like you're making empty claims. Let them know you have given this careful thought—perhaps even worked out a new personal budget. Also let them know what motivates you besides money so they'll see that you would find other rewards from the work and thus not leave the new job after a few months in search of a bigger paycheck.

If you aren't willing to take a pay cut but want them to see that you are worth the money you deserve, talk about how you can save them money and give examples of how you have done so in the past.

In addition to the money issue, claiming that you are overqualified might also mean that the employer is worried that you'll be bored and will leave, or that you'll get antsy to be promoted sooner than is convenient for them. This is particularly common when you are making a major career change and are willing to start at the bottom—or at least on a low floor—in the new field. You have to alleviate employers' concerns by conveying the amount of thought that has gone into choosing the new target job. Also try to think of tasks on your past jobs that correspond to those of the prospective lower-level job. Explaining that you not only know what you're getting into, but that you have performed similar duties in the past with no complaint might be a way to deflect their objections.

You're underqualified

Often, labeling you as underqualified is a legitimate call. You might not have the experience, skills, credentials, or content knowledge needed for success in a position. If this is true, your best recourse is to discuss the assets that you do bring to the table. These might balance out the deficits. Also, don't just say, "I'm a quick learner" when talking about how you would boost your qualifications. Give examples of how you've gotten up to speed quickly in the past when a situation called for doing so.

Another option is to offer to work on a trial basis for no pay for a period of weeks or months to prove yourself. Or, you might ask to work as an intern or apprentice of sorts while simultaneously getting the necessary skills through courses or other means (and while working in another full-time or part-time job just to pay the bills). Sometimes, getting from where you are to where you want to be in your career requires having a "patchwork" life for a while. The point is to be creative and persistent and not give up.

Bright Idea

If an interviewer is concerned that you lack direct experience required for the job, point out the benefits of the fresh perspective you would bring coming from a different industry or sector.

However, if there is just no chance of working in any capacity for the employer who has labeled you as underqualified, you can at least take from the experience new insight into how you might improve your candidacy elsewhere. Ask the employer to be specific in describing your deficits and to suggest ways you might overcome them. And, who knows, if you accept the rejection gracefully and show a willingness to work on your professional development, you might be successful in applying with that same employer in the future after you boost your qualifications.

You're just not the right fit

This might be a legitimate objection if it is based on concern about the nature of your experience, your tangible qualifications (such as your skills and expertise), or your education and training. If that is the case, you need to find out which aspects of your qualifications are seen as deficits and discuss how you can make up for those deficits. Talk about how you can take classes, attend seminars, teach yourself on your own time, or speed up your on-the-job learning by putting in extra hours. As with the problem of being underqualified, you should also reiterate your asset statements to remind the interviewer how your transferable skills might make you a good fit.

Be aware, however, that saying you just aren't the right fit can be a euphemism for saying they want someone more attractive, older or younger, of a different race, or some other discriminatory criterion. The discussion of illegal questions later in this chapter will help you identify lines of questioning that might clue you in to some bias.

Anticipating objections

To ensure that you won't be caught off guard when an employer raises an objection, consider completing a form like the one that follows to help you prepare. With some careful advance planning, a well-crafted counter argument, and a positive, confident attitude, you can overcome most interviewers' objections. As long as you have other assets that would be of value, most employers will forgive a few hiccups in your past. If they won't, then you have a decision to make. You can keep beating your head against a brick wall trying to reason with an unreasonable hiring manager or recruiter, or you can cut your losses and move on. Throwing in the towel after you've done everything in your power to alleviate their concerns is often the best thing you can do for your search.

The questions you ask

You are probably already aware that in addition to anticipating certain questions to be asked of you, you need to prepare questions you will ask. Many job seekers dread getting to the point of the interview when they hear, "So, do you have any questions for us?" It can be difficult to come up with questions to ask because many will have already been answered by your pre-interview research or throughout the interview. This is particularly true in a conversational interview in which the interviewer is likely to have told you everything you need to know about the position and the organization—and then some. So how do you ask intelligent questions when you don't really have any in mind? Or, how do you know whether questions that you do have in mind are appropriate? Consider the following tactics:

- Avoid the problem altogether by asking questions throughout the interview rather than waiting until the end of the meeting.

- Don't ask anything that you should know already, such as information easily available in an organization's online or print publications.

- Ask questions that a consultant would ask, such as questions about the organization's needs, problems, competition, challenges, plans, and goals.

- Don't ask about money and perks, such as salary, health benefits, vacation time, sick leave policy, and the like. You'll have time to find out about those things after an offer is on the table.

- Ask questions that help you get a clear picture of what the job would really be like day-to-day instead of the glossed-over image the interviewer might portray.

- Similarly, ask probing questions about the organization so that you can assess its stability and strength and can see whether the direction it is heading matches your own career goals.

Questions you should ask fit into three basic categories: the position, the organization, and next steps in the hiring process. Questions about the next steps in the hiring process are discussed in Chapter 15, which discusses follow-up strategies to land the offer. Questions to ask about the position for which you're interviewing and the organization you're seeking employment with are listed here.

Questions about the position

Depending on what is relevant to the position at hand and what has already been addressed by the interviewer, consider rounding out your knowledge of the job by asking these questions. Note that I've grouped related questions together.

 Bright Idea

If you ask questions about an organization's problems, plans, and goals early in an interview, you'll be able to structure the rest of the conversation around how you can meet those needs.

Questions Typically Asked of Students and Recent Grads

How did you choose your college/graduate school?

Why did you select a major in . . . ?

Tell me about your senior project/thesis/dissertation/ other major project.

How has your college experience prepared you for a career?

Why did you decide to attend graduate school?

Describe your most rewarding extracurricular experience in college/graduate school.

If you had to do it over again, how would you plan your education differently?

Are your grades representative of your abilities?

What was your worst grade, and how did it happen?

What are your standardized test scores? (SAT, GRE, LSAT, and so on)

Who was your favorite professor, and why?

Which teaching styles do you learn from best?

Tell me about your internships and part-time jobs.

Why didn't you work during college/graduate school?

Why didn't you hold any leadership roles in college/ graduate school?

How did you pay for school?

How much did you study during college/graduate school?

How would your classmates describe you?

As an alum, how do you plan to be involved in your school?

- Where does this position fit into your organizational chart?
- To whom would I report?
- Who else reports to that person?
- How long has that person been with the company?
- With which other groups or departments would I interact?
- What are the future plans for this department?
- What are the biggest challenges facing this department?
- What is a typical career path for this position, or is there one?
- How will my performance be measured/evaluated?
- Why is this position open?
- How long has it been open?
- How long was the last person in this position?
- How many people have held this position in the last X# of years?
- What qualities are needed for success on this job?
- What are you really looking for in a candidate?
- Are you considering any internal candidates?
- What percentage of my time would be spent in the various duties?
- What are the top priorities for this position in the first six months/year?

You should leave the interview with a clear picture of what the job would entail, what's needed to do it well, and what daily life on the job would be like. If you are meeting with someone who is only doing a preliminary screening of you and isn't familiar with the day-to-day intricacies of this position, ask who will know these answers and whether that person will be part of the interviewing process down the road.

Questions about the organization

Just as you are being evaluated as a job applicant, you need to evaluate the potential employer. Just remember not to ask about anything that should be obvious and easily researched. These questions can help you learn more about the employing organization itself:

- **What are the organization's plans/goals for the future?**

- **What resources are being deployed to reach those goals or objectives?**

- **Are there plans to expand/consolidate/discontinue current products or services?**

- **Is any change of ownership planned?**

- **What is this company's exit strategy? (if a privately-held company)**

- **How well is this company/organization capitalized/ funded?**

- **What are the biggest challenges facing this organization?**

- **Which of your competitors pose the biggest threats these days?**

- **How would you describe the working environment here?**

- **What do you most/least like about working here?**

Develop additional questions that arise out of the pre-interview research you conduct. You might read something about the organization, either on its own Web site or in trade or news publications that you want to discuss. Don't hesitate to ask probing questions, although consider reserving the more sensitive, touchy questions for a later interview as you don't want to raise controversial topics in a first interview. Wait until you have an offer or are near an offer to ask about matters that might be sensitive or negative.

Just the facts

- Don't be thrown by off-the-wall interview questions—the ones that make you uncomfortable of force you to bring up awkward issues. Think about what the question is getting at and keep your cool. Err on the side of candor when replying, but don't shoot yourself in the foot by saying too much.

- Know your legal rights so that you can recognize discrimination and know what information you are required to divulge. If faced with a question that you know is illegal, you have the choice of answering it or dodging it tactfully.

- The best way to deal with interviewers' objections is to anticipate them before they come up and to prepare a succinct, nonapologetic counter-argument in advance.

- To overcome an interviewer's objection, keep a level head, don't get defensive, understand the root of the objection, and don't make it a bigger issue than it needs to be.

- Don't wait until the end of the interview to ask questions yourself. The more questions you ask early in the interview, the more easily you can build a case for why you're the best candidate.

GET THE SCOOP ON...
Why interview follow-up really starts during the
interview ▪ Thank-you letters that clinch the
deal ▪ How to follow up without being a pest ▪
Evaluating and confirming job offers ▪
Negotiating the best compensation package

Clinching the Deal

Chapter 15

O ne of the biggest mistakes job seekers make is
to sit back after an interview and wait for the
phone to ring. Strategic interviewing doesn't
stop at the parting handshake; the efforts you make
after the interview are just as critical as those made
before and during it. If your encounter with an interviewer was less than magical, effective follow-up might
turn the tables and salvage your candidacy. Or, if your
interview went well, but you face stiff competition,
the contact you make afterward with the prospective
employer can set you apart from other candidates.

Then, when the offers do start coming in, it's
important that you're prepared to evaluate and
negotiate each offer to make the right decision and
get the best deal. This chapter offers tips for handling this critical stage of the process.

Starting your follow-up before the interview ends

Follow-up actually begins before you ever leave the
interviewer's office. If you ask the right questions

and cinch the rapport as the interview comes to a close, you build a solid foundation on which to base your later follow-through efforts.

Imagine you had an interview three weeks ago and now you're sitting by the phone hoping to get a call. Let's say you mailed a thank-you note the day after the interview and left two phone messages the following week but have not received a call back. The three weeks since the appointment seem like an eternity, and you're so tired of waiting that at this point you wouldn't even mind receiving a rejection letter in the mail. You just want an answer, even if it's "no." You're left in the awkward position of not knowing whether you should call or write again.

Two simple things can prevent this scenario. The first is obtaining adequate information about the employer's decision-making timeframe. If you had found out how long the employer plans to be interviewing candidates, then you would know whether to be concerned about no contact for three weeks. The second thing to do is to leave the interview on a confident, positive note with good rapport established so that you will be perceived as something closer to a newfound friend than a pest when you make your follow-up calls or send notes.

Questions that build a foundation for follow-up

As an interview draws to a close, ask questions that help you know how and when to follow up and where you stand. These include:

- **What is your timeframe for making a decision?**
- **How many more candidates do you expect to interview?**
- **When do you need someone to start in this position?**
- **Is there anything else you need to have a complete picture of my qualifications?**

Bright Idea

Get complete contact information for everyone you interview with so you can follow up promptly and efficiently. Remember that all this information might not be on someone's business card (such as an email address or direct phone line), so check for missing data before you tuck the card away.

Establish rapport so you can maintain rapport

Establishing rapport does not mean becoming the interviewer's new best buddy; it simply means connecting in some meaningful way. The rapport you establish opens good lines of communication and helps you avoid awkwardness when you attempt to stay in touch after the interview.

Close the interview with confidence

A confident departure is one in which you not only thank the interviewer for his or her time but also spell out why you think you're right for the position. You restate your asset statements in a concise pitch to reinforce the case you've been building. Leave a strong last impression, not just a good first impression.

What to do within 24 hours after an interview

You might think that all you need to do immediately after an interview is write a thank-you note. Although the note is important, two steps must take precedence because they will help you write a more powerful thank-you note—or, as it is called in this book, "follow-up letter."

First, evaluate the interview experience, then seek feedback on it from key members of your network. This should be done within 24 hours after the interview. Then you can write the follow-up letter and make plans for further follow-up—two things that should also be taken care of within 24 hours, or at least within 48 hours.

Watch Out!

Be objective when assessing a potential job and employer in the first hours or days after an interview. If the experience was pleasant on a social level, you might paint a rosier picture of the opportunity than is warranted. Objectivity now helps you better evaluate a job offer later.

Evaluate the interview experience

You might leave an interview feeling like you're walking on air or trudging through quicksand—or something in between—but there's nothing like an objective, logical analysis of the experience to complement those gut reactions. While the encounter is fresh in your mind, it's important to jot down some thoughts on how you did, what the employer's main needs and interests were, and where you think (or know) your candidacy stands. Also make note of any tidbits of information that can work to your advantage during the follow-through, such as pet concerns or hobbies of the individual interviewer, or interests you have in common.

These notes not only aid in the follow-up stage but can also serve as criteria on which to base a decision, should you end up receiving a job offer. Use the Interview Evaluation Form that follows as a way to structure your notes. You might photocopy the form or create your own on your computer so that you can complete one for every interview.

Consult with your network for interview feedback

Conducting the interview evaluation helps you lay a foundation for your follow-up letter and other post-interview communication, but it's just the first step. Next, you need to speak with people who can help you interpret things the employer said and take an accurate read on your assessment of the experience. Consider whether any of the following categories of people could be of help to you:

Headhunters

If your interview was arranged through a staffing agency or search firm, the first place to turn for feedback is to the recruiter you are working with. In many cases, the prospective employer will let the recruiter know how you did on the interview and where your candidacy stands. The extent to which the employer is forthcoming with such information depends upon the nature of the relationship he or she has with the recruiter, so what you're able to learn will vary from place to place.

Other employees at the prospective employer

If you know anyone who works at the organization where you interviewed, don't hesitate to contact that person to get an insider's insight into your chances. Also ask for advice on what steps you should take next. If you had an initial screening interview followed by additional interviews with different people, you should consider contacting the person who conducted the first interview. He or she may be willing to serve as an advocate of sorts for you with the other hiring authorities.

Your career consultant

If you have been—or plan to start—working with a career development professional, be sure to debrief your interview with that person. Career consultants know the right questions to ask to identify any red flags you might not have spotted.

Other members of your network

If you aren't working with a career counselor or job search coach, there may be other people—friends, family, or professional colleagues—who can give you the same kind of objective read on your description of the interview.

 Moneysaver

As often as possible—and when appropriate—follow up with employers via email rather than racking up big expenses from long-distance calls and faxes, or from postage and stationery.

Interview Evaluation Form

Interview date:

Interviewer name:

Company/organization name:

Address:

Email:

Tel:

Fax:

A. My Performance

1. How did I do? (generally)
2. How was the balance of power? Did I come across as a potential peer?
3. Asset statements I used:
4. Questions I had difficulty answering:
5. Points I forgot to make:
6. Things I said that might have been misunderstood:

B. What I Learned About the Employer

1. The organization's most pressing needs or problems:
2. Anticipated areas of growth for the organization:
3. Other organizational goals:
4. Which skills, content knowledge, and personal qualities are sought?

C. Do I Want the Job?

1. How did the culture/work environment seem?
2. What would the work schedule be?
3. What would my responsibilities be?
4. What did I learn about salary and benefits?
5. How does this position/employer fit with my short-term goals?
6. . . . with my long-term goals?

7. Does this position/employer seem right for me in general?

8. What are my specific concerns, if any, about the suitability of this position/employer for me?

D. What Are My Chances of Getting an Offer?

1. Did I get a straight answer about my candidacy?

2. What were my strengths?

3. What concerns did the interviewer express about me?

E. Questions for Follow-up

1. What did I learn about the interviewer's personal and professional interests?

2. Over which work-related or non-work-related topics did we bond?

3. To which communication/personal style did the interviewer seem most receptive?

4. Is there some information or materials the interviewer expressed a need for or interest in that I can send?

5. When do they expect to make a decision?

6. How many more people are going to be interviewed?

7. When do they need someone to start?

8. How did the interviewer respond to my request to stay in touch after the interview?

9. Did the interviewer offer any guidelines for when and how he or she prefers that I follow up (for example, How often? Via phone or email?)?

Watch Out!

Never usurp the authority of an executive recruiter or employment agent by following up directly with the prospective employer when the interview was set up through the headhunter. With rare exceptions (and with permission from the headhunter), you have to let the recruiter or agent do the talking for you.

Sending a follow-up letter

After you have evaluated the interview—both on your own and with the help of objective third parties—you're ready to send your follow-up letter. This letter should be more than a thank-you note; it is a letter that either clinches the deal or encourages the employer to have you back for more interviews.

Most of your fellow candidates will send letters that do nothing more than express their appreciation for the interviewer's time and reinforce their interest in the position. To set yourself apart from the pack, you must do those two things but also use the letter as your chance to have the last word, to address any concerns the interviewer might have had with you and to further strengthen your case.

Your letter should include the following sections, roughly in this order:

1. An expression of your thanks for the opportunity to interview. If the interviewer expended any extra effort on your part—perhaps speaking to you at length, introducing you to others, or giving you a tour of the facility—be sure to note your appreciation for that effort.

2. A very brief recap of your assets, focusing on those most relevant for the position or in which the interviewer expressed most interest.

3. A straightforward, nonapologetic counter-argument to any concerns the interviewer openly expressed about your qualifications. Don't raise any worries that don't already exist!

4. A statement of your interest in the position and enthusiasm for the employer.

5. A subtle reminder of the next steps you agreed upon, such as, "As you suggested, I will call you next week to see where you are in the decision-making process."

Keep the letter concise, but be sure to touch on each point described. A thank-you note that consists of only two or three lines is a waste of time. On the other hand, don't go overboard and send a letter that is longer than one page. You should be able to state your case succinctly in just three or four brief paragraphs.

If you had a panel interview or met with multiple people on the same day, be sure to send a personalized letter to each person you met. The letters need not be drastically different from each other (the recipients are not likely to have time to compare notes with each other), but they should vary slightly.

When your letter is ready, you can send it through email, regular mail, express mail, or fax—or you can hand-deliver it. Traditionally, follow-up letters have been sent by regular mail to conform with proper business etiquette. Over the past few years, however, is has become common and acceptable to send your thank-you letter by email. Avoid hand-delivering or express-mailing the letter unless it is particularly urgent to get it to the hiring authorities before a decision is made. Sending a follow-up letter should look effortless, not like a major ordeal. You also want to keep up the image of having more important things to do with your time than to run around town dropping off letters.

 Bright Idea

When sending your follow-up note, encourage further communication by enclosing something the interviewer might feel obligated to thank you for or comment on: a magazine or newspaper article, a link to a Web site, or anything else relevant to the interviewer's personal or professional interests.

Sample Interview Follow-up Letter

Mr. Loren Woods
National Sales Director
AAA Wireless, Inc.
111 East Elm Street, Suite 100
Anytown, NY 00000

March 26, 2005

Dear Mr. Woods:

I enjoyed meeting you yesterday and appreciated the opportunity to discuss how I could contribute to your turn-around efforts on the East Coast as a Regional Manager of Sales. I was impressed with the degree of professionalism in everyone I met at AAA Wireless and am excited about the possibility of joining your team.

Now that I've learned more about your objectives, I'm confident that I have what you need. As we discussed, the challenges you're facing at AAA are very similar to the initiative I led at XYZ Company where I brought a failing region from lowest rank in the company to second highest, increasing sales revenue by 39% to $200 million in 18 months.

I look forward to continuing our discussions and will also follow up with your VP of Human Resources, Lynn Baker, regarding next steps. Thank you again for your time and consideration.

Sincerely,

Barbara Peters

Schedule your next steps

After your letter is on its way, you need to plan the next steps in your follow-up. A typical scenario in a job search is that you have a first interview, send a follow-up letter or email within a day or so, and then stay in touch with the employer (usually by phone or email) until you are invited to return for a follow-up interview or are told that you are not in the running for a position.

Secrets of persisting without pestering

When you're waiting to hear the results of a hiring decision, questions inevitably arise about how assertive—or even aggressive—to be in chasing after those results. Although you do need to do everything you can to produce a favorable outcome—to get an offer—there is a fine line between being persistent and being a pest. You might be all too familiar with those awkward moments when your hand is on the phone, but you just aren't sure whether you should leave the employer yet another message—even though it's been two weeks since your interview. You might have one voice inside of you saying, "Be bold, make the call," and another cautioning you not to be a pest. Or, you may consider emailing or faxing a note to be less obtrusive, but you aren't sure what to write. Staying in touch after an interview requires as much strategy as the interview itself. Follow-up that is done haphazardly or half-heartedly is worse than no follow-up at all. Let's look at the rationale behind your persistence—as well as some guidelines for it.

Why your follow-up efforts are so important

Getting employers to return your calls or reply to your emails can be an incredibly frustrating process. Sometimes matters are made even worse when you do finally get through to them and find that they are not forthcoming with information, are noncommittal, or—at worst—are downright rude. Despite these frustrations, following up is critical for the following reasons:

Getting a job is your priority, but filling a vacant position might not be the employer's priority

Or perhaps, there's a fairly urgent need to bring someone on board, but the hiring manager is busy putting out fires somewhere else. By following up, you turn yourself into their priority.

Some employers test candidates by seeing who follows up and shows the most interest

This is especially common with positions such as sales, in which you would need to be aggressive and persistent.

Out of sight is out of mind

Sometimes jobs go to the person who happens to call on the day that the hiring authority feels like extending an offer—not to the one who is better qualified.

Post-interview phone calls and written correspondence let you alleviate concerns the employer might have about you

Sometimes the follow-up letter sent immediately after the interview isn't sufficient; you might need to talk with the employer directly to address those concerns.

Being persistent gives you a sense of power over the outcome

A job search can be stressful, so to keep your sanity during it, you need to retain as much control as possible. Even if you're not getting any immediate results from your efforts, at least you know that you're doing everything you can.

 Watch Out!

Keep in mind that you need to be yourself during your search. If being assertive is not in your nature, make yourself to be that way just enough to get the job done, but don't try to make a 180-degree switch to being an extremely aggressive person. Your actions will come across as contrived and phony.

Guidelines for considerate but assertive follow-up

To take a proactive approach to your follow-up but not be seen as a pest, consider the following guidelines.

Let your follow-up efforts be guided by what, if anything, you found out during the interview

If you know the position might not be filled for two months, then there is no need to harass the employer with daily or even weekly phone calls.

Don't get hung up on exactly how frequently you should try to reach someone who's not returning your calls or email

There is no magic formula. Use your common sense and imagine that you were the person receiving the voice mail or email. You probably wouldn't want to be called five times a day, but you might not mind a call or two per week, depending on the overall timeframe.

Consider the nature of the position, the organization, and the industry as well as the style of the people there

Is aggressiveness likely to be not only valued but expected, or are you dealing with people who are more low-key?

When you do reach someone on the phone, don't sound like you're just going through the motions of placing the requisite follow-up call

There's no point in making the call if you're merely going to say something like, "I'm just checking in to see whether you've made any decisions." You'll sound passive, disinterested, and possibly like a nuisance. Instead, connect on a human level and also use the opportunity to build your case further.

Remember how hiring decisions are made, as described in Chapter 2, "How Employers Think"

You might be dealing with a process that is disorganized, or one in which multiple decision-makers must come to a consensus, or one that involves some wild card variables that are out of your control.

Be sure you're following up with the right person

Don't waste your time chasing down someone who has little authority in the hiring decision.

Know when to give up

If your follow-up reaches the point of absurdity (if it goes on for months and you're pushing the limits of common courtesy with the number of times you've called and written), then you may need to cut your losses and move on.

If you have reached the end of your rope and need an answer, consider faxing a letter instead of leaving yet another phone message or sending yet another email

Politely but firmly state that you need to have an answer so that you can pursue other opportunities, and you would appreciate a call or email letting you know where your candidacy stands— even if the answer is "no." Note that you would typically only do this if you had more than one interview and know that the employer had seemed very interested in you, perhaps to the point of insinuating that an offer might be forthcoming.

If you do find out that you're being turned down for a position, see whether you can get any feedback on why you didn't get the job

Be aware that many will be reluctant to offer any. The issue of giving feedback is an extremely controversial one among human resources professionals and hiring managers. Some feel they have no business acting as your career coach, but others believe you deserve an honest critique.

Evaluating and negotiating the offer

A job offer usually will be extended verbally by telephone or in person. The hiring manager or human resources representative will—or should—state the position title and salary being offered and might recap what your responsibilities would be. You do not have to give an answer on the spot, but you should express enthusiasm and appreciation for the offer and tell them when you will give your response (or ask how long you can take to make your decision). You then use that time to evaluate the offer and prepare your negotiating strategy to make it a more attractive offer. In doing so, you need to remember one of the guiding principles of this book: You are not a desperate job seeker. Employers need you as much as you need them. Coming from that position of strength can help you approach the negotiations with confidence and the decision making with a clear head.

If you've ever tried to work a puzzle like a Rubik's Cube, you know how frustrating it is to move one piece of the puzzle into the right position, only to find that another one gets shifted out of place and sends you back to square one. Negotiating and evaluating job offers is a little like that. No job or employer is going to fit your interests and needs perfectly. One position might offer the money you want but would require an extra hour a day of commuting. Another may be just around the corner from home and offer a little more money, but would have a boss who seems like a loose cannon.

Accepting a job offer usually involves some degree of sacrifice and compromise. You might settle for less of a salary increase and more volatility in your boss in exchange for the convenience of walking to work. Or, you might say that the personality of the people you work with is of utmost importance, so you'll take the other job and find a way to live with the commute. The way to feel comfortable with these trade-offs is to make a careful assessment of your priorities and to get a complete picture of exactly what the job will entail and what the employer has to offer. Of course, to avoid having to make many

Watch Out!

Never accept an offer immediately and try not to enter into negotiations immediately. Ask for some time to consider the offer. This time also gives you a chance to prepare your negotiating strategy.

sacrifices or compromises in the first place, you need to negotiate favorable terms of the offer. The steps involved in negotiating and evaluating an offer are as follows:

1. Identify your priorities so that you have solid criteria on which to base a decision.

2. Scrutinize the offer so you know exactly what you're getting into and so you feel confident that you're getting a fair deal.

3. Determine whether the offer satisfies your priorities.

4. Negotiate more favorable terms, if necessary.

5. Decide whether to accept or decline the offer.

The sections that follow take you through each of these steps.

Step one: identify your priorities

One of the biggest mistakes people make when evaluating a job offer is to do just that: evaluate the *offer*. They learn everything they can about the position's responsibilities, the stability of the employer, and the salary and benefits, but they neglect to evaluate their own priorities. Sure, they might assess what they would like out of a job—more money, interesting new challenges, or opportunity for advancement, perhaps—but they don't define which of those desires take precedence over the others.

If you take this approach, you will be evaluating the offer in a vacuum. You'll know everything there is to know about the job, but you won't know how it satisfies your needs. This problem becomes particularly evident when you are evaluating more than one offer and must compare the advantages and disadvantages of each. The pros and cons might balance out to make the

Watch Out!

In the excitement of getting a job offer, it's easy to be lax when it comes to scrutinizing an offer. Don't let the flattery that comes with receiving an offer cloud your good judgment. Get out the magnifying glass and see whether it's really as great as it seems.

offers about equally attractive, so you don't know which to choose. In that case, you might find yourself in a situation of comparing apples and oranges, unable to make a decision because the nature of the pros and cons differs.

Now is the time to go back to the "Deciding What You Want" section of Chapter 3, as well as the "Job Search Wish List" in that same chapter. You've already identified your priorities, so now all you have to do is determine how a job offer you're faced with satisfies those priorities, which leads you to Steps Two and Three.

Step two: scrutinize an offer

Have you ever made a careful career decision only to find that when you actually started the new job or ventured into the new profession, the reality didn't match your expectations? Part of the problem may have been that you had not adequately clarified those expectations in the first place. If you did not clearly identify your priorities before making the move, you might have taken a job that didn't satisfy what you needed. The problem also might have resulted from insufficient information about what the job would entail. The heading for this section uses the term "scrutinize" for a reason: It's not enough to have a vague idea of what a job would entail or what an employer has to offer. You must read between the lines, second-guess, investigate, be suspicious, and leave no stone unturned. In other words, you have to find out what you're getting into.

Become a job offer detective

Knowing what you're getting into requires some detective work. Just as you conducted research before your interview, you now need to combine print, electronic, and people resources for clues to the quality and suitability of an offer. The following are ways to find the information you need to scrutinize any offer:

Refer to your pre-interview research

Take another look at the Information Gems worksheet you completed in Chapter 11 as well as any other notes you've taken about the employer and the job in question.

Refer to the interview evaluation form you completed after the interview

Look for observations you made about the position and the employer while the interviewing experience was still fresh in your mind.

Talk to your network

Get input from anybody and everybody on the prospective employer. You might come across some inside scoop that could sway your decision significantly.

Do a keyword search on the Internet using the employer's name to find the most recent information on the organization

You can also do searches related to the industry as a whole if you are deciding among job offers from employers in different industries.

Ask to talk to the person who recently held the position you are being offered

This is usually only possible if that person is still employed at the same organization, having been promoted or transferred, as opposed to leaving the company entirely.

Ask tough questions

Don't hesitate to ask the recruiters or hiring managers involved in the process any questions that will elicit the information you need. If they really want you, they'll be forthcoming.

Indicators That a Job Offer Might Be an Offer You *Can* Refuse

- The organization is in a major state of flux due to reorganization, rapid expansion, lay-offs, mergers, or other significant activity.

- The changes described in the previous point are not yet happening at this organization but are rampant elsewhere in the industry as a whole.

- This position has had frequent turnover.

- The employer keeps emphasizing the need for someone who can hit the ground running. Could be a euphemism for "We can't train or support you."

- Your prospective boss is very new and, therefore, an unknown, untested, quantity.

- Your prospective boss has been with the company since before time began and, therefore, might be burned-out or tuned-out.

- The job is in a start-up company or new division of an established company with no clear pipeline of funding or revenue.

- The position is project-based with contracts and, therefore, budget lines not yet finalized.

- You are not given the opportunity to meet and talk privately with your prospective co-workers.

- The interviewing and hiring process is disorganized and inefficient, which could signal a lack of professionalism in other areas of the organization.

- The offer was made quickly before they had a chance to get to know you thoroughly.

- You have been subjected to a too-good-to-be-true sales pitch for the organization.

Step three: compare the offer with your priorities

In addition to your Job Search Wish List from Chapter 3, the Job Acceptance Criteria worksheet that follows is a helpful tool for evaluating an offer. The worksheet lists 25 factors that might or might not be critical to your satisfaction on a job. The objective is to rate each factor on a scale of 1–10 according to how important it is that your next job satisfy that criterion. A high rating—such as 8, 9, or 10—would indicate that this factor is extremely important to you. Low ratings of 1, 2, or 3 reflect factors that you really don't care much about, and the middle ratings reflect criteria that you feel some degree of indifference toward or might like to have met but that aren't essential. The questions that follow each criterion can help you decide how important that factor is to you. In the space provided after each set of questions, you might find it helpful to jot down some specific thoughts to give your numeric ratings more meaning, particularly for those you rated as 6 or higher. For example, after the skills criterion, you might list some of the actual skills you would like to utilize or develop. After the perks criterion, you could list actual perks you care most about.

Step four: negotiate the best deal

Rarely do you have to accept the first offer you are given. Room almost always exists for negotiation—with some exceptions, such as union or government positions in which the compensation, job title, and responsibilities are fixed at a particular grade or level. (Even then, however, you might be able to propose that you come in at a slightly higher grade than the one offered.) With those exceptions, most employers expect you to negotiate, so don't hesitate to give it a try.

Principles of savvy negotiating

With the following guidelines, you'll be able to negotiate a favorable offer like a pro:

Do your homework

As with an interview, a negotiation session involves building a case for yourself and your needs, as well as showing the employer what you bring to the table. To negotiate effectively, you need to prepare that case in advance by doing sufficient self-assessment and market research.

Define your deal-points and breaking-points in advance

Know which issues are important to you (based on your priorities identification) and which ones are so critical that you would rather decline the offer than to have to concede them.

Be yourself

Negotiating strategies usually fall somewhere on a spectrum from aggressive to cooperative in style. If you try to go to one extreme or the other in a way that doesn't fit your natural style, the negotiations will not only be difficult for you to pull off, but they are not as likely to work in your favor.

Approach negotiations with the mindset that both parties are there to reach a win-win conclusion

It need not be adversarial. After all, these are the people with whom you will be working.

Negotiate with a style that reflects the position, the employer, and the industry or profession

Adopt a more aggressive or more reserved approach as befitting the setting and the person with whom you are negotiating. In either case, however, never be rude or overbearing. Tact and consideration will take you far.

 Watch Out!

When identifying your priorities, be sure they reflect what you really want out of a job or career, not ones that family or friends want you to consider important or that are socially desirable.

Be fair

Skilled negotiators know that it's not about winning at the expense of the other parties involved but about coming to terms that are satisfying for both sides. So, don't play dirty or rough; doing so won't get you anywhere.

Be truthful

Don't tell lies to win points. If you mislead the prospective employer about your salary history, qualifications, or anything else, you will most likely get caught in the lie and might have the offer retracted—or be fired if you're caught after being hired.

Be flexible

Negotiations require that you give to get. You must be prepared to make concessions on some points to gain ground where it really matters to you.

Negotiate more than salary

Keep in mind that you are discussing the terms of the offer as a whole. Although the money factor may be important to you, the negotiation is a chance for you to shape an employment opportunity that will be satisfying to you in more ways than the impact on your bank account.

Be resourceful

There's often more to gain from negotiation than just dollars. For example, if an employer cannot go up on your salary because the amount must be equal to that of your co-workers, think of ways you could be rewarded that would not be so obvious as to cause ill will among your colleagues. Could you get extra vacation time, a signing bonus, or some other perk?

Don't let 'em see you sweat

Keep your cool, no matter how tough the negotiations get.

Never be hesitant

The only way to make your case convincingly is to do so in a persuasive, confident manner.

Bright Idea

If you're trying to get a higher salary than one you've ever earned, cite your previous salaries as aggregates of bonuses, commissions, and even the value of the benefits packages so that you're talking total annual income, not just base wages.

Use leverage

If you receive another bonafide offer prior to—or while in negotiations with—one employer, play the offers off each other to see who can ultimately give you the best deal.

Be patient

Some employment negotiations take time. You might have to conclude a first conversation without agreement and then revisit the issue in a subsequent phone call or face-to-face meeting. Don't try to rush the process, or you'll only do yourself a disservice.

Be willing to hold out for what you deserve

Although it is important to be flexible and let the other side save face occasionally, you do deserve to get an offer that is fair—or even more than fair. Walking away from an offer is a tried-and-true tactic that works. The employer realizes you mean business and sees that you must really think you deserve a better offer. Just be prepared, however, to lose out on the job if the terms you are refusing to accept actually are the employer's best and final offer.

Getting the money and benefits you deserve

Although all the negotiation tactics described previously apply to the issue of salary and other compensation, keep a few guidelines in mind when it comes to just the money part of your negotiations:

Don't speak until spoken to

Try not to speak first when it comes to discussing salary. Fortunately, most employers will tell you what the salary is at the time that they extend an offer. You then are expected to accept that salary or negotiate for more.

Redirect the conversation

If an employer asks point blank what you are looking to make without stating a salary first, try to redirect the conversation by saying something like, "I think my salary requirements are in line with what is typical for positions like this. Why don't we look at the terms of the offer as a whole and then get into the specifics of the money?"

Talk in broad brush strokes

If an employer won't let you brush off a question about salary and pushes for a specific figure, limit your reply to a general salary range with a statement like, "I'm looking for something in the 50s or 60s, but exactly where in that range depends on other aspects of the compensation, benefits, and nature of the position." Or, talk in terms of broad periods in your salary history, such as, "My annual compensation for the past few years has ranged from $50,000 to $65,000." Doing so will keep you in the running with employers who can pay only $50,000, but it won't cut off your chances of getting $65,000 or more.

Know your figures

Part of the homework you do for the negotiations must include a look into typical salaries for the type of position and employer in question. Through research and the input of knowledgeable people in your network, you should be able to get a sense of typical salary ranges and what amount you could command within that range.

 Moneysaver

Look for hidden costs in an employer's benefits package. Some require that you contribute a portion of your pre-tax earnings to your health plan, life insurance, or other benefits, whereas others foot the entire bill for you.

Watch Out!

When negotiations come to a close and all parties make it clear that they accept the results, the case is closed. If you try to re-open negotiations after receiving written confirmation of your terms of employment, you will be seen as unprofessional and could jeopardize the offer.

Do the math

Another important aspect of preparation is to determine in advance how various salaries play out in reality. For example, you might negotiate for more money per year only to find out that it bumps you into a higher tax bracket. You also need to know how various incomes affect your daily life and personal budget. One job might offer $100 more of discretionary income a month than an offer with a lower salary, but it would require that you spend $75 more a month on gasoline, tolls, and parking because of the job's location. When you get into the thick of a negotiation, you might not have time to think through all the implications of various dollar amounts, so try to do so in advance.

Look at the compensation holistically

You must know how the entire pay plan works, not just what the annual salary or hourly wage is. Take into account any commissions, year-end bonuses, signing bonuses, relocation expenses, overtime policy, and schedule for performance reviews.

Don't leave the fringe benefits on the fringes

Be aware of what a boon a good benefits package can be to your overall financial state. The money you save in medical bills or that you earn in pension plans and stock options can help you view that weekly or monthly paycheck in a new light. See the Benefits Checklist for a thorough look at the extras a job might offer.

Benefits Checklist

Medical insurance
Dental coverage
Optical coverage
Life insurance
Short- and long-term disability insurance
Pension/retirement plan, e.g., 401(k)
Paid vacation
Federal or religious holiday closings
Floating holidays or personal days
Sick leave
Maternity or parental leave policy
Profit sharing/stock options
Relocation expenses
Tuition reimbursement
Company car
Paid parking
On-site daycare
Off-site child care subsidy
Health club membership
Meals
Entertainment expense account
Corporate discounts(for sports events, theater, movies)

When your negotiations of compensation and other terms of the offer reach a satisfactory conclusion, you will most likely be ready to accept the job. Keep in mind, however, that you are still not obligated to accept the offer. If the terms are not favorable to you, or if you have simultaneously negotiated offers at more than one employer, then you may still have a tough decision ahead of you.

By the way, never mislead an employer by accepting an offer, then entering into negotiations, and then reneging on the offer because you were also in talks with another organization and received more favorable terms with that other employer. Before getting deep into negotiations, you should make it clear that you are not accepting the offer but are merely interested enough to try to work out a mutually satisfying agreement, and that your acceptance of the offer is contingent upon that successful conclusion to the negotiations.

Job Acceptance Criteria Worksheet

Read the questions that follow each criterion, and decide how essential that factor is to you. Write a number between 1 and 10 in the space next to each criterion, with 10 indicating utmost importance and 1 indicating little importance.

1. Interests met: the job   Rating: _____
   How important is it that the responsibilities of my next job fit my interests? Do I need to find the content of my work highly interesting?

   _____

   _____

   _____

2. Interest factor: the employer   Rating: _____
   How important is it for me to be interested in the products and services of the next organization that employs me?

   _____

   _____

   _____

3. Skills utilization   Rating: _____
   Which skills do I want to use on my next job?
   _____
   _____
   _____

4. Skills development   Rating: _____
   Which skills would I like to develop on my next job?
   _____
   _____
   _____

5. Learning opportunities   Rating: _____
   In which subjects, content areas, or topics—as
   opposed to tangible skills—would I like to gain
   more expertise or acquire more knowledge on my
   next job?
   _____
   _____
   _____

6. Personality fit   Rating: _____
   How necessary is it that my next job fit my personality? Am I willing to alter my natural, preferred way
   of acting to fit the job?
   _____
   _____
   _____

7. Work environment/
   organizational culture   Rating: _____
   How essential is it that the "culture" at my next job
   fit with my concept of an ideal work environment or
   style of employer?
   _____
   _____
   _____

8. Co-workers   Rating: _____
   How important is it that I work around the types of
   people I consider to be ideal co-workers?

   _____

   _____

   _____

9. Supervisor(s)   Rating: _____
   How important is it that my boss(es) have a management style, personality, and/or background that
   fits my ideal?

   _____

   _____

   _____

10. Nature of the responsibilities   Rating: _____
    How much do I care about the content of my work?
    Am I looking for new challenges or familiar tasks?
    Do I want to deal with particular subject matters?

   _____

   _____

   _____

11. Formal training   Rating: _____
    How important is it to me that I receive formal
    training on the job or through seminars or classes?

   _____

   _____

   _____

12. Stability of the organization   Rating: _____
    Do I care if the prospective employer is financially
    and structurally secure, or am I willing to tolerate
    some volatility in exchange for exciting possibilities?

   _____

   _____

   _____

13. Growth potential of the
    organization   Rating: _____
    Would I prefer to be with a well-established organi-
    zation that might not experience much expansion
    more than one that is rapidly growing?

    _____

    _____

    _____

14. Advancement potential   Rating: _____
    How important is it that the employer offer clear
    opportunities for promotions, increased responsi-
    bility, or lateral transfer into an area in which I hope
    to work? (Remember that advancement doesn't
    always have to mean moving up!)

    _____

    _____

    _____

15. Schedule   Rating: _____
    How important is it that the schedule of my next job
    (hours, days, overtime) fit with my preferred way of
    working?

    _____

    _____

    _____

16. Impact on personal/professional
    life balance   Rating: _____
    Do I need my next job to satisfy a desire for a bal-
    anced life, or does the job take precedence at this
    point in my life?

    _____

    _____

    _____

17. The commute   Rating: _____
    Do I care how long it takes me to get to work and
    what modes of transportation I must take to do so?

    _____

    _____

    _____

18. The location   Rating: _____
    How important is the geographic location of the job?

    _____

    _____

    _____

19. The office itself   Rating: _____
    Do I care what the organization's overall facilities
    are like, as well as the size, style, and location of my
    actual workspace?

    _____

    _____

    _____

20. Travel involved   Rating: _____
    How important is it to me that my next job require
    the amount of travel I desire, whether that's no
    travel, a little, or extensive travel?

    _____

    _____

    _____

21. Salary and other monetary
    compensation   Rating: _____
    How important is the salary and any bonuses, com-
    missions, or other monetary rewards of my next job?

    _____

    _____

    _____

22. Benefits   Rating: _____

How important are the benefits? Do I have specific
needs regarding health insurance, amount of vacation, or other benefits?

_____

_____

_____

23. Perks   Rating: _____

How much do I care about perks? Is having a company car, an expense account, access to a VIP box at
the sports stadium, or other perks a real plus to me?

_____

_____

_____

Step five: make the decision

Good decision-makers know that only they can make the ulti-
mate decision; no one else can do it for them. They also know,
however, that they can't do it alone. A wise choice is based on
input from others, through research and networking. They also
know that the decision-making process must combine objective
and subjective information. You collect all the data you need
but also let your heart or gut have a say in the matter. Good decision-makers also are methodical. They don't fly by the seat of
their pants, but instead they follow a step-by-step process to get
from indecision to decision. Let's look at those steps as well as
some guiding principles for decision making.

Seven steps to making a good decision

1. *Look for the magic answer.* Yes, sometimes there really is one.
   Before you settle down for a long winter's night of decision making, prepared to agonize, hypothesize, and strate-
   gize, see whether you already know the answer. Quickly

but thoroughly run through what you know about the position and employer and then listen to your instincts and see whether a clear answer emerges. In other words, don't make the process more difficult than it has to be.

2. *Evaluate the quality of your information.* Try to determine whether you have all the facts. Do you know everything you need to know about the offer? Can you go through that list of questions on the Job Acceptance Criteria Worksheet from earlier in this chapter and answer them all for the jobs you are considering? Is your data comprehensive and accurate?

3. *Connect the dots.* If there are gaps in your knowledge, as discovered in Step 2, do the necessary research to gather the information you need. Look to the Internet, library, or notes you took on research already conducted to find answers to your questions, or call the employer back to say that you need some more answers before you can make your decision.

4. *Get outside opinions.* Consult with advisors in your network—both formal ones such as mentors, career consultants, or headhunters and informal ones such as friends and family—to put your choices in perspective and get input into your decision.

5. *Do a systematic evaluation.* Even if you're the type of person who prefers to listen to your heart rather than your head, you must do some sort of systematic—even quantitative— evaluation of your options. Get the pros and cons down on paper, and see what insights jump off the page at you. Read through your Job Evaluation Priorities form step by step, seeing how the job in questions holds up against your priorities. As long as you get the issues down on paper in some way, you'll make a better decision than if you try to make sense of the random thoughts floating around in your mind.

6. *Adjust your priorities as needed.* You'll recall from the earlier discussion of priorities that you might have to adjust the ratings or rankings of your priorities when considering them in the context of specific offers. Money may become more important when you're tempted with the big bucks, or location might become more important when you think about what a long commute would really mean to your daily life. At this step in the decision-making process, it is important to be flexible and to realize that your original take on your priorities might shift slightly now that reality is in the picture.

7. *Listen to your instincts.* After you have completed a systematic evaluation of the options based on objective data, see how it all feels. Your heart or your gut—whichever way you prefer to label that subjective part of decision making— does deserve to have a say in the process. If an offer that looks good on paper doesn't feel right, you need to take a second look at the data and reconsider the job's suitability for you. As long as you don't take the subjective approach too far and make a decision that is rash or haphazard, the heart and gut can be reliable sources for the right answer.

As you go through those steps of decision making, keep in mind that you are deciding about what you want to do, not what others want you to do. You are the one who will have to live with the decision, so make it for you.

Also, if you are dealing with any major personal transitions, such as a wedding, new baby, death in the family, building a new home, etc., while also trying to make a transition in your career,

 Bright Idea

To avoid getting pressed for time when an employer expects an answer from you regarding a job offer, do as much advanced preparation as possible. Identify your priorities, ask a lot of questions, and get input from your network when you believe an offer is imminent.

Watch Out!

Don't assume you'll be signing an employment contract before starting a new job. The employment laws of some states, as well as the nature of many positions, dictate that you be hired at-will, meaning that you or the employer can terminate the arrangement at any time and are not bound by a contract.

you might feel overwhelmed and unable to approach your career decisions with a clear head and good judgment. In that case, the best plan may be to delay making any major decisions about your career until the other matters are settled. Of course, if unemployment or underemployment—or being unhappily employed—is the cause of one of the other problems (such as those in the financial or health areas), then you must take care of the job problem before the others can be resolved.

Confirming the offer

To avoid any potential disputes or misunderstandings, it's important to confirm the offer in writing. In many cases—particularly at organizations with well-organized human resources functions—you'll receive a confirmation letter or letter of agreement to approve and sign. A sample of such a document is provided in the Appendix, "Action Verbs and Sample Résumés." This letter should state the job title, start date, and salary. It might also outline the terms of your probationary period and benefits package and remind you that your offer is contingent upon satisfactory results of reference and background checks, if they weren't done already. No details of the document should come as a surprise to you, as the letter should reflect the results of your negotiations. Nevertheless, you must read the letter carefully and don't hesitate to ask for clarification of any part of it.

If your new employer does not have a policy of issuing written confirmations, you need to initiate the process yourself. Compose a letter including the same information but using phrases such as, "It is my understanding that. . ." or "As we agreed, I will. . ." The letter should be businesslike and to the point, but you can convey your enthusiasm for the position and express your appreciation for the offer.

If multiple people were involved in the hiring decision, you should send copies of the letter to each person. The letter is typically addressed to the human resources representative who extended the formal offer and who handles the administrative aspects of your hiring and orientation. Copy the hiring manager of the department in which you will work. (This is often your new boss.)

Note that for senior-level positions you might be asked to sign a more formal employment agreement. Treat this as you would any legal document: read it carefully and consult with an attorney for assistance.

Just the facts

- Build a foundation for your follow-up efforts before you leave the interview. Ask questions about the decision-making timeframe, what your chances are, and how you should follow up.

- Don't waste your time sending a thank-you letter that does nothing but express your appreciation for the interviewer's time. Make it a true follow-up letter, in which you get the last word by restating your assets and addressing any concerns the employer might have.

- Err on the side of persistence and assertiveness in your follow-up efforts, but always with courtesy and tact.

- The key to evaluating a job offer is to identify your priorities so that you know how the job can satisfy your interests and help you reach your goals.

- To make a good decision about a job, you need have a clear picture of what it would entail, and you should look for red flags indicating potential problem areas.

- To be sure you're getting a fair deal when it comes to salary and other compensation, conduct thorough research.

- Negotiation is a win-win proposition, not an adversarial encounter.

- Always confirm a job offer in writing before starting.

Action Verbs and Sample Résumés

This appendix provides an action verb list to help make your written self-marketing tools more powerful along with sample résumés to give you ideas for how your own résumé might look and sound.

Action Verb Lists

Feeling speechless when trying to write your résumé or cover letters? The lists of verbs and verb phrases that follow might come in handy for writing those as well as when developing your asset statements, bio, and other self-marketing tools.

The verbs are grouped into broad skill set categories. The rationale behind these groupings is that they make it easier for you to find the words you need than if they were in one long alphabetical list. The groupings aren't perfect, however, as not all skill sets are represented, and some verbs could easily be categorized into more than one group. In some cases, I have repeated a word in more than one category where I thought it was particularly important to do so, but you should check all categories to find the word you need.

Note also that the verbs are listed in past tense as most of your résumé will include past work experience. Of course, if you're currently employed, be sure to convert these verbs to present tense when describing your current work.

Accounting/Finance/Quantitative

analyzed

appraised

bought

budgeted

calculated

compiled

computed

counted

estimated

examined

financed

forecasted

priced

projected

purchased

quantified

quoted

tabulated

valuated

valued

Adminstration/Production/Logistics

adapted

administered

allocated

arranged

assembled

assisted

balanced

carried out

catalogued

centralized

classified

collected

compiled

complied

contributed

coordinated

delivered

disbursed

dispatched

disseminated

distributed

enforced

ensured compliance

executed

expedited

focused

formalized

fulfilled

gauged
handled
hosted
implemented
installed
maintained
manufactured
organized
paid
planned
prepared
processed
procured

produced
recorded
reorganized
reported
routed
scheduled
streamlined
structured
supported
synchronized
synthesized
systematized
updated

Coaching/Training/Helping

acclimated
advised
advocated for
aided
assisted
attended
coached
consulted
counseled
developed
educated
encouraged
explained
facilitated
familiarized
fostered
guided
helped
informed

inspired
instilled
instructed
introduced
lectured
listened
mentored
motivated
oriented
presented
proctored
provided
settled
spoke
taught
trained
treated
tutored

Communications

addressed

answered

apprised

arbitrated

asked

authored

briefed

built relationships

clarified

collaborated

communicated

composed

conducted presentations

contacted

conveyed

convinced

copy edited

corresponded

created

defined

demonstrated

described

designed

developed

dissuaded

documented

drafted

edited

examined

explained

expressed

facilitated

illustrated

inquired

interpreted

lectured

listened

mediated

narrated

negotiated

persuaded

presented

proofread

provided customer
   service

published

replied

reported

responded

served as a liaison

spoke

summarized

translated

wrote

Creativity/Innovation

accelerated

activated

altered

amended

automated

changed

charted

conceived

conceptualized

inspired

converted

instituted

created

invented

designed

modernized

developed

originated

devised

overhauled

displayed

perceived

drew

pioneered

effected change

revamped

established

revised

fashioned

revolutionized

illuminated

shaped

imagined

started

improved

tightened

inaugurated

updated

initiated

visualized

innovated

Leadership/Management

allocated

directed

appointed

elected

approved

enlisted

authorized

governed

built teams

held responsibility for

chaired

hired

challenged with

initiated

charged with

inspired

conducted

instituted

controlled

judged

cultivated

led

cut

managed

decided

moderated

defined

motivated

determined

negotiated

operated

orchestrated

ordered

oversaw

planned

presided

produced

promoted

recruited

reduced costs

spearheaded

supervised

Problem-Solving

acted resourcefully

addressed

analyzed

anticipated

ascertained

assessed needs/situation

brainstormed

consulted

corrected

debugged

identified

pinpointed

resolved

revealed

salvaged

saved

solved

troubleshot

uncovered

Research/Analysis

analyzed

assessed

assured

audited

checked

classified

conducted analysis

critiqued

defined

detected

determined

diagnosed

discovered

documented

evaluated

examined

gathered

graded

grouped

identified

integrated

interpreted

interviewed

inquired

inspected

monitored

observed

perceived

planned
ranked
recognized
re-evaluated
researched
reviewed
screened
searched

solved
sorted
structured
surveyed
synthesized
tested
validated
verified

Results

accomplished
achieved
added
advanced
attained
augmented
awarded
boosted
broadened
built
concluded
condensed
consolidated
contributed
decreased
demonstrated
distinguished by
doubled
eliminated
exceeded
excelled
expanded
gained
generated

grew
honored with/by
improved
increased
mastered
minimized
obtained
produced
raised
reached
recovered
rectified
restored
resulted in
retained
revitalized
rewarded with/by
saved
secured
strengthened
surpassed
tripled
won

Sales/Marketing/Customer Service

acquired	managed relationships
advertised	marketed
attracted	negotiated
bargained	persuaded
capitalized	promoted
captured	publicized
closed	pursued
cold-called	resolved
consulted	secured
convinced	sold
cultivated	solicited
launched	targeted
maintained relationships	

Sample Résumés

The résumé samples that follow are intended to give you an idea of both the content and overall look of effective résumés. These are based on résumés of actual clients with whom I've worked, but all names, contact information, employer names, and other identifying information have been changed for anonymity. These samples were chosen as representative of solid, well-rounded résumés from which anyone in any profession or industry can learn. If you want to see more samples related specifically to your field, check out the books listed in the "Résumés–Specialized" section of Bonus Appendix 2: Recommended Reading List at www.wiley.com/go/michelletullier. Also, don't forget to review Chapter 5, "Résumés," for further guidance on how to put yours together.

The following samples are organized in four sections: chronological format; functional format; executive-level; and an e-Résumé.

Chronological Résumé Samples

The three résumés that follow demonstrate the most traditional style of résumé, the chronological format.

RICHARD BLAKE

333 Sienna Lane   H: 222-333-8888
Albuquerque, NM 44444   rblakeNM@email.com

OPERATIONS MANAGER

Process Re-engineering   Cost Control   Team-building
Spearheaded two major turnarounds for global Fortune 500 leader

Results-driven leader who quickly identifies operational issues and designs/executes solutions that improve across-the-board performance. Respected manager who thrives on challenge, leads by example, champions employees' development and inspires teams to top performance. Consistently improves performance, productivity, quality, service, safety, and profits.

PROFESSIONAL EXPERIENCE

SOUTHWEST DELIVERY, INC.   19XX–20XX
Operations Manager, 19XX–20XX
Selected to turnaround under-performing operations in Albuquerque and Phoenix. Led areas to exceed corporate objectives in all measurable facets of operation. Full responsibility for the planning, scheduling, and organizing of 200 employees. Provided extensive employee development through training, coaching, and motivation with eight direct reports promoted to management positions. Responsible for reconciling station cargo claims. Repeatedly recognized for solid leadership skills, cost control, and customer service.

Accomplishments in Phoenix, 20XX–20XX, include:

- Led facility from last to 1st of 33 business units.
- Improved employee satisfaction rating from 75% to 99% (vs. 75% company goal).
- Propelled service performance from 94% to 99.8%.
- Delivered $400,000 annual savings through safety improvements and productivity gains.
- Improved workgroup productivity from 70% to 99% (vs. 98% station goal).

Accomplishments in Albuquerque, 19XX–20XX, include:

- Drove one of five worst performing business units to #1 in district and #3 in region.
- Slashed $1.2 million annual theft problem by 97.5%.
- Boosted customer service rating from <94% to 99% (vs. 98% corporate goal).
- Reduced monthly accidents and injuries, saving $384,000 annually.
- Improved employee satisfaction rating from 60% to 95% (vs. 75% company goal).

Courier / Team Leader, 19XX–19XX

AWARDS

- Ranked in top 5% of managers out of approximately 300 company-wide, five consecutive years in a row on annual leadership survey.
- Earned Chairman's Award four times for superior performance and contributions.
- Two-time recipient of Global Leadership Award for outstanding people skills.

EDUCATION AND CERTIFICATIONS

Bachelor's degree studies, Business, Phoenix Community College–Phoenix, AZ
Certified Management Development Practices Trainer
Professional development in safety, continuous improvements, DOT regulations

MARCIA VELEZ

4653 Barrington Rd.
Houston, TX 11111
M: 333-222-5555
mvelez@email.com

OBJECTIVE

Challenging senior administrative position utilizing proven organizational skills and diverse experience from several corporate cultures to add value to a dynamic company.

QUALIFICATIONS SUMMARY

Accomplished executive assistant with 10+ years administrative experience. Adept at meeting and event planning for both small and large events. Skilled in interpersonal communication and noted for ability to brief senior management and handle sensitive information with a high degree of professionalism. Demonstrated achievements in:

Administrative Skills: typing/word processing (100+); copy editing and proofreading; meeting coordination, event planning, and travel arrangements.

Project Management: sets priorities and works independently while handling heavy workloads; high degree of resourcefulness and follow-through skills.

Computer Software: proficient in Microsoft Word, Excel, and PowerPoint. Working knowledge of Access.

Personal Qualities: dependable, high-energy, and efficient; very personable, positive attitude, loyal, and honest. Builds business relationships on all levels.

PROFESSIONAL EXPERIENCE

Company 1– Houston, TX   **199X–20XX**
Leading retailer with 400 stores nationwide.
Executive Assistant
Supported the Senior Director and 10 managers in field offices throughout the southwestern United States.

- Directly influenced decision-making by acting as a liaison among department employees, Senior Director, and corporate headquarters.
- Selected to manage national award program with $100,000 budget responsibility. Maintained monthly reports regarding status of store openings and closings, as well as expense report tracking and approval. Consistently met budget.
- Supported annual national convention (4,000 attendees) and six regional meetings (300 attendees) with average budget responsibilities of $40,000.
- Effectively controlled Senior Director calendar by scheduling all meetings, conference calls, administrative time, and coordinating travel arrangements.

PROFESSIONAL EXPERIENCE (continued)

Company 2– San Antonio, TX   199X–19XX
Global provider of commercial HVAC and industrial refrigeration/process cooling.

Office Manager/Administrative Assistant

Assisted President, Vice President, and five sales representatives in daily office functions including typing sales quotes, letters to customers, and technical data. Maintained office equipment and supplies, phone system, petty cash, meeting plans, and travel arrangements.

- Developed a freight system to streamline shipping of products (2-100 ton units).
- Established and maintained company 401(k)/profit sharing program.
- Created a manageable system to track and maintain personnel records.
- Collected and analyzed time and material data in relationship to the gross margin of unit profit, contributing to successful cost reduction effort.

Company 3–Houston, TX   19XX–19XX
Global provider of indoor HVAC systems for residential, commercial, and industrial needs.

Executive Secretary

Assisted Vice President of Service in all aspects of customer relations, personnel, and office administration. Hired and supervised collections and clerical staff. Composed invoices, service documents, and lengthy service quotes.

- Planned and administered annual 10-day seminars for 300+ customers.
- Effectively maintained uniform and literature program for 25 service technicians.
- Organized and actively participated in annual budget planning meeting with senior management.

Prior experience includes clerical, customer service, and administrative positions of increasing responsibility. Detailed work history available upon request.

EDUCATION

Associate of Arts Degree–DuPree Business College–Houston, TX
Included: Business, Economics, Accounting, Public Relations, and Humanities.

LANA BROWN

888 Spring Avenue   (222) 444-6666
Richmond, Virginia 11111   LBengineer@email.com

OBJECTIVE

A **database administrator or software architect/software development position** where strengths in oral and written communication, teamwork, and business knowledge will be utilized to develop systems that support corporate goals.

QUALIFICATIONS SUMMARY

Accomplished software development professional with experience in all disciplines of mainframe and PC platforms. Proven track record of delivering quality results on schedule. Exceptional analysis and programming skills and extensive experience with **Microsoft SQL Server, performance measurement and capacity planning**. Effectively delivers technical training.

TECHNICAL SKILLS

Platforms:	WINDOWS XP, WINDOWS 2000, WINDOWS NT
Productivity Tools:	MICROSOFT WORD, EXCEL, POWERPOINT
Software Environments:	CLIENT SERVER AND BROWSER (MICROSOFT INTERNET EXPLORER), UNISYS A-SERIES, UNISYS 2200
Software Methodology:	ISO 9000/9001, SEI/CMMI, RATIONAL UNIFIED PROCESS
Languages:	POWERBUILDER, T-SQL, COBOL, VISUAL BASIC, ALGOL, DASDL
Databases:	MICROSOFT SQL SERVER, UNISYS DMSII
APPLICATIONS:	Manufacturing, Distribution, Banking, Accounts Payable, General Ledger, Human Resources, Accounting

EXPERIENCE

SYSTEMS CORPORATION–Richmond, VA   20XX–20XX

Software Engineer, 20XX–20XX

Designed and developed software for bank branch automation system and customer relations management (CRM) package, in both client server and browser environments.

- Member of team that converted a dissatisfied client into a referenceable site. Package later sold to other bank clients. Received cash bonus achievement award.
- Designed Microsoft SQL Server database for CRM package.
- Designed and consulted on implementation of database replication system.
- Tested and implemented successful upgrades of Microsoft SQL Server databases from version 6.5 to 7.0 and from version 7.0 to 2000.
- Designed, coded, tested, and implemented system for both batch and on demand real-time data downloading from mainframe database to SQL Server database.
- Developed and facilitated transfer of information class on existing CRM software system for offshore developers.
- Worked with personnel to successfully transfer CRM system maintenance and support offshore.

(SYSTEMS CORP. CONTINUED)

Systems Analyst, 19XX–20XX
Integral member of team for large mainframe accounting package. Converted large IBM mainframe accounting package including HR, AP, GL, and other modules to A-Series, V-Series, and OS2200.

- Package required several releases per year with mandatory regulatory deadlines that were all met ahead of schedule.

- Identified problems with vendor's software quality, communicated problems to management, and worked three months on vendor's site to resolve problems and improve procedures. Reduced number of critical bugs found in the code delivered by vendor in succeeding year by 43%.

ALLIED SUPPLY COMPANY–Virginia Beach, VA   **19XX–19XX**
Database Administrator
Maintained database and system software for leading southeastern plumbing, heating, and air conditioning distributor.

- Converted night batch runs to automated process that could run without operator supervision. Eliminated need for night operator shift, reducing employee expenses by more than $20,000 annually.

- Selected, implemented, and trained programming staff on new 4GL programming system.

SLEEPEASE CORPORATION–Richmond, VA   **19XX–19Xx**
Database Administrator, 19XX–19XX
Maintained database and system software for national bedding manufacturer.

- Redesigned and rewrote existing system to allow real-time and batch systems to run simultaneously on east and west coasts. Saved more than two hours of run time per night.

- Planned, tested, and implemented data center disaster recovery plan. Analyzed and revised backup procedures. Worked with third-party disaster recovery site to ensure adequate hardware in the event of a disaster. Led disaster recovery plan test team.

Lead Programmer/Team Leader, 19XX–19XX

- Led team that developed real-time order processing system

EDUCATION

MA, Computer Science, Parkland University, Richmond, VA   19XX
BS, Mathematics, Hilldale College, Wichita, KS   19XX

CERTIFICATIONS

Microsoft Certified Professional
Exam 229–Designing and Implementing Databases with Microsoft SQL Server 2000 Enterprise Edition
Exam 228–Installing, Configuring and Administering Microsoft SQL Server 2000 Enterprise Edition
Exam 029–Designing and Implementing Databases with Microsoft SQL Server 7.0
Exam 028–Administering Microsoft SQL Server 7.0

Functional Résumés Samples

These résumés are in a functional format, which downplays the actual work history and highlights accomplishments. Note how the "Lana Brown" résumé that you just saw in the chronological samples has been converted to a functional format, so that you can easily see the differences and similarities in the two styles.

LANA BROWN

888 Spring Avenue   (222) 444-6666
Richmond, Virginia 11111   LBengineer@email.com

OBJECTIVE

A **database administrator or software architect/software development position** where strengths in oral and written communication, teamwork, and business knowledge will be utilized to develop systems that support corporate goals.

QUALIFICATIONS SUMMARY

Accomplished software development professional with experience in all disciplines of mainframe and PC platforms. Proven track record of delivering quality results on schedule. Exceptional analysis and programming skills and extensive experience with **Microsoft SQL Server, performance measurement and capacity planning**. Effectively delivers technical training.

TECHNICAL SKILLS

Platforms:	WINDOWS XP, WINDOWS 2000, WINDOWS NT
Productivity Tools:	MICROSOFT WORD, EXCEL, POWERPOINT
Software Environments:	CLIENT SERVER AND BROWSER (MICROSOFT INTERNET EXPLORER), UNISYS A-SERIES, UNISYS 2200
Software Methodology:	ISO 9000/9001, SEI/CMMI, RATIONAL UNIFIED PROCESS
Languages:	POWERBUILDER, T-SQL, COBOL, VISUAL BASIC, ALGOL, DASDL
Databases:	MICROSOFT SQL SERVER, UNISYS DMSII
Applications:	MANUFACTURING, DISTRIBUTION, BANKING, ACCOUNTS PAYABLE, GENERAL LEDGER, HUMAN RESOURCES, ACCOUNTING

SELECTED ACCOMPLISHMENTS

• Member of team that **converted a dissatisfied client** at Systems Corporation into a referenceable site by designing and developing software for a bank branch automation system. Effectiveness of package enabled Systems Corp to sell additional packages. **Received achievement award.**

• Demonstrated **strong interpersonal and organizational skills** through successful transfer of CRM system maintenance and support offshore.

• As systems analyst converted large IBM mainframe accounting package to A-Series, V-Series and OS2200. Package required several releases per year with **mandatory regulatory deadlines that were all met ahead of schedule.**

• Identified problems with a vendor's software quality, communicated problems to management, and worked three months with vendor to resolve problems and improve procedures. **Reduced number of critical bugs found in the code delivered by vendor in succeeding year by 43%.**

• As database administrator with Allied Supply, converted night batch runs to automated process that could run without operator supervision. Eliminated need for night operator shift, **reducing employee expenses by more than $20,000 annually.**

• Redesigned/rewrote existing system software at SleepEase to allow real-time and batch systems to run simultaneously on east and west coasts. **Saved two+ hours of run time per night.**

LANA BROWN   PAGE TWO

WORK HISTORY

SYSTEMS CORPORATION–Richmond, VA   **20XX–20XX**

Software Engineer, 20XX–20XX
Designed and developed software for bank branch automation system and customer relations management (CRM) package, in both client server and browser environments.

Systems Analyst, 19XX–20XX
Integral member of team for large mainframe accounting package. Converted large IBM mainframe accounting package including HR, AP, GL, and other modules to A-Series, V-Series and OS2200.

ALLIED SUPPLY COMPANY–Virginia Beach, VA   **19XX–19XX**

Database Administrator
Maintained database and system software for leading southeastern plumbing, heating, and air conditioning distributor. Selected, implemented, and trained programming staff on new 4GL programming system.

SLEEPEASE CORPORATION–Richmond, VA   **19XX–19XX**

Database Administrator, 19XX–19XX
Maintained database and system software for national bedding manufacturer. Planned, tested, and implemented data center disaster recovery plan. Led disaster recovery plan test team.

Lead Programmer/Team Leader, 19XX–19XX

Led team that developed real-time order processing system

EDUCATION

MA, Computer Science, Parkland University–Richmond, VA   **19XX**

BS, Mathematics, Hilldell College–Wichita, KS   **19XX**

CERTIFICATIONS

Microsoft Certified Professional
Exam 229–Designing and Implementing Databases with Microsoft SQL Server 2000 Enterprise Edition
Exam 228–Installing, Configuring and Administering Microsoft SQL Server 2000 Enterprise Edition
Exam 029–Designing and Implementing Databases with Microsoft SQL Server 7.0
Exam 028–Administering Microsoft SQL Server 7.0

ROBERT LAFEVRE

413 Revere Street, #2A   H: 777-888-0000
Boston, MA 66666   RLafevre2@email.com   M: 777-555-6666

OBJECTIVE

Management position where strengths in project management, marketing communications, and problem solving will be utilized to increase market share and strengthen customer loyalty.

PROFILE

Dedicated leader with 11+ years of diverse experience and achievements in marketing, project management, vendor relations, business development, communications, and customer service. Highly motivated team player who gets the job done. Analyzes, prioritizes, and identifies creative solutions. Functions effectively under pressure while maintaining a positive demeanor. Excellent communicator with strong presentation skills, high level of technical knowledge, and outstanding reputation for details.

SELECTED ACHIEVEMENTS

Project Management

• Selected to manage the relocation of a major corporation's sales and marketing department due to an acquisition. Selected new location, negotiated lease terms, secured office equipment, and organized the final move. **Completed within the mandated 30-day goal at 5% under budget.**

• Developed and implemented a customer incentive sales program to focus on retaining customers after the acquisition. **Resulted in 85% customer retention and sales increase of 28%. The 20XX program is on target for a 30% growth in sales.**

• Managed distributor incentive sales programs from conception through final execution for nine consecutive years. Successfully executed all programs within budget. Implemented plan to offset the corporation's Olympic participation costs, **saving the Commercial Division more than $250,000.**

• Developed, implemented, and managed the distributor Advisory Council. Worked with Executive Management to select the appropriate members and create strategy. **The Advisory Council continues to be the company's best resource for exchanging ideas and gathering feedback** on new product ideas and company policies and procedures.

Marketing Communications

• Based on proven, intense attention to detail, was selected by the Director of Marketing to develop and implement a process to reduce the unnecessary costs of reprinting marketing collateral. **New process produced $20,000 annual savings.**

• Used knowledge of database marketing and electronic communications to decrease communication time with customers and reduce the need for using costly outside vendors and services. **Produced $100,000 annual savings and dramatically increased customer satisfaction.**

• Selected to serve as Marketing/Communications representative on three acquisition teams due to successful involvement with prior acquisitions, allowing for a smooth and error-free transition. **Defined the expectations and mapped critical business processes to lead the company through the rapid transition period.**

• Devised a solution and coordinated a team effort to present to management to reduce costs of annual trade shows. **Resulted in more than $50,000 annual savings without eliminating any shows from the company's yearly calendar.**

SELECTED ACHIEVEMENTS (continued)

Event Management

• Managed the successful onsite execution of distributor and sales incentive trips worldwide for nine consecutive years. **All programs received an outstanding rating from 98% of attendees.**

• Managed the creation and execution of six national sales meetings with more than 200 attendees each, and two meetings only three months apart. **Executed all meetings within budget, met predetermined goals, and energized the sales force.**

• Developed and managed customer sports hospitality programs resulting in enhanced customer relationships with strategic customers leading to additional business. **Creatively organized each event by matching customers to the nearest available event, resulting in lower travel costs.**

• Arranged and organized annual customer appreciation galas with more than 400 people each from planning phase to conclusion. Each gala was executed within budget and met predetermined goal of enhancing the customer's perception of the new company.

PROFESSIONAL EXPERIENCE

PAPERPRODUCTS, INC.–Framingham, MA   19XX–20XX

    Marketing Communications Manager–Tissue Division, 20XX-20XX

    Market Development Manager–Tissue Division, 20XX-20XX

    Associate Market Development Manager–Commercial Products Division, 19XX-20XX

    Sales Promotion Coordinator–Consumer Products Division, 19XX-19XX

    Trade Promotion Coordinator–Consumer Products Division, 19XX -19XX

    Customer Service Representative–Consumer Products Division, 19XX -19XX

EDUCATION

Bachelor of Business Administration   19XX
Boston University–Boston, MA
Major: International Business (Marketing emphasis)

Executive Résumé Samples

Although résumés for senior-level management or executive positions do not have to differ a great deal from other résumés, you will note some differences in these samples.

LANCE WILLIAMS

333 York Road   (404) 666-5555
Atlanta, Georgia 30306   LWilliams@email.com

PROFILE

Enthusiastic senior executive with a passion for results and track record of growing businesses in
Fortune 500 companies and early-stage ventures. Skilled at designing and implementing innovative
business development, marketing, and sales initiatives that align with corporate capabilities,
strategies, and goals. Dynamic leader who energizes and motivates teams.

Areas of expertise include:

- Strategic planning
- Customer acquisition-focused marketing
- Business development
- P&L management
- Product development and management
- Mergers and acquisitions
- Change management
- Staff recruitment and development

PROFESSIONAL EXPERIENCE

SECUREWARE, INC. – Atlanta, GA   **20XX-present**
Chief Marketing Officer

Lead all aspects of marketing activities including analyst relations, brand strategy, channel
programs, direct marketing, marketing communications, product marketing and public relations.
Manage staff of twelve and $4 million budget.

- Created and implemented comprehensive marketing plan resulting in 200% growth in 20XX
  and 100% growth in 20XX.
- Effectively scaled lead generation to grow business from $15 million to $34 million run rate
  in nine months.
- Oversaw analyst and public relations effort that secured significant awards and reviews
  including *Atlanta Biz Publications* Pioneer Award, Dodd & Bell Fastest 50, and *InfoWire*
  "Excellent" rating.

GLOBELINK, INC. – Tampa, FL   **20XX–20XX**
Executive Vice President, Marketing, 20XX–20XX

Business unit P&L responsibility for GlobeLink's mobile wireless businesses. Developed and
executed business case and market strategy to extend business beyond the personal computer.
Managed budget of $150 million and 160 direct reports in business development, channel sales,
marketing, operations, product development, and product management, as well as an overseas
subsidiary.

- Launched and grew business to 210,000 customers generating $55 million in revenue in
  22 months.
- Managed laptop services and negotiated agreement for Wi-Fi network access.
- Services recognized by Able Computing in October 20XX as best in class.
- Engineered acquisition of XYZ Corporation via a bankruptcy proceeding and ZYX
  Corporation via a tender offer.

Senior Vice President, Narrowband Services, 20XX

Oversaw call center sales, channel sales, field marketing, loyalty marketing, and product
management. Managed budget of $130 million and staff of more than 200.

- Created and implemented GlobeLink and HandSpring merger-related branding strategy.
- Led GlobeLink and HandSpring product integration efforts.

HANDSPRING ENTERPRISES, INC. – Atlanta, GA   **19XX-20XX**
Executive Vice President, Sales and Marketing, 19XX–20XX

Set and implemented overall growth strategy for business and consumer offerings. Handled all
marketing functions including advertising, business development, corporate communications,
channel sales, customer loyalty, direct marketing, field marketing, product development,
product management, and strategic alliances.

PROFESSIONAL EXPERIENCE (continued)
(Handspring, Executive Vice President of Sales and Marketing, continued)

- Exceeded 19XX plan, growing revenues to $328 million, a gain of 182%.
- Surpassed 19XX plan, growing revenues to $115 million, a 117% gain.
- Built customer base from 341,000 to more than 1.3 million users.
- Effectively scaled annual marketing expenditures from $10 million to $93 million.
- Recognized as one of Computer Marketing's "19XX Marketers of the Year."

Vice President, Business Development, 19XX–19XX
Led team of 20 in quest to obtain new customers. Responsible for achieving revenue plan in excess of $50 million and controlling $4.7 million departmental budget. Directed acquisitions, field marketing, OEM sales, and retail sales functions.

- Exceeded 19XX new customer goal while lowering average subscriber acquisition cost by 22%.
- Established national business development strategy and leveraged strategic partnership opportunities.
- Personally negotiated and closed key distribution agreements.

Market Development Manager, 19XX–19XX
Analyzed metro market potentials and recommended target areas. Developed market opening process. Pursued media barters that provided a local marketing presence. Built retail channel through sales agency program. Ran consumer trade shows. Purchased advertising and managed marketing budget. Negotiated subscriber acquisitions from competitive ISPs and managed transition processes.

- Spearheaded expansion efforts throughout the Southeast, growing the company's marketing footprint from six to 41 markets in less than six months.
- Built top performing team accounting for 80% of company revenue.
- Achieved 125% of plan target.

MILLARD CHEMICAL COMPANY, PLASTICS DIVISION–Lexington, KY   199X-199X
District Sales Manager, 19XX–19XX
Product Manager, 19XX
Sales Representative, 19XX–19XX (Hoboken, NJ)

ADDITIONAL PRIOR PROFESSIONAL SALES EXPERIENCE,   19XX–19XX.

EDUCATION
M.B.A., Georgia Institute of Technology–Atlanta, GA   198X
B.B.A., with honors, University of Georgia–Athens, GA   198X

PROFESSIONAL DEVELOPMENT
Mergers & Acquisitions Seminar, Harvard School of Business–Cambridge, MA   20XX
Directors' College, Terry College of Business, University of Georgia–Atlanta, GA   20XX

COMMUNITY LEADERSHIP
Kimball Arts Center, **Board Member**   20XX–present
Technology Development Center, **Volunteer Mentor/Instructor**   20XX

THOMAS ALLMAN

88 Lake Drive • Los Angeles, GA 11111 • 770-594-1738 • tallman@email.com

SENIOR MANAGEMENT EXECUTIVE

Positioning Service as a Key Driver to Revenue, Profit and Market Success
for Fortune 500 and Rapid Growth Enterprises

Recognized as the "go-to" executive to build, transform, and energize customer service, account management, and operations organizations to be the key competitive differentiator in consumer and business-to-business markets. Provides strategic and tactical leadership to define customer relationship management and creates successful revenue and cost structures for customer service, technical support, field Support, and operations.

Delivered significant results across multiple industries and customer support channels as a leader in Big Company One, Big Company Two, and Big Company Three as well as two "new economy" ventures. MBA degree.

PROFESSIONAL EXPERIENCE

BIG COMPANY ONE – Century City, CA   20xx–20xx
  Senior Vice President – Operations
Senior executive recruited to build service and operations organization to be leveraged as the competitive advantage for a new business unit launched to develop and sell information services directly to consumers via the internet and through business partners. Responsible for customer service, business partner management, operations and Marketing/Technology interface for website and product development.
- Instrumental in growing revenue 192%, to $70 million from $24 million in two years.
- **Developed and implemented customer relationship strategy to position customer service as the cornerstone of the company's value proposition to increase revenue through repeat purchases.**
- Generated 10% of business unit revenue through multi-channel marketing contacts to customer base of six million. Product renewals increased to 52% while industry standard was 30%. Repeat purchase index rose to 70% from low 50%.

BIG COMPANY TWO – Los Angeles, CA   20xx–20xx
  Senior Vice President – Customer Service & Technical Support
Challenged with upgrading service delivery quality of the 6th largest [nature of business] company and creating a customer relationship focus that transcended sales, technical support, and customer service. Led organization design, process implementation, and employee development.   Contributed to successful company acquisition by Micron Electronics and led integration task force. Managed $155 million budget.
- Consolidated customer service and technical services, which increased customer responsiveness 60% and reduced expenses by 40%.
- Personally visited or contacted top 100 customers soliciting input regarding support expectations, then shifted the service organization from reactive to proactive philosophy that anticipated customer needs and offered immediate solutions for over 1000 major accounts.

START-UP COMPANY – Marina del Rey, CA   199x–20xx
  Vice President – Customer Service
  Built a national client support organization from the ground up for this pre-IPO
  broadband communications company. Leveraged service as a driver of revenue and
  market expansion in the highly competitive, shared tenant services market.   As a
  corporate officer, engaged in establishing the strategic direction, go-to-market plan and
  rapid ramp-up of the business.

- Developed a customer relationship management model for a support organization
  committed to customer service excellence. Recruited, trained, and supervised client
  service management placed in 27 new markets within six months.

- Engaged teams in multi-level relationships with commercial office building managers
  and end-userswhose only market differentiator was the quality of the service they
  received for voice, data, and cable.

- Contributed to the successful IPO of the company in March 20xx and supported 85%+
  revenue growth to $14 million based on a value proposition driven by proactive
  customer service in the local markets.

BIG COMPANY THREE – Chicago, IL   19xx-19xx
  Director – Customer Service, 19xx-19xx
  Challenged to build the first teleservices organization for North American Division,
  consolidating 43 locations into three call centers. Outlined the business model,
  organizational structure, and resource/technology requirements to build a world-class call
  center organization that grew from 500 to 1400 employees and handled 18 million calls
  per year with a $45 million budget.

- Launched customer service centers generating $120 million.

- Improved customer satisfaction to more than 92% while driving 28% productivity
  improvements. Instituted quality-driven processes and metrics leading to ISO
  9000 Certification.

- Initiated strategies to incorporate electronic service into traditional teleservices to
  provide first multichannel service model.
  Regional Manager – Consumer Sales and Service, 19xx-19xx
  Key leader in developing world-class service and sales organizations. Transcended service
  and sales to transform cost centers into revenue centers and drive sales to new and
  existing customers through proactive account management. Led 100-employee customer
  service center and then directed 1600 sales and service professionals in four consumer
  sales and service centers.

- Ranked as the #1 region out nine regions by exceeding all objectives by up to 120%.

- Developed account management strategies that enabled the first-ever targeted sales
  effort aimed at the existing customer base. Generated 10% organic revenue growth
  while lowering customer churn from 5% to 2%.
  Manager –Marketing Support, Customer Service, Operations
  Recruited into a leadership role only six months into fast-track management training
  program.

EDUCATION

MBA, Northwestern University–Chicago, IL   19xx
BS, Business, Loyola University–Chicago, IL   19xx

Electronic Résumé Samples

Chapter 10, "Online Job Hunting," provides a step-by-step guide to creating a résumé for various electronic or Internet-based uses. The "Lana Brown" résumé that you've seen in chronological and functional format is now turned into an e-Résumé in the sample that follows.

LANA BROWN
LBengineer@email.com

OBJECTIVE
A database administrator or software architect/software development position in which strengths in oral and written communication, teamwork, and business knowledge will be utilized to develop systems that support corporate goals.

KEYWORDS
Software Development. Software Design. Software Engineer. Database Administration. Systems Analyst. Team Leader. Team Lead. Developer. IBM Mainframe. PC Platforms. CRM. Analysis. Programming. Programmer. Microsoft SQL Server. Performance Measurement. Capacity Planning. Vendor Relations. Offshore. Microsoft Certified Professional. BS degree. Master's degree. Computer Science. Technical Trainer. Mentoring. A-Series. V-Series. OS2200.

TECHNICAL SKILLS
• PLATFORMS: Windows XP, Windows 2000, Windows NT
PRODUCTIVITY TOOLS: Microsoft Word, Excel, PowerPoint
• SOFTWARE ENVIRONMENTS: Client Server and Browser (Microsoft Internet Explorer), Unisys A-Series, Unisys 2200
• SOFTWARE METHODOLOGY: ISO 9000/9001, SEI/CMMI, Rational Unified Process
• LANGUAGES:
PowerBuilder, T-SQL, COBOL, Visual Basic, ALGOL, DASDL DATABASES: Microsoft SQL Server, Unisys DMSII
• APPLICATIONS: Manufacturing, Distribution, Banking, Accounts Payable, General Ledger, Human Resources, Accounting

EXPERIENCE
SYSTEMS CORPORATION-Richmond, VA, 20XX-20XX
Software Engineer, 20XX-20XX
Designed and developed software for bank branch automation system and customer relations management (CRM) package, in both client server and browser environments.
• Member of team that converted a dissatisfied client into a referenceable site. Package later sold to other bank clients. Received cash bonus achievement award.
• Designed Microsoft SQL Server database for CRM package.
• Designed and consulted on implementation of database replication system.
• Tested and implemented successful upgrades of Microsoft SQL Server databases from version 6.5 to 7.0 and from version 7.0 to 2000.
• Designed, coded, tested, and implemented system for both batch and on demand real-time data downloading from mainframe database to SQL Server database.
• Developed and facilitated transfer of information class on existing CRM software system for offshore developers.
• Worked with personnel to successfully transfer CRM system maintenance and support offshore.

Systems Analyst, 19XX-20XX
Integral member of team for large mainframe accounting package. Converted large IBM mainframe accounting package including HR, AP, GL, and other modules to A-Series, V-Series and OS2200.
• Package required several releases per year with mandatory regulatory deadlines that were all met ahead of schedule.
• Identified problems with vendor's software quality, communicated problems to management, and worked three months on vendor's site to resolve problems and improve procedures. Reduced number of critical bugs found in the code delivered by vendor in succeeding year by 43%.

ALLIED SUPPLY COMPANY-Virginia Beach, VA, 19XX-19XX
Database Administrator
Maintained database and system software for leading southeastern plumbing, heating, and air conditioning distributor.
• Converted night batch runs to automated process that could run without operator supervision. Eliminated need for night operator shift, reducing employee expenses by more than $20,000 annually.
• Selected, implemented, and trained programming staff on new 4GL programming system.

SLEEPEASE CORPORATION-Richmond, VA, 19XX-19Xx
Database Administrator, 19XX-19XX
Maintained database and system software for national bedding manufacturer.
• Redesigned and rewrote existing system to allow real-time and batch systems to run simultaneously on east and west coasts. Saved more than two hours of run time per night.
• Planned, tested, and implemented data center disaster recovery plan. Analyzed and revised backup procedures. Worked with third-party disaster recovery site to ensure adequate hardware in the event of a disaster. Led disaster recovery plan test team.
Lead Programmer/Team Leader, 19XX-19XX
• Led team that developed real-time order processing system

EDUCATION
MA, Computer Science, Parkland University, Richmond, VA, 19XX
BS, Mathematics, Hilldale College, Wichita, KS, 19XX

CERTIFICATIONS
Microsoft Certified Professional
Exam 229-Designing and Implementing Databases with Microsoft SQL Server 2000 Enterprise Edition
Exam 228-Installing, Configuring and Administering Microsoft SQL Server 2000 Enterprise Edition
Exam 029-Designing and Implementing Databases with Microsoft SQL Server 7.0
Exam 028-Administering Microsoft SQL Server 7.0

A

action verbs, 443–450

actions, asset statement scripting, 100–101

American Staffing Association, 211

anxiety and interviews, 302–307

aptitude testing warnings, 63

areas for improvement interview question, 369

assessments

additional skills, uncovering, 69–70

aptitude testing, 63

business & management skills, 63–64

career assessment tests, 60

cognitive skills, 64

content knowledge, 60–62

creative skills, 65

data collection and, 49–50

interpersonal skills, 65–66

oral communication skills, 66

organizational skills, 67

personal qualities, 70–72

quantitative skills, 67

sales skills, 68

technical skills, 68

transferable skills, 62–69

written communication skills, 69

asset statements, 17, 92–112, 140–141

assets, listing in cover letter, 165–166

Association of Executive Search Consultants, 211

attire. *See* dress

attitude

adversity and, 7–9

expectation setting, 13–14

genuineness, 10–11

honesty and, 11–12

interview preparation, 286, 299–307

introduction, 5–7

power perception and, 9–10

self-talk and, 7

thank yous and, 12–13

B

behavior-based interviews, 310–312

benefits, 427–431

biography, self-marketing packages, 21

block style of cover letter, 177

breaking-points in offer negotiation, 425

business & management skills, checklist, 63–64

business cards, self-marketing package, 20

C

Campbell Interest and Skill Survey, 60

candidate selection, data collection, 47–50

CAO (context-action-outcome) formula, asset statements and, 92

career advice, Internet-based job search, 254